Robert Boodey Caverly

Annals of the Boodeys in New England

Together with lessons of law and life, from John Eliot, the apostle of the Indians

Robert Boodey Caverly

Annals of the Boodeys in New England
Together with lessons of law and life, from John Eliot, the apostle of the Indians

ISBN/EAN: 9783337304263

Printed in Europe, USA, Canada, Australia, Japan

Cover: Foto ©ninafisch / pixelio.de

More available books at **www.hansebooks.com**

OF

THE BOODEYS

IN NEW ENGLAND,

TOGETHER WITH

LESSONS OF LAW AND LIFE,

FROM

John Eliot, the Apostle to the Indians.

BY

ROBERT BOODEY CAVERLY,

COUNSELLOR-AT-LAW, POET, AND AUTHOR OF BOOKS.

LOWELL, MASS.:
PUBLISHED BY THE AUTHOR.
1880

To the

REVEREND CLERGY OF NEW ENGLAND,

AND TO THE

Teacher and Advanced Student in the Sabbath School or Church,

THESE

LESSONS OF LAW AND LIFE, HISTORIC,

ARE INSCRIBED.

Faithfully, Thine,

ROBT. B. CAVERLY.

CENTRALVILLE, Feb. 22, 1880.

ILLUSTRATIONS.

TABLE OF CONTENTS.

6   TABLE OF CONTENTS.

ELIOTS IN ENGLAND.

INTRODUCTORY.

BEFORE advancing to obtain Lessons from John Eliot, the Apostle, we turn to his ancestry. There is no test, in bringing to light the merits of a man, better or more conclusive than to exemplify the blood that moves him. True it shall be found, that the life-current which fed the Evangelist had flowed auspiciously in England through many a successive channel for more than seven hundred years, leaping forth and meandering in all its life-inspiring elements, and from the pure original fountains of good-will, social gladness, and progressive manhood.

SIR WILLIAM.

When William the Conqueror, in the year 1066, with his army, in seven hundred ships, then landing on the shores of England, at Pevency, he had on board an *Eliot*,—not an apostle, but the remote ancestor of our New England evangelist. It was no other than *Sir William De Aliot*, a military officer under the great Conqueror, then valiant, and then in high command.

History bears record that the landing of that vast army was made without resistance; that the archers landed first, that they wore short habits, and had their hair cut close; that the horsemen next followed, wearing steel head-pieces, tunics, and cuirasses, and with long, heavy spears, and straight, two-edged swords; and then, to the shore, next came the workmen of the army, pioneers, carpenters, and smiths, who unloaded on the strand, piece by piece, prepared beforehand, three wooden castles already framed.

The Conqueror being the last of all to touch the English shore, in the setting of his foot upon it, made a false step, and fell in the mud upon his face; at which there went up a murmuring cry, "God preserve us! God preserve us! This is a bad sign!" But the duke, rising to his feet (with hands full of mud), cried out, "See, seigniors! I have seized England with both hands! See, seigniors! All is our own!"

Then one of the men, running forward, and snatching a handful of thatch from the eaves of a hut, turned to the duke and exclaimed to him, "Sire, come forward, and receive seizen of this land! I give you seizen! This land is yours!" The duke answered aloud, "I accept it! I accept it! May God be with us!"

Thus landed the first Eliot, eight hundred years ago, on England's shores, — a valiant officer, in the midst of an army of conquerors. According to history, Sir William, our Eliot's remote ancestor, then and there addressing the duke, and swearing fidelity, declared that "at the hazard of his life, he would maintain the rights of his lord, the Conqueror, to the vast sovereignty of England."

For this avowed fidelity, the Conqueror at once added to the Eliot coat-of-arms a canton (on a field of azure), an arm and sword as a crest, with the motto, "*Per saxa, per ignes; fortiter et recte,*" — "Over rocks, through fires; bravely and honorably."

Ever since the Norman conquest, England's places of honor and trust have constantly called them out. Especially since the reign of James the First (1625) the Eliot name stands on the record highly honored. Independent of royal appointments, generalships, and other high places, no less than thirty Eliots, both from England and Scotland, represent the realm as members of Parliament.

DESCENDANTS.

From that noble knighthood have descended Maj.-Gen. George Augustus Eliot, honored as Lord Heathfield; Sir Gilbert Eliot, the Earl of Minto; and most, if not all, the many thousands of distinguished Eliots who have since lived in England, including those who, within the last two hundred and fifty years, have landed and lived on these our New England shores.

And proud may the race be, that the same heroic blood that moved one of the old conquerors, is fruitful of inspiration in the veins of the generous Eliots in this our day. For more than fourscore years, it came, — coursed and moved the Apostle, inspiring life and light and love divine, on his mission to the heathen tribes of the wilderness.

Aside from the Eliot ancestry in England, now unremembered, unknown, in spite of oblivion, which in stealth creeps in, overwhelming the generations of earth, the Eliot name everywhere still adorns the English annals.

Sir John Eliot.

This noble knight, born in 1590, was a member of Parliament from Newport, and afterwards representing Cornwall, — was a leader in the House in the latter part of the reign of James II and the first part of Charles I. Repeatedly he had made himself prominent in opposition to the king's assumed prerogative; and finally, among other things, he strenuously led off in opposition to the levying of tonnage and poundage by the king himself, without consent of the House of Commons.*

Being an active man, and a decided enemy to favorites and their encroachments, Sir John was appointed by the House a manager in the impeachment trial of the Duke of Buckingham. By reason of his action in this, he, with his associate Digges and others, was committed to the Tower by the king, but was soon afterwards released.

In 1628 he was again imprisoned, with others, for his alleged parliamentary misconduct, and for his refusing to answer for it before the Privy Council; and yet he was again released.

Again the king having persisted in the aggressions above named, and Sir John, in concert with other members, having

---

* Among the many great men associated with Sir John Eliot, were Sir Edward Coke, Sir Edwin Sandis, Sir Robert Philips, Sir Francis Seymour, Sir Dudley Digges, and Sir Thomas Wentworth, the noble Earl of Strafford. —Hume's Hist., Vol. V, pp. 33, 34, 59, 60.

at length framed a remonstrance against the levying of tonnage
and poundage by the king without consent of the House, presented it to the clerk to be read; but the clerk refused.   Thereupon Sir John arose, and read it to the House himself.

The question being called for, the speaker objecting, said he
had a command from the king *not to put any question*, but to
adjourn the House; and, rising up, leaving the chair, an uproar
ensued.

The speaker was pushed back into his chair, and was forcibly
held into it by Hollis and Valentine, until a short remonstrance
in writing was framed by Sir John, which, without vote, was
passed by acclamation.   In this, Papists and Arminians were
declared by the House capital enemies to the commonwealth, as
well as those who had been concerned in levying tonnage and
poundage.   The doors at this time being locked, the usher of
the House of Lords, sent by the king, could not obtain admit-
tance, until that remonstrance on the motion of Sir John Eliot
had been carried through.*

POSITION OF THE KING.

These proceedings of the House were denounced by the
throne as seditious, and on this account several members of
the House were imprisoned, but were afterwards, with much
difficulty, released.

SIR JOHN IN COURT.

This member, with Hollis, Valentine, and others, was (May 29,
1628) summoned to his trial before the King's Bench for "seditious speeches and behaviour."   Sir John was charged of having
declared, in the House, that "the council and judges conspired
to trample under their feet the liberties of the subject and the
privileges of Parliament"; and being arraigned before a tribunal
inferior to his own, as asserted, he refused to answer.   Thereupon the King's Bench condemned him to be imprisoned in the
Tower at the king's pleasure, and to pay a fine of £2,000.   His
parliamentary associates received less, but similar, sentences.

---

* Hume, Vol. V, p. 59.

The king, in the midst of embarrassment, offered them a release on the terms of concession, to which they would not yield, nor would they accept of bail generously offered; but for the cause of liberty they cared not for the bonds that held them. Under this imprisonment Sir John Eliot died in the Tower Nov. 27, 1632. This was announced throughout the realm as the death of a martyr, and it was not very long afterwards (1648) when his royal oppressor also died, beheaded.*

THE APOSTLE IN ENGLAND.

The first now known of our John, the Apostle, is, when he was at school with Rev. Thomas Hooper, at Little Baddow, in Essex,† as an usher, or assistant teacher; and tradition has it, that he was also schooled for some time in the University at Cambridge, but of this last statement there is some doubt.‡

The Apostle, as well as his brothers Philip and Jacob, was once supposed to have originated at Nasing, in Essex; but a special historian has journeyed to that town, and upon diligent search, finds no evidence of it. Nor does it in any way appear that the Apostle ever saw that town.

In 1631, the year previous to Sir John Eliot's death in the Tower, the Apostle and his two brothers, disgusted at the then oppressive papacy, and at the royal misrule as affecting themselves and kindred ties, had made up their minds to desert England.§

ABOUT TO EMBARK.

Being about to leave the realm, these Eliot brothers must needs advance to take final leave of favored friends. So doing,

---

* Hume's History of England, Vol. V, pp. 59, 60, 371.

† Hooker was suspended from the ministry by reason of his hostility to papacy and royalty as then administered; and years afterwards, in 1640, left England in the ship "Griffin," with two hundred others (among whom Oliver Cromwell started, but turned back), and finally settled in Connecticut, and was honored as the "Moses" of that State.

‡ Eliot Gen., p. 35.

§ Life of Eliot, by Francis, pp. 6, 7, and note. Hist. of Puritans, Vol. II, p. 245.

we seem to see them on the way, hurriedly advancing in and
along the narrow highways of London to its Tower, on a visit
to their dear old uncle, Sir John Eliot, the Martyr. They pass
incognito. Their sympathies concentre at the Tower. They
know and feel the injustice of the imprisonment, and the cruelty of that royal power which holds him within its walls.
Foremost, as they advance, the great white fortification heaves
in sight, and then next its outstanding twelve towers, and then
a spacious moat or canal that surrounds it. Here, then,
a fortress, terrible in its history, and awful in its frowning
strength and power, now stands before them. They gaze
glancing upon its embattled watch-towers, and upon its heavy,
time-stained, stately walls.

Up the Stairway.

Permitted by "the warder, or yeoman of the guard," they
pass the gateway into the outer ward, and farther onward
enter within and along up the heavy stairway from the inner
ward, and still higher along between the various dismal
dungeons and solitary apartments of the great white Tower.

Tools of Torture.

On their winding way upward, step after step, on either side
are seen, in various forms, the many implements of cruelty and
death of long-gone years. Here is seen the collar of torment;
there the thumb-screw; there the rack and the stock that
destroyed the limbs of men, and the block that held the heads
of queens. There, too, among thousands of other dread implements, is the broad, bloody axe which, one after another,
all the way through England's reign of terror, had left kings
headless and many a noble heart lifeless. As they move upward, gazing, wondering, the splendor of royalty and the
beauty of queens fall oft upon their vision. The dazzling
insignia of royalty and the glittering power of princes are
exemplified. Found high up in one of the towers, in all their
value and beauty, they behold

ENGLAND'S JEWELS.

These diadems are grouped. The crown of the sovereign consists of a cap of purple velvet, enclosed in hoops of silver, surmounted by a ball and cross, all brilliant in diamonds. In the centre of the cross is the inestimable sapphire; and in front is the heart-shaped ruby once worn by the Black Prince. .

St. Edward. — One of the group is the crown of this prince, made of gold, richly embellished with emeralds, pearls, and other precious gems.

Prince of Wales. — The crown of this prince is of pure gold, unadorned. It is a crown which usually is placed before the seat of the heir-apparent in the House of Lords.

Ancient Queen's Crown. — This is used at coronations, for the queen's consort.

Queen's Diadem. — This is adorned with large diamonds and pearls.

St. Edward's Staff. — Made of beaten gold; it is four feet seven inches in length, and is surmounted with an orb. It is carried before the king at the coronation.

The Royal Sceptre. — This, with the cross, is usually carried before the Archbishop of Canterbury at the coronation. It is of gold, adorned with jewels.

Rod of Equity. — This sceptre is placed in the hand of the sovereign at the coronation. Made of gold, it has an orb, and a dove with expanded wings.

Ivory Sceptre. — This was the sceptre of "Queen Marie De Estie."

The Golden Sceptre. — This seems to have originated from Queen Mary, of William the Third, and is the last of the group.

These, to the brothers, were indeed "glittering generalities."

INSCRIPTIONS, OFFENCES, AND CRUELTIES.

Next they enter various other departments, encased with huge walls, upon which now and then are deeply engraved the many sentimental sayings, inscribed in plain letters, — some in English, some in Latin, and others in other languages, —by the many heroic victims, men and women, who in by-gone ages had perished in the Tower.

On one side, over the fireplace, is found the name "Philip Howard." Philip was the son of the Duke of Norfolk, who in 1572 had been beheaded for the grave offence of having aspired to the hand of the dear Mary, Queen of Scots. This was the duke's offence. Philip's own crime proves to have been an ardent devotedness to the church of his choice, at which Queen Elizabeth had taken offence. Philip, seeing his danger, tried to escape into exile; but, detected, was seized and sent to the Tower, where, upon its walls, over his name (immortalized), he engraved the following words : —

" *Quanto plus affectiones pro Christo in hoc secula plus gloriæ cum Christo in futuro.*   *Philip Howard.*

"*Arundell, June 22, 1587.*"

The interpretation of this declares that, "The more suffering with Christ in this world, the more glory shall be obtained with Christ in the world to come."

Philip's Sentence.

This same earl, being found guilty of high treason, was condemned to death, but having been convicted on religious grounds, was not beheaded, but, doomed, was held a prisoner for life. Worn with sorrow, he expired in the Tower, "1595, aged 39." In person he was tall, of a swarthy complexion, but "had an agreeable mixture of sweetness and grandeur of countenance, with a soul superior to all human considerations."

Next they come to the inscriptions made by Arthur Poole, on the north side of his cell, to wit: "*Deo servire penitentiam inire fato obedire Regnare est.*   *A. Poole, 1564 I. H. S.*"

It seems that Arthur was in the belief that "to live penitently, yield to fate, and serve God, is to reign."

And again, the same prisoner leaves on the walls other words, "I. II. S. A passage perilous maketh a port pleasant." "A. 1568." "Arthur Poole." "A. C. sue 37 A. P."

In another place in the walls are found, from his brother, the following: "*I. II. S. Dio semin . . . in lachrimis exultatione mater. A. E. 21 E. Poole 1562.*" "That which is sown of God in tears is to be reaped in joy."

Under one of the autographs of Edmund Poole is the word "*Iane.*" This is said to have been the royal title of Lady Jane Gray; and as appears, Lady Jane herself, while imprisoned in the Tower, left an inscription scratched upon the wall with a pin, as follows:—

> "To mortals' common fate thy mind resign,
> My lot to-day, to-morrow may be thine."

IMPRISONMENT AND DEATH.

It was in 1640, when Sir Thomas Cromwell, for his Reformation sentiments, was cast into the Tower, and afterwards was beheaded on Tower Hill. About this time, in the midst of heresy and delusion, the dungeons were filled with learned divines.

In 1546, Anne Askew, a lady of merit, for denying in conversation the doctrine of transubstantiation, was tortured in the Tower, and then burnt at the stake in Smithfield.

The offence of Margaret, the Countess of Salisbury, mother of Cardinal Pole, was that she was of royal blood. When brought to the scaffold on the green, she refused to lay her head upon the block, saying, "So do traitors use to do, and I am no traitor." An awful scene followed. At length the headsman dragged the countess by her long, frosty locks to the block. Thus perished the last full blood of the Plantagenets.

Sir Walter Raleigh, once an inhabitant of the New World, was afterwards seized in England, charged of being concerned in the plot of placing on the throne Lady Arabella Stuart. For this he was held a prisoner in the Tower twelve years. Released, he went to Guiana in search of gold; but failing in that enterprise, on his return, for the original offence, he was again remanded to the Tower, and without reason was beheaded in 1618.* While in the Tower that noble Raleigh wrote a history of the world.

---

* Hume, Vol. IV, p. 452.

Thomas Wentworth, * Earl of Strafford, one of England's most eminent sons, was incarcerated in the Tower for trying to withstand the popular current, which was concentrating to a revolution, and in 1641 was beheaded, to the intense grief of his sovereign.

STATUARY AND WEAPONS.

Present to the brothers, as they advance, are also other unnumbered victims of despotic vengeance in the by-gone centuries. They behold, in deep thought, the emblematic banners which floated over heroes like Edward I, Edward III, the Black Prince, and many others, such as had been fanned by "the whirlwinds of war and by the crimson wing of conquest." Here, too, on the right and left as they pass, are the crossbows, with their stocks curiously carved, used in the sixteenth and seventeenth centuries. Here, also, is the carved steed, bearing away upon himself, in his pride, Elizabeth, Queen of England. Here, too, fronting the queen, is the equestrian statue of a noble knight wielding in his hand a tilting lance, clad in the closest armor. Also, farther upward, is the figure of an archer in a brigandine jacket; and there, too, is a crossbow used in the days of our remote Eliot and William the Conqueror, with groups of spears on all sides of it. Next to be noticed are rugged shields, with scenes from the story of Hercules; helmets and breast-plates, ancient firearms, matchlocks, etc., innumerable. Still farther upward are groups of arms and armor, iron skull-caps, and various figures of statuary; effigies of noble knights on horseback, very common, among which appears Charles the First on horseback in the same gilt armor which he had received as a gallant gift from the city of London. All these, and immensely more, excite the senses of our Eliot brothers on that day in the heart of their native England, and in the proudest city of the world.

Now, half halting, our young Apostle, breaking silence, thus addresses Philip and Jacob: —

---

* Sketches of the Tower, p. 39.

ROYAL OUTRAGES.

These, as you see, are but the emblems that have come down from a wild, unjust, untutored ambition, whence dread heresies, and the thirst for power, have, through carnal weapons, been allowed to gain the ascendancy over a Christian civilization as found in the laws of God, and which forever must needs be enforced, pursuant to "the great God's Golden Rule." Thus in this our English fathers have failed. England, beautiful England, whose mountains have been made vocal with the high-born Hoel's harp and soft Llewellyn's lay, hath suffered all this. Indeed, a better era shall follow her. Then shall her kings and queens reign in righteousness; and "then shall her princes decree justice."

Next, now, as the brothers pass, are pointed out to them the various dungeons which long previously had been filled with the mighty men of Scotland. For here it was that King Baliol was imprisoned in 1297; where, also, the noble Wallace suffered imprisonment and death in 1305; where the gallant earls of Ross, of Athol, and of Monteith, in 1346, King David Bruce's time, all perished;* and where, also, the six hundred Jews must have been quartered, who inhabited the Tower, prisoners in the reign of Edward the Third, and during the military career of "Sir Hugh Calverly, the *chevalier verte*," who first used guns in England's wars.†

In 1406, in the reign of Henry IV, the boy Prince James, son of Robert III, King of Scotland, when on a sea-voyage to France to obtain an education, driven by storm and tempest, was cast upon the shores of England. Now, for reason that Scotland was then at war with King Henry, this infant prince was seized, as if by a wrecker, and was consigned to the Tower of London, and was there held imprisoned eighteen years. He educated himself there, and in after life, crowned, he at length became renowned " for consummate wisdom and virtue."

---

* See Harmon's Sketch, pp. 32, 33.

† These Jews, for this, their offence of having adulterated the coin of the realm, with their entire nation, were finally released from the Tower, by being banished from England. See Hume, Vol. II, pp. 124, 131, 256–282, 337.

It was in the Tower that the Black Prince, then in the fifteenth century, the pride and delight of England, fell a prey to "the wolf-like passions of rival factions." At this period were seen the tyrants' darkest deeds. Then it was that royal cousins, in wrath, struggled for the crown, now and then dooming the unhappy aspirant to a dismal dungeon, or to a dread assassination. Rampant for power, they increased the traffic in tools of torture, in the building of scaffolds, and in deeds of blood.

Here (seen by the brothers) is the image of Queen Anne, consort of Richard II, on her knees pleading in tears at the feet of her lord, for her dear king's own friend, Sir Simon Burley, all in vain; and Sir Simon, "that noble Knight" (1388), was made the first victim beheaded upon the new scaffold at Tower Hill. Discontent follows Richard II, and soon he resigns his kingdom to his relative Bolingbroke, in language as follows: "Fair cousin Henry, Duke of Lancaster, I give and deliver to you this crown, and therewith all the rights thereto depending." Richard himself was then committed to the Tower, and thence to Pomfret Castle in Yorkshire; and to this day a sable veil conceals his death.

Nor was the reign of Bolingbroke peaceful. Ah! how truthful the poet sings,—

> "Gives not the hawthorn bush a sweeter shade
> To shepherds, looking on their silly sheep,
> Than doth a rich embroidered canopy
> To kings, that fear their subjects' treachery?"

It was here, in 1485, when in front of St. Peter's Chapel, Lord Hastings was doomed to instant death at the mandate of Richard III. And from here, from within the Tower's dismal recesses, the renowned Sir John Oldcastle, Lord Cobham, after a long imprisonment for religious opinions (1417), was carted away, and at the fields of St. Giles was burnt at the stake. And here during the reign of Henry the Eighth, when Rome was at its height in persecutions, and the populace were frantic in charges of heresy, the broad gates of the Tower of London were wide open swung in the reception of innocent hearts.

Under statutes that empowered the "Bishop to imprizon any

one suspected " of heresy, the dungeons of the Tower were soon filled with pious convicts. The illustrious Lord Chancellor, Thomas More, and Fisher, the venerable Bishop of Rochester, covered as he was with the frosts of eighty winters, were held here as heretics, thus to pine away their otherwise useful lives in solitude and sadness, until death at length relieved them. They were held under the wrath of King Henry, the professed head of the church.* This old bishop, while there, in a letter to one of the lords, complains : "I have neither shirt nor sute to wear, but that be ragged, and rent so shamefully—and my dyett also, God knoweth how slender it is at meny times."

In 1533, Anne Boleyn was the pious queen of Henry VIII. She was escorted to him by the Lord Mayor of London, arrayed in scarlet and clad in golden chains, "amidst the great melody of trumpets and divers instruments, and a mighty peal of guns." In 1536 her home was in the Tower. The traitor gates opened wide to receive Queen Anne; she came attended by her jailers; her fair fame had departed, and the gloom of death overshadowed her. Charged of unfaithfulness to her king, and arraigned before the Duke of Norfolk, she was condemned to death, at which she exclaimed, "O Father! O Creator! Thou who art the way, the truth, and the life, Thou knowest I have not deserved this death." On the 19th of May, 1536, a mournful procession passed over the green. Anne Boleyn, dressed in black, surrounded by a retinue of sympathetic maidens, was on the way from the Tower to the scaffold, there in person transcendently beautiful, "mournfully brilliant." Here ended the earthly career of a generous queen.

In 1553, dread royalty again is seen in the Tower, during the ten days' reign of Lady Jane Grey, who, as it often is told, fell a victim to the unholy ambition of the Duke of Northumberland. Her husband, Lord Guilford Dudley, was executed about the same time, on Tower Hill. Lady Jane, as declared by Fuller, "had the innocense of childhood, the beauty of youth, the learn-

---

* Parliament conferred on the king, power as a supreme head of the church of England.—Hume's Hist. of Eng., Vol. III, pp. 189-197, 490, 491.

ing of a clerk, the solidity of middle life, the gravity of old age, and the soul of a saint." She, like many others, died a victim to a low ambition under a thirst for power, and against all law, true religion, and common decency.

AT THE CELL OF SIR JOHN.

Here the brothers, conducted, have at length arrived. With eager eyes they glance at their kind uncle, the martyr, in silent solitude. The old man, startled at their footsteps, rising up, turns himself hither and thither like a caged lion, as if from a deep slumber, or from an absorbing reverie. A long imprisoned beard rests loosely upon his breast; the frosts of dreary winter hang, spread wide, upon his shoulders; yet there is the blood of an Eliot in the long, pale, furrowed cheek, and a flash of fire, glimmering, still twinkles in the old man's eye.

The brothers draw near; and oh! with what gladness, what love and thankfulness, does the oppressed martyr meet and greet them, separated only by intervening bolts and bars. The old knight, after an interchange of greetings, pauses, listening to a brief detail of their designs for the future, as they were now about to leave their native land, to sojourn for life in a wilderness afar off, beyond the high seas, breaking silence, advises them thus: "For the just liberties of the realm I remain here. This Tower is my home. But, for you, full of life, England in its distractions, having become offensive, it is but wise that the Puritan should leave it. Full of vigor, you may as well go to the New World. Accept of no office there. Trust to your own strength in the faith of God. Divulge not incurable difficulties. Keep your own councils, that the disadvantages of this sad Old World may not encumber you there in the New; observe the law and keep the faith."

The brothers are silent, sad. An extended hand, a half-suppressed adieu, is had, and then an heart-felt, old-fashioned farewell is extended and returned. Sadly away the brothers turn; the old knight sinks back into his couch, again thoughtful, silent, at rest.

By this the shades of night are beginning to becloud the Tower, and the brothers, turned, are beginning to tread downward the various stairways that wind in and about its dark dungeons and lofty walls. Descending cautiously, the terrible apparitions of England's royal cruelties, with unseemly sights of her sainted subjects slain within this fearful fortress, fall constantly upon their vision. At every footstep, the hollow, sepulchral rotunda resounds with the agonizing sighs and groans, as the spectral victims of regal rage and power of the past seem constantly to give unearthly utterances. From the ceiling, from every step and stairway, the complaints of sainted souls, whose blood had been shed here, and whose dust hath been trampled under the foot of princely power, seem everywhere audible. From the pores of the pilasters and crevices of the eternal walls, the innocent blood of men and women, in the midst of sepulchral accents, seems to ooze out. Nay, behind every statue or image of royalty, behind the bloody block, or rack of torture, or statue, as they pass, unseemly ghosts of kings, or of queens, or of martyred innocence, strangely appear, peeping out.

Thus, to the Apostle and brothers in the Tower, while rambling in the midst of its terrible emblems, did injured humanity, and the dread maledictions of a just God, move their Puritan minds into a sad melancholy. Out of it, advancing to the archway of the traitor's gate, there they pause, but to reflect, how oft had royalty and grandeur passed beneath its portals; how often here had "the dreams of honor and glory," and "the brilliancy of courts," been exchanged for the dungeon, the torture-room, and the scaffold. Advancing farther out, they reach the Bloody Tower, where, near it, is the iron railing upon the green, which encloses the block at which Lady Jane Grey last kneeled, yielding up her life.

Thence backward they glance, taking a comprehensive last look at that old vast white fortress, and the twelve great towers, with embattlements, that stand around it; and thence, not far away, to behold that ancient St. Peter's chapel, within which the bodies of fated prisoners numerously in the silent dust moulder.

LEAVING THE TOWER.

Now, with heavy hearts, but with lightsome step, leaving, the Eliot brothers hasten away on their half-bewildered, backward return. And now the pale moon, amid the bright stars of heaven rising, beholds them wandering, first nearing the old College of Heraldry, which records the valor of England's best blood; and then next near the towering walls of St. Paul; and then round through the stately gateway of Temple Bar, which to this day marks the entrance through the once-frowning walls of the first London; and thence away they wander, to the ship "Lyon," which on the morrow is to waft them away, — away from conflicting powers; away from unholy, oppressive dynasties; away from a bewildered populace and a distracted representation; away from an insane kingdom, driven to terrible extremes by unhallowed, cruel conflicts.

On board the ship, after taking the required oaths of "allegiance and supremacie," the brothers, in their bunks, tired, all night long in dreams are thoughtful, both of the past and of the future. Morning, now breaking in upon them, adorns the world with uncommon glories; and the big ship on the way is now beginning to brave the broad billows. The sweet breezes of heaven, promising freedom, prosperity, and progress, are whispering in the rigging like the harp of a David, the thrilling, peaceful acclaim of an evangelist, or like the seraphic song of congregated angels; and away that brave old bark, as if in the care of a God of Love, moves straight onward, westward.

Another night has cast her lights and shades over the vast expanse, bringing back again the beauteous morn, when a voice from the high deck is heard, —

> "Come aloft, my companions, the billows are beauteous,
>   To the God of creation devotedly duteous."

Obediently all are aloft. And now the boundless ocean, rolling up her billows to the sky, and the brilliant azure of the God-given sunlight playing upon the wild waters, the ship's canvas, and the clouds, inspires the world.

"Ah!" says the Apostle to his comrades, " this is life, in its progress; life foreshadowed! Still, indeed, there are storms and gales and even tempests on the way. This highway vast is fraught with doubt and dread dangers; yet through faith and trust and trial, we will reach the New World. Nay, as we advance farther onward in life's journeyings, not less of storm and of tempest will beset us on the way, advancing to that beautiful land above, of which our dear old father had in fervent faith advised us."

"Be heedful, my brother," said Philip. "Remember, when in the Tower, our Sir John advised caution, that neither our town of nativity nor the name of the dear father be disclosed."

"Yes," said the Apostle, " that name, always dear at heart, needs never to be expressed.

> ' O, no, I 'll never mention him,
> That name shall ne'er be heard;
> My lips are hence forbidden to speak
> That once familiar word.' "

Back now to the cabin the brothers return. The old ship, keeping her course onward, the breath of heaven swelling the sails auspiciously, outrides the storm and tempest, and at length, after many days, beneath brighter skies, lands her freight of valiant hearts at Plymouth on the shores of New England. Philip had come, as if for the defence of liberty, being soon found in the gallant ranks of the "Ancient and Honorable," at its origin, and then next in the honored halls of legislation. Jacob, also, a Puritan gentleman, had come, making himself highly useful in support of a laborious industry, and in the furtherance of the benign rules of law and justice. John was here also, to proclaim the divine law, — Love to God, and love to the red-man in the wilderness.

LESSONS OF LAW AND LIFE.

"It is wise to recur to our ancestors. Those who do not look upon themselves as a link connecting the past with the future, do not perform their duty to the world."—DANIEL WEBSTER.

SIR FRANCIS DRAKE.

First White Man on a New England Shore (Chronology: Drake, 1586; Pilgrims, 1620;
John Eliot, the Apostle, 1631.)

John Eliot, the Apostle.

CHAPTER I.

Nothing in the acquisition of knowledge shall prove more profitable than the study of the lives and characters of great and good men. Such men, like an index, . serve to lead the way to an improved civilization, and to a more devoted fidelity to God and to mankind. To study and know them is wisdom; to follow their precepts and examples, bespeaks an abundant success in this life, and the gain of a glorious reward beyond it. The lessons thus to be learned are practical; tending to manliness, to sobriety, to a stern integrity, to a diligent industry, and to a fervent faith.

I therefore invoke the attention of my readers, for a brief period, to such light and learning as may be obtained from the extraordinary life and character of John Eliot, as seen in and through his evangelical mission to the Indian tribes of New England. For two centuries, Eliot, with the faith and fruits of his mission, hath been estimated as the common property of all New England. Like, as from a province of real estate, held jointly, the generations have hitherto been constantly benefited by his exemplary productive life and character.

Still onward, in this light of history, Eliot's force —

his holy aspirations, his labors of love, his vast undertakings, and his valiant perseverance in the midst of opposition, still exist, and shall afford to the intelligent reader pleasure and profit forever.

The obstacles which encumbered his way were hazardous and fearful, — yet valiantly he advanced. History points to no one man of so much force, against such embarrassments; of so much perseverance, against such discouragements; of so much patience, under such provocations; of so much laborious industry, with an apparently slender constitution; of so much endurance, under severe hardships and keen sufferings; and with so much faith and consecration to his God and to his fellow-man, — never failing, never faltering.

Such was the man who made our English Bible speak the Indian language; who raised up missionaries; and who, for forty years, preached the Gospel to the wild man of the wilderness; and who thereby had turned many hearts from a savage life Zion-ward. And when the dread conflict with Philip had come, and civilization in New England, as against barbarism, seemed quivering in the scale, yet, protesting against the use of carnal weapons, Eliot held the balance of power, and thus, in the end, served to tip the scale to the side of civilization — lost the tribes, but saved the white man, who still pursued, leaving the lone Indian mother to her lamentations : —

> " I will go to my tent, and lie down in despair;
> I will paint me in black, and dishevel my hair;
> I will sit on the shore where the hurricane blows,
> And will tell to the God of the tempest my woes.
> I will weep for a season, on bitterness fed,
> For my kindred have gone to the mounds of the dead;

But they died not of hunger, nor wasting decay, —
The steel of the white-man hath swept them away."

That balance of power, which the Apostle, in his mission, held, was none other than the power of Christian love.

LIFE AND DEATH.

John Eliot first lived in the far-off England, in the year 1604. He left this world of care and conflicts, at Roxbury, Mass., May 20, 1690, at the venerable age of eighty-six years.

In personal appearance (if we may judge from his portrait), he was a little above medium height, in form slender, and in features not entirely unlike the honest face of Abraham Lincoln.

After completing his education in England, Eliot embarked for the New World, — landed in Boston in November, 1631, — and there, at the age of twenty-seven, raised the banner of the Cross.

Soon, a train of neighbors and friends followed him. They settled near him, at Roxbury; and the next year they called him there, to be their minister.*

Obeying their call, he took his final stand at Roxbury, as if upon the loftiest part of Zion's walls, and he held his station there all the way onward, through the remainder of his long life.†

INTOLERANCE.

That want of toleration, which had driven the Pilgrims over here, eleven years previously, probably had much influence, inducing Eliot also to sever the social

---

* Bacon's Hist. of Natick, ch. 2, p. 12; ch. 15, p. 152.
† Memoir of Eliot, pp. 8, 9, 10.

ties, to forsake the friends of his youth, and, far away over the great deep, to cast his lot among the sons of strife.

Thus, over here, as if at the command of God, "Go ye into all the world," the Apostle began his work. He began it — where every man ought to begin to labor, to wit, at the main obstacle to be overcome — where the most good can be done, or where the noblest ends in life may be accomplished.

The Position.

Looking back, we seem to see the evangelist, as in full life, standing on the highest point of that Zion's hill of his, as if, at the outset, to look the landscape over. Afar off before him, in the distance, the lofty mountain-peaks tower up towards heaven ; — they stand there, against the sky.

His sharp vision seems to descry the Connecticut, the mighty Merrimac, and the Saco, as they, in ten thousand rills, leap forth from the mountains, forming these rivers, up to that time unmeasured of the white man, and which, ever since the Creation, had been rolling and meandering downward, through a wild old wilderness, to the sea.

Indian Nations.

In the dense forest, and in and about these rivers of water, and along the shores of the sea, are thirty nations of native Indians, numbering, in all, fifty thousand. These nations, organized under laws unwritten, wander in tribes, as all the inhabitants of the world, before civilization dawned, did wander in tribes.

The Pilgrim Fathers are at Plymouth and vicinity,

and the scattered Puritan settlements are beginning to make openings in the landscape.

The field was to be the world; and this New England world, thus spread out before him, was thenceforth to be Eliot's field, — a field, then a wilderness, full of ferocious beasts, and of ungodly, unbridled red-men; and yet a field which, through the Evangelical leadership of John Eliot, is to be cleared up and cultivated; and which, in the far future, under the sunshine of heaven, is to become a flowery field, bearing upon it, everywhere, not carnal weapons, but the sweet fruits of a Christian civilization.

And now, at this distant day, although there are secluded corners in the field, where the generations have gone down, —in which many of us have sometimes been made to weep; yet it is plain to be seen that, through the leadership of Eliot, in God's ministry, those corners, all over New England, have been made to our people as the very gateways to heaven. Plain it is, that this New England field, with all its gates and guide-boards heavenward, although two hundred years have passed away, now remains, and, through all the generations yet to come, shall remain, still to flourish and bear fruit, as having descended, with all its vernal glories, from that same ancient, original Christian proprietor, John Eliot, the Evangelist.

His First Work.

At first the Apostle, in preparation for his final great effort, directed all his sermons to the white man, — seeking to build up strong exemplary churches in the hamlets held by English settlers, at his own Roxbury, and elsewhere.*

---

* Dearborn's Sketch of Eliot's Life, p. 13.

His habits were like this: Every second Sabbath of his ministry he preached away from home, to the white settlers of the neighboring towns.*　And thus onward, for the first fifteen years of his ministry; while, in these same years, he was educating, as well as he might, his Indian young men and others, who, in due time, were to be his preachers, his printers, his proof-readers, and interpreters; and who, in the wilderness, were to aid him in the vast undertaking of evangelizing the tribes.

During all these years he was at work with his pen, — by pamphlet, by letter, and by many books, — shaping and concentrating public opinion to the great plan of his operations. Also, by prayer and petition, at home and abroad, he from the commencement, and from time to time, continually obtained material aid and encouragement for the carrying out of his design.

His Apparel.

Again, let us glance for a moment at the Evangelist, as he appeared two hundred and thirty years ago, when about to move upon his Indian mission.

We will imagine him still there, on the high hill at Roxbury, — in his common costume, an English dress-coat or sack; small clothes, long boots, and a slouched broad-brimmed hat.

There he stands, as if divinely meditating, as if contemplating the long labors of life, in that vast field of which we have spoken, and which the God of Nature had spread out before him.

---

* History of Natick, ch. 1, p. 12.

LOCATION OF THE TRIBES.

From thence, away to the west of him (as he could but discover), there are six nations of Mohawks, made up of many tribes, leading useless, wayward, wandering lives.

Northeast of him, on the Sagadahock, and all along towards the eastern borders of Maine, he calls to his vision those troublesome warlike tribes, the Tarratines, or Abanaquise, who twenty years previously had come up here from the East, wielding weapons of war; and, accelerated by the plague of 1617, had destroyed the entire Patuxet nation, leaving their bones to be bleached upon the hills and in the vales, — seen often, doubtless, of Eliot, as well as of the Pilgrims.

Not far away from him, on the left, are the ashes of that great Indian fort, on the Mystic, where, as appears, through the weapons of war and flames of fire, a hostile Pequot nation had in one night (1637) all perished by the English sabre.

To the southwest of him, as he there stands, are the Narragansetts, in Massachusetts and Rhode Island, led of Canonicus, and of that fated, but brave old chief, Miantonimo.

From the same height, away to the left, are the flagrant Mohegans of Connecticut, at the head of which Uncas reigned as chief, — wild in all of his infidelity and barbarism.

Then next, more immediately in front of the Apostle, as he looks northward, in contemplation, are the Nipmuck tribes, roaming and hunting all over that tract of country which lies between the great rivers Connecticut and Merrimac. Hence, all of us who happen to reside southwest of the Merrimac, if natives, might be denominated Nipmucks.

Northward, at Concord, and along the banks of the Merrimac, wandered the peaceful Pennacook and the Wamesit tribes, then led by that venerable sachem and necromancer, Passaconaway, whose people, at a later period, were ruled for several years by his son, Wonalancet.

Though a peace-maker, once, in a time of hostilities, this chief, with becoming prudence, established an Indian fortification at Fort Hill, on the east of the Concord River, at Wamesit.*

ELIOT'S FIDELITY.

The soul-trying incidents of the forty years of the Apostle's life, then yet to come, beginning to be disclosed, are now breaking in upon his vision. There are lions, terribly ferocious, prone, lurking along his pathway, in prospect, all the way onward, with all their devouring threatenings.

Yet he must advance, must move onward, to the responsible, the noble, and soul-trying duties of an evangelist, in the midst of unlettered savages.

Whatever there may be of trouble on the way or in the field of operations, he is constantly, duteously to be

---

* We suggest, that on Fort Hill there ought to be erected two statues,—one to John Eliot, the Apostle; and another to the peaceful Wanalancet, holding the fort. Such statues in our *Wamesit*, proclaiming peace on the one hand, and a Christian civilization on the other, while they would evince the magnanimity of our people, would tend, for a thousand years, to inspire the generations to a becoming peacefulness, to a diligent industry, to a truthful fidelity to mankind, and to a stronger faith in Him whom the Apostle so devoutly loved and served.

there. What though the very elements are to conspire
to hedge up the way; what though the wintry blasts of
snow and hail and tempest, as they were wont to come,
sweeping away "the honors" of a thousand years, from
that vast old wilderness, — John Eliot is to be there,
and there, too, in a fervent faith, — faith that the same
God, who tempers the wind to the shorn lamb, would
also be there; and *he was there.*

Nay, even though the thunders of war, in their threatenings, begin to break forth from a New England sky,
such in their terrors as were never known on earth
before (save in the bloody tragedies of a Homer) even
then John Eliot must be there, holding out a healing
hand divine, and bearing aloft the beautiful Christian
banner of peace and love.

And though destruction is impending, and a threatened
distraction may be about to fall upon his native churches,
driving and carrying his Indian Christian people into
exile and imprisonment; yet the Apostle, like the good
shepherd, is to follow the flock, is to stand between the
fires, is to administer comfort, and is to bind up the
broken heart.*

Nay, aside from the carnal conflicts of war, when its
tearful terrors have waned away, there are to the
evangelist terrible trials still.   And what of all this?

What though strong men refuse "to bow themselves,"
heeding not the way? What though the bowl, and the
wheel, and "the pitcher, be broken"? What though, in
the events of this New World, the sun and moon and
the stars are to be darkened? What even, if all "the

---

* Dearborn's Sketch of Eliot's Life, p. 15.

keepers of the house" are trembling? List! list! High above all, the tribes are to hear the clarion voice of the evangelist, fearlessly proclaiming the word, — faithfully seeking to save that which seemed to be lost.

For Eliot knew, as we know, that "man goeth to his long home"; that his "dust must return to the earth as it was"; and that his never-dying spirit must go back to the God who gave it.

TROUBLES IN ENGLAND.

Eliot had left the Old World, as we have seen, in 1631, when the unfortunate Charles the First was king, and at the time when the religious creeds of the realm were distracted, all in dread conflict; when the King was at war against Parliament, and Parliament was angry against the King; when our English government was powerless to advance, its wheels being clogged up, the kingdom throughout broken down, and falling apart into factions. It was then the religious and political rights of the realm were being trampled down under the feet of tyrants,* and the armies of England, Scotland, and Ireland in conflict were making sad havoc on bloody fields of battle.

Eliot left England, and in leaving forsook, as we have seen, the comrades of his youth, among whom there was a strong young man, whose valiant heart, like his own, was full of republicanism. That man, disgusted with the English government in its distracted condition, had with other refugees, packed up his trunks to embark for our New England shores, but was prevented. It was

---

* Hume's History of England, vol. 5, pp. 85–434. Rush., vol 2, pp. 409–418.

OLIVER CROMWELL.

But the God of governments, as if for wise ends, turned the intent of Cromwell, to still remain in England; * while John Eliot was led, for another wise purpose, to seek his field of apostolic labors in the wilderness of a new world.

At that time, as we have seen, the English government was fast falling to pieces through its internal religious and political infirmities, which resulted in the downfall of King Charles the First, who, at length, was beheaded at the decree of about seventy judges.

Thus, while Cromwell became the great Protector in the Old World, John Eliot came over here, and became renowned as the great primeval leader to a Christian civilization among the settlers and Indian nations of the New.

MATERIAL AID.

He was encouraged to advance upon his mission through influences brought to bear upon the universities of Oxford and Cambridge, and upon a missionary society in his native England, as well as upon our own Colonial government at home.

Cromwell, as appears, encouraged Eliot, and Eliot, in his way, tried to obey and sustain the English government, under him, as the great Protector of both countries.

THE BOOK.

During the existence of Cromwell's government, seven

---

* "Urged by his wants and his piety, he had made a party with Hamblen, his near kinsman, who was pressed only by the latter motive, to transport himself into New England, now become the retreat of the more zealous among the Puritanical party; and it was on an order of Council which obliged them to disembark and remain in England." — Hume, vol. 5, ch. 61, p. 437.

years, — up to the end of his (the Protector's) life, Sept. 3, 1658, — Eliot had written a work entitled "The Christian Commonwealth," in which he planned, and bestowed praise upon, and chalked out a republican form of government. But, alas! Before the book issued extensively from the press, Cromwell dying, the government, in a year or two, changed back to a kingdom; and then Charles the Second (a son of the beheaded Charles), being crowned king, and becoming apparently dangerous, as against the active adherents to Cromwell's administration, is filled full of exasperation against all ideas of republicanism.

This event exposed the Apostle's head to great danger, by reason of his having written that "Christian Commonwealth," which indirectly assailed the Crown. The Colonial government became anxious, and advised the suppression of the book; and for the sake of his great cause and of his life, Eliot suppressed the manuscript, and the book never issued.*

These were times of trial in both countries. The tide in tyrannical events rolled high.† All of the Cromwell adherents were narrowly watched.

The regicide judges, who had sat in the trial of the late king, — some of them, caught in England, were beheaded there; some of them escaped to foreign countries. Three of them at least, coming to Boston in 1660, were followed, and were pursued here, in Connecticut, in and about Hadley, Mass., and other places, by the king's constables. Fortunately, by flight and concealment, from place to place, in the caves of the wilderness, they escaped violent death.

---

* Eliot's Life, by Francis, p. 210.　　† 5 Hume, p. 434.

Thus, more than two hundred years ago, did John Eliot foreshadow our republican form of government in his "Christian Commonwealth," thus suppressed; yet his cautious plans and suggestions became popular, and lived to be adopted and sustained, by a noble nation, an hundred years after his death.

> " Truth crushed to earth shall rise again,
> The eternal years of God are hers."

ELIOT AND THE KING.

Still he takes courage. Invoking the angry king, Eliot makes him his friend, and also a contributor, in the carrying forward his mission to the Indian nations. With long and eloquent letters, he presented to the king translations of our English Old and New Testaments into the Indian language, and thereby obtained favor and patronage from the throne itself.*

REPUBLICAN GOVERNMENT.

The Hebrew commonwealth, organized and officered by Moses of old, undoubtedly had some influence upon the Apostle's action, in the forming of a commonwealth. In this respect, he could but see Moses had his seventy-two elders, which would answer to our U. S. Senate; his twelve tribes of Israel may be likened to the original thirteen United States; and his congregation of the people, as appears, may be taken to accord with our House of Representatives.

Moses himself, occupying the place of president, presided over the whole. Such a government is supposed

---

* Life of Eliot, pp. 258, 259.

to be the best, if not the strongest, of all. In this, Moses and Cromwell and Eliot and Washington all seem to agree.

ELIOT'S ORDER.

In all his operations, the Apostle was exact, and full of discipline. A civil officer, Major-General Gookin, a wise, conciliatory man, usually attended him. Gookin had been clothed, by the Colonial government, with a power of organization over the people, — a power, to a certain extent, both judicial and executive. So, it appears, Gookin appointed civil officers; sat as judge, holding courts; and issued commissions to the Indian rulers of hundreds or of fifties or of tens, as the tribes, under the Apostle, saw fit to elect them, and as the good of the Indian church, from time to time, seemed to require.*

Thus Eliot and Gookin, moving together, constituted an efficient, peaceful, executive power; and, at the same time, prudently led the way to a progressive Christian civilization.

LAW.

Believing order to be the first law of heaven, it was one of the axioms under which Eliot, in his economy, always moved. From his life and example we gather these rules:

1. There must always be a ruler, or leader, to every organization.

2. That a ruler, or leader, is never to be ignored, but

---

* Bigelow's His. of Natick, p. 22. Sketch of Life of Eliot, p. 17.

is always to be respected and followed, for the office' sake, if for nothing else.

3. That the first great maxim in a kingdom, to wit: that "the King can do no wrong" (though that may not be true in fact), is sound in principle, and unless revolution is intended, must be observed and followed throughout, from the king down to the humblest parent of a family.

RULERS.

A leader, once known, whether appointed of man or of God (as in case of a parent), *must* be recognized, and must always be followed. Everything else would be disorder; everything else is grief; everything else is revolution, distraction.

To illustrate this: take the leader of the family, and then the leader of a church organization, and then the leader of a town, or state, or of the United States, as may be seen in a President. Now every one of these, for the peace, safety, and well-being of the respective bodies which they severally represent, must be recognized as such, and followed.

For instance, our President,* although many may disapprove some of his acts and measures, yet, in a general sense, he must be upheld and sustained. What if he was not well chosen? He was so declared to be by the united force and voice of this great nation. Hence he must needs be sustained, otherwise anarchy, confusion, and general distraction would follow.

What if he did (as some have alleged) bargain away the rights of others, — tending to cripple the political liberties of the freed-man? What if he did extend a
* 1879.

conciliatory compromise to a Ku-Klux Clan, then armed offensively with thousands of rifles, threatening violence and blood? Even if all this be true, by the laws of God and the rules of government, it is but wise and just in the people to sustain him to the end of his term. Otherwise anarchy, distraction, and confusion would follow, and thousands of hearts would be made to bleed all over the land.

Hence, duteously, as Eliot would say, we must always follow the leader, — in the country at large, in the state, and in the family.* Thus, under the Apostle for the Indian church, as elsewhere, you would always find a leading ruler, with a teacher, and oftentimes an interpreter, having a watchful care over *ten* Christians, or over *thirty*, or over *fifty*, as the peace and prosperity of a Christian civilization might require. And to the praise of the red-men of the forest, Eliot's rules and ordinances were generally observed, respected, and obeyed as such by them.*

Although the Apostle, under the ordinations of God, with the discreet Gookin at his side as a magistrate, thus ruled, yet he never seemed to rule.

TEACHERS.

O that the spirit of John Eliot, in the sight of all these subjects, like the light of heaven at early morn, might break in upon us, to inspire our teachers to prepare themselves, that they may train the rising generations to the true science and economy of life; that we may all be trained to a becoming servitude, — to a code of genuine

---

* Cotton Mather's Magnalia, 3d B., Art. 2, p. 494.

good manners; without which there can be no substantial success in the world; that they may train their pupils, male and female, to love labor, industrious, ardent, economical labor, without which there can be no sound health, nor solid, enduring comfort; that we may be trained to fervent, lofty aspirations; that henceforth the wanderer may be reclaimed, and led upward in life to a more congenial condition, and thence onward to a glorious immortality.

Yes, let us be trained, if leaders, to lead justly, kindly, and judiciously. If mere servants we remain (and we are all more or less servants in this world), let us serve heartily and faithfully over everything, — throwing bread upon the waters, helping the needy neighbor first, and then ourselves, as Eliot would do.

Bear in mind, that man, in his best economy, lives, by helping others to live; and remember, there are roads enough to honor, and highways enough heavenward, "for all to go up, without crowding one another."

CIVIL POWERS.

All the way along in the Apostle's progress, there were many elements of power which had to be respected.

First of all, there was the parent English government at London, then distracted, as we have seen, by terrible conflicts. Then, there was the colonial government at Boston; and then, the loose, the rude, and undefined governments of the Indian nations. The rights and rules, habits and customs, of all these, at all times, were to be heeded and respected. For there is no nobler reward in this life, than the consciousness of having "rendered to all their dues."

CHAPTER II.

DISCIPLES.

Eliot had many pupils, first and last, — some in preparation for the ministry, some for teachers, interpreters, etc. Many of them were schooled at the Indian college at Cambridge, among whom there were Sassamon [*] and Ephraim, James the Printer, Daniel, Waban,[†] Piambo, Speen, Oonamo, Tukaperwillin, Ohatawan, Capt. Tom, Old Jethro, Numphow, John Thomas, Solomon, Samuel Peter, Nesutan,[‡] and many others. Among his white assistants, as clergymen, teachers, rulers, etc., there were Rawson, Gookin, Thracton, Dettins, Bandit, Noyes, Cotton, Mahew, Bourne, and some others.

ELIOT TAKES COURAGE.

From his lofty position, thus far he had been advancing, anticipating the obstacles which at times would roll in to hedge up his way, and which already were often encumbering him with many difficulties.

---

[*] Sassamon was murdered by Philip's Indians. — Memoirs of Eliot, ch. 14, p. 86.

[†] Waban served as Justice of the Peace at Natick, and held courts as such. One of his warrants reads thus: "You, You, big constable, quick you catch Jeremiah Offscow, strong you hold um, safe you bring um beffore me.

"WABAN, *Justice of the Peace.*"

[‡] Slain in battle fighting for the English at Mt. Hope. — Drake's American Indians, B. II, p. 51.

But now, in sight of the prospect, he is said to have broken out in the pathos of his warm and glowing heart: "I see [in the distance] the day-breaking, or the sun-rising, of the Gospel of Christ in New England."

INDIAN SERMON.

Among the many places where the tribes were wont to congregate, when they came up from their fishing and hunting excursions, was a place near Natick in Newton, called *Nonantum.* This, in Indian language, means a place of rejoicing. An intellectual Indian chief occupied it, by the name of *Waban.** And Waban's tent was there.

Previously a proclamation had been sent forth, that Eliot, on a given day, would preach to the native nations at Nonantum. Accordingly, on the twenty-eighth day of October, 1646, Eliot stood forth there, for the first time, an *Evangelist,* in the midst of the assembled sachems, powows, sanaps, necromancers, the red-man in his plumes, and squaws, women, and little children, painted and adorned, as in primeval life, with rustic beads and rings, and other appendages, fashionable and ornamental. Eliot stands forth, above them, proclaiming his text (Ezekiel xxxvii, 9): "Prophesy! unto the wind, prophesy, son of man! and say to the wind, — Thus saith the Lord God, Come from the four winds, O breath; and breathe upon these slain, that they may live!"

All are silent. Above, as he stands over the multitude, there is an open sky. The bleak winds of heaven are moving the brave old tree-tops into silent, secret

---

* Life of Eliot, pp. 27, 28, 79, 80. Sketch of Life of Eliot, p. 13.

whisperings. The voice of infidelity, the war-whoop, the Indian wood-cry, and the howlings of the wild beast, are hushed for the time being. The Apostle's prayer went up to the God of the Red-man! They sung a song of Zion, — a sermon from that text, and from that trumpet-toned, apostolic voice, reverberating, fell upon the hearts of the then heathen inhabitants of this New England world, for the first time.

Next? There 's something strange in the sun, — something strange in the earth and in the skies.

What ails that sanap out there? What ails the soothsayers, and the necromancers, that the pipes they were smoking have unconsciously fallen from their lips? Out yonder, what ails that young squaw upon the leaf-covered ground, with little children about her, that tears, forbidden, are falling from her eye-lids? And afar off, what ails the brave old Waban, at the door of his tent, weeping?

What is it but that a live coal from the altar of God hath touched Waban's heart?

Ah! how true! how propitious! Waban is beginning to sing that new song, which no man of his race ever had sung in New England, from the beginning of the world.

Thence, that point, that place in the wilderness, emphatically had become a place of rejoicing, ever afterwards to be held sacred. Indeed, it had become to the tribes a temple of worship, a gateway to heaven.

NATICK.

Near to Nonantum, Eliot obtained a gift (or exchange) of lands, on which to build up and organize an Indian town, which they called *Natick*, and which, in their language, means "a place of the hills."

This Indian town was peopled, organized, and officered by Indians, — all the affairs of which were conducted in a perfectly orderly manner, by its Christian Indian inhabitants, for nearly a century, all through the remainder of the Apostle's life, and for nearly fifty years afterwards.

At Natick, Eliot, often attended by his Indian ministry, continued to meet the assembled tribes of red-men, up to the end of his days, as well as in other Indian towns, then fast becoming civilized, within his spacious fields of labor.

Praying Indians.

These numbered (up to the commencement of King Philip's war, 1674) 1,150; first and last, in all, as some say, 3,600.

Infidelity.

Many of the English settlers, from the beginning of Eliot's undertaking, professed to have no faith in the effort to civilize an Indian.

This, at the outset, tended to embarrass and afflict the Evangelist. The desperado, thus aided by the weak and jealous white man, who ought to have known better, obtained encouragement.

And thus, oftentimes, his progress was retarded by a secret foe within the camp. Yet the labors and achievements of John Eliot were more than equal to those of ten ordinary active men put together, and his great mission moved onward.

He soared so far above the mediocrity of his fellow-laborers in the vineyard, that the musketry of "the sappers and miners," who are always combining and advancing, in pursuit of great and good men, to traduce them, never could reach him.

SUNSHINE AND THE CLOUD.

Many years of his mission had now passed away. Through storm and sunshine, he had already labored among the tribes (from 1646 up to 1674) twenty-eight years. In the mean time, our English Bible had been made, by the Apostle, to speak the *Indian* language. And our then New England wilderness, in its openings, had been dotted with little Christian churches.

But, alas! there is a war-cloud in the heavens. King Philip is angry, meditating war and blood. John Sassamon, an Indian pupil and preacher, who had been schooled in the Indian college at Cambridge, hath been murdered by Philip's men.

Sassamon, heedlessly, while serving with Philip as an interpreter, etc., had divulged to the English Philip's secret purpose of making war against them.*

King Philip, obtaining knowledge of this supposed treachery of Sassamon, instigated three of his Indians to murder him; and this gave rise to the trial of these murderers in an English court. All this tended to hasten a dread conflict. The war-trump is sounding. It comes like the rushing of a terrible tempest, threatening devastation and death all over this western New England world. The tomahawk and scalping-knife, on

---

* Hubbard's Indian Wars, pp. 78, 79, 80. Bacon's History of Natick, pp. 29, 30.

the one hand, and the English bayonet and the deadly sabre on the other, are beginning to be sharpened.

Alas! as against the vengeance of conflicting races, as against ten thousand carnal weapons, upraised, threatening extermination, indeed, what is to become of the faithful old Eliot and his Christian churches?

Ah! when the beautiful oriole, down from a leafless, wintry sky, animated by the sun-beams of spring, hath hung her nest to a branch of the tree-top on high, she takes joyful pleasure in that little church-like charge of hers, which she holds at the hand of nature's God — her joys are the joys of Heaven.

But there is a cloud in the sky; and there are fearful mutterings beyond the mountains; and the tempestuous gale howls; and, coming down, sweeps away the tree-top, madly dashing that dearest little family of hers to the deadly earth!

Now, in the agonies of despair, she flies from place to place, afflicted; and she mourns — mourned, as we now have it, the dear old Eliot, in prospect, thus doomed, must mourn.

But when the clouds had cleared away, and when time, that great healer of hearts that bleed, had brought another lovely day, that little mother dried her tears (if tears they have), and she turned again to her duteous labors, bringing sticks, and strings, and other material things, and builds aloft another habitation; and soon rears, and faithfully takes charge of, another little God-praising, parent-loving family.

In this similitude, I briefly foreshadow that part of John Eliot's life, which, among other things, coming as lessons from his exemplary wife, will be elaborated in my next chapters.

Still there is a cry without — King Philip is on the war-path! Murder! murder! Sassamon is murdered of Philip's Indians! The terrible trump of war, afar, is blowing its blast, with dread alarms, reverberating all over the settlements!

Meanwhile, the three Indian murderers — Mattashunanamo, Wam-pappaquam, and Tobias — arrested by English officers, are brought into court at Plymouth, to be tried by English judges.* The judges are there, and the jury is there, with five red men added to it, as advisers, or as a mere show of fairness; and the Indian prisoner, above named, are there, standing, trembling, doomed, upon an indictment, to be tried for their lives. An allegation in the indictment reads as follows: —

" *For that being accused, that they did with joynt consent vpon the 29 of January anno 1674 att a place called Assowamset pond wilfully and of sett purpose and of malice fore thought and by force and armes murder John Sassamon another indian, by laying violent hands on him and striking him, or twisting his necke, vntil hee was dead; and to hyde and conceale this theire said murder att the tyme and place aforesaid did cast his dead body through a hole of the ice into the said pond.*"

It is now that the much-suspected, much-feared King Philip enters that court; and, denying the right of the English to try his own Indian subjects, for the killing of an Indian, promulgates his own notions of law and right, in language purporting, in substance, to be a plea to their jurisdiction; if we may speak in poetic form, substantially thus: —

---

* Hubbard, Hist. of Indian Wars, pp. 80–82. Hist. of Natick, pp. 29, 30.

What right, what law, these prisoners to arraign,
Have Englishmen, in this, my own domain ?
What lease of venue, from allotted lines,
To make invasions, and to adjudge of crimes!
Why seek the Indian's life, in guile forlorn,
Of these three men, of native mothers born?
Who one and all, with Sassamon, the slain,
Were my liege subjects, bound by laws the same,
Which governed tribes a thousand years ago,
But which, evaded, brings an endless woe.
What mind, what project, points your boundless sway,
But hence to drive the red-man, far away
From this fair land, his birthright and his wealth,
And hold these regions vast, through royal stealth!
With flagrant wrong, the tribes will ne'er concur,
And to your bold intrusion, I demur!
My subjects here, an English court may try, —
By spurious judgments, they may fall and die;
Yet *vengeance*, dread, shall point the red-man's steel,
And to the God of battles I 'll appeal!
Philip withdrew, and ne'er returned again;
His truthful talk was uttered but in vain;
The prisoners held, and thus condemned to die,
Brought darkness, gathering o'er this western sky;
The bloody sunset, and the forkèd light,
That broke the curtain of that fearful night,
Awaking English matrons, 'mid alarms,
To hug sweet infants with tenacious arms,
Foretold gross carnage of successive years,
And devastations in a land of tears.
True to his word which danger thus defied,
Philip the pilgrims fought, and fighting died;
With countless victims by the self-same blade
Which mutual madness had in folly made.*

---

* From my Epics, Lyrics, and Ballads, p. 344.

7

CHAPTER III.

IN the foregoing chapters we have spoken of the lessons which ought to be learned from John Eliot's life and character; have alluded to his birth in England, to his education there, and to his arrival at Boston in the month of November, 1631; and in the narration have told of his former friends landing here in the following year, and settling at Roxbury; how he then and there became their pastor, and remained their minister to the end of his long life; how, for the first fifteen years, he preached solely to the white-man; how, during that time, he was educating Indian boys to the English language, and white men's boys to the Indian language; and how, in the same period, he had prepared many young men for the ministry, that they might, in the Indian .dialect, preach to the tribes of the wilderness; and how, at the same time, he had begun to make our English Bible speak the Indian language. And when he had prepared his young ministry to follow him in succession to the apostolic work, he then, Oct. 20, 1646, amid the Indian wigwams in the wilderness, preached his first sermon to the assembled tribes at Nonantum. How Natick was obtained of the government, for the organization of an Indian town; how it was officered by Indians, who administered the government of it, as Christian citizens, for nearly a century. How our apostle, from the first, advanced as a leader, a law-giver, and as an evangelist; how he wrote up his "Christian Commonwealth," favoring a republican government under the great Protector, Oliver Cromwell; how Cromwell, then dying (1658), and before the book effectually issued from the press, Eliot, at the frown of the king, and at the command of our colonial government, suppressed it, and thus saving his mission, and perhaps his own head, he appeased the wrath of Charles the Second, who had then been crowned king of the reinstated kingdom under which our fathers lived. His two letters to the king, the one written in 1661, and the other in 1663, are given below.

To the High and Mighty Prince Charles the Second, by the Grace of God, King of England, Scotland, France and Ireland, Defender of the Faith, &c., the Commissioners of United Colonies in New-England with increase of all happiness, &c.

MOST DREAD SOVEREIGN : —

If our weak apprehensions have not misled us, this work will be no unacceptable present to your Majesty as having a greater interest therein, than we believe is generally understood, which (upon this occasion) we deem it our duty to declare.

The people of these four Colonies (confederated for mutual defence in the time of the late distractions of our dear native country) your Majesty's natural born subjects, by the favor and grant of your father and grandfather, of famous memory, put themselves upon this great and hazardous undertaking, of planting themselves at their own charge in these remote ends of the earth, that, without offence and provocation to our Brethren, and Countrymen, we might enjoy that liberty to worship God, which our consciences informed us was not only our right, but duty; as also that we might (if it so pleased God) be instrumental to spread the light of the Gospel, the knowledge of the Son of

God, our Saviour, to the poor barbarous heathen, which by his late Majesty, in some of our Patents, is declared to be his principal aim.

These honest and pious intentions have, through the grace and goodness of God, and our kings, been seconded with proportionable success;

That other part of our errand hither hath been attended with endeavors and blessing, many of the wild Indians being taught, and understanding the doctrine of the Christian religion, and with much affection attending such preachers as are sent to teach them, many of their children are instructed to write and read, and some of·them have proceeded further, to attain the knowledge of the Latin and Greek tongues, and are brought up with our English youths in University learning. There are divers of them that can, and do read some parts of the Scripture, and some catechisms which formerly have been translated into their own language, which hath occasioned the undertaking of a greater work, viz., the printing of the whole Bible, which (being translated by a painful labor amongst them, who was desirous to see the work accomplished in his day) hath already proceeded to finishing the New Testament, which we here humbly present to your Majesty, as the first fruits and accomplishments of the pious design of your royal ancestors.

" Sir : — The shines of your royal favor upon these undertakings, will make these undertakings to flourish, notwithstanding any malevolent aspect from those that bear evil will to this Lion, and render Your Majesty more illustrious and glorious to after generations.

The God of heaven long preserve and bless Your Majesty with many happy days, to his glory, — the good and comfort of his Church and people. — Amen."

LETTER II.

MOST DREAD SOVEREIGN : —

As our former presentation of the New Testament was graciously accepted by your Majesty, so with all humble thankfulness for that royal favor, and with the like hope, we are bold now to present the *whole Bible*, translated into the language of the natives of this country, by a painful laborer in that work, and now printed and finished, by means of the pious beneficence of Your Majesty's subjects in England; which also by your special favor hath been continued and confirmed, to the intended use and advancement of so great and good a work as is the Propagation of the Gospel to these poor barbarians in this (erewhile) unknown world.

Translations of the Holy Scriptures,—the Word of the King of kings,—have ever been deemed not unworthy of the most princely dedications; examples whereof are extant in divers languages. But your Majesty is the first which hath received one in this language, or from the American world, or from any parts so remote from Europe as these are, for aught that ever we heard of.

Publication also of these sacred writings to the sons of men (who here, and here only, have the ministers of their eternal salvation revealed to them by the God of heaven) is a work that the greatest princes have honored themselves by.

But, to publish and communicate the same to a lost people, as remote from knowledge and civility, much more from Christianity, as they were from all showing, civil and Christian nations,—a people without law, without letters, without riches, or means to procure any such thing,—a people that sat as deep in darkness and in the shadow of death as (we think) any since the creation. This puts a lustre upon it that is superlative, and to have given royal patronage and countenance to such a publication, or to the means thereof, will stand among the marks of lasting honor in the eyes of all that are considerate, even unto after generations.

And, though there be in this Western world many Colonies of other European nations, yet we humbly conceive, no prince has had a return of such a work as this; which may be some token of the success of your Majesty's plantation of *New England*, undertaken and settled under the encouragement and security of your royal father and grandfather, of famous memory, and cherished with like gracious aspects from your Majesty.

Though indeed the present Poverty of these plantations could not have accomplished this work had not the forementioned Bounty of England lent Relief; nor could that have continued to stand us in stead, without the Influence of Your Royal Favor and Authority, whereby the Corporation there for Propagating the Gospel among these Natives hath been established and encouraged, (whose Labor of Love, Care and Faithfulness in that Trust, must ever be remembered with Honor;) yea, when private persons, for their private Ends, have of late sought Advantages to deprive the said Corporation of Half the Possessions that had been by Liberal Contributions, obtained for so Religious Ends. We understand that, by an Honorable and Righteous Decision in your Majesty's Court of Chancery, their Hopes have been defeated, and the Thing settled where it was and is; for which great favor and illustrious fruit of Your Majesty's Government we cannot but return our most humble thanks in this Public manner; and as the result of the joint Endeavors of Your Majesty's subjects, there and here, acting under your Royal Influence, We present You with this work, which upon sundry accounts is to be called *yours*.

Religion is the End and Glory of mankind, and as it was the professed End of this Plantation, so we design ever to keep it in our eye as our main design, (both to ourselves and the natives about us,) and that our products may be answerable thereunto. Give us therefore leave, (Dread Sovereign) yet *again* humbly to beg the continuance of your Royal Favor, and of the Influences thereof, upon this poor plantation, The United Colonies of New England, for the securing and establishment of our Civil Privileges and Religious Liberties hitherto enjoyed; and upon this Good Work of Propagating Religion to these Natives, that the Supports and Encouragements thereof from *England* may be still countenanced and confirmed.

May this Nursling still suck the Breast of Kings, and be fostered by your Majesty, as it hath been by your Royal Predecessors, unto the preservation of its Main Concernments. It shall thrive and prosper to the Glory of God and the Honor of your Majesty. Neither will it be any loss or grief unto our Lord the

King, to have the blessing of the Poor to come upon Him, and that from these Ends of the Earth.

The God by whom Kings Reign and Princes Decree Justice, Bless Your Majesty and establish your Throne in Righteousness, in Mercy and in Truth, to the Glory of His Name, the Good of His People, and to your own Comfort and Rejoicing, not in this only but in another World."

PROGRESS.

I have already spoken of the New England landscape as seen in 1631; of the location of the various Indian nations, then roaming upon it, wild hunters of the wilderness. We come now to speak more particularly of Eliot's perseverance and progress in the fourteen Indian towns, of his care, and of his 3,600 praying Indians, up to 1674, when the tearful terrors of Philip's war began to becloud New England, bringing dread dismay to the souls of men, women, and children. How previously, in 1648, the four colonies heedlessly, and perhaps unintentionally, retarded Eliot's mission of love, by permitting the use of carnal weapons, with all their appalling consequences, as against Christianity; and by giving their unjust assent to the same, as may be seen in the murder of that life-long Englishman's friend, the brave old Miantonimo.* Thus many instances of cruelty and of crime came like clouds, floating in, polluting the atmosphere, all tending to hedge up Eliot's highway to civilization and Christianity.

Yet in spite of these terrible happenings; in spite of all the carnal outrages on the one side and on the other, —of war, of conflagration, of skirmishes, and murders

---

* My Duston, and New England Wars, pp. 160-169.

in the midst of his people, Eliot's mission of love had prospered all the way through. Up to 1674, he had made constant, fruitful progress.

His Care for Schools.

From the first, Eliot had evinced uncommon interest towards the rising generations. Cotton Mather bears testimony to his strong force in that direction.

At one of the synods held in Boston, Mather says: "I heard Eliot pray: 'Lord! for schools everywhere among us;* that our schools may flourish; that every member of this assembly may go home, to procure a good school to be encouraged, in the town where he lives; that before we die, we may all be happy to see a good school established in every part of the country.'"

Indian Schools.

So it was, by his resistless force of character, as time advanced, an Indian college at Cambridge, being erected, was supplied with students for the ministry; and thus his disciples, both red and white, were schooled to be his successors in the vast undertaking of evangelizing the red-men of New England. Up to 1674, Eliot's mission had advanced, and his progress had been favored, apparently, by the great Head of the Church.

Rulers and Ministers.

Many assistants, as well as successors, were needful to his mission. Proceeding to the translation of the Bible into

---

* Memoirs of Eliot, p. 74. Adams' Life of Eliot, p. 51.

the Indian tongue, scholars, well tutored in the languages, both Indian and English, had become a necessity. Hence, many had been raised up as volunteers, to enter his field of progress, as teachers, as rulers, as printers, as translators, and as ministers, to supply the various towns where the Apostle had established churches, or Indian preaching stations.

In all this, as we have seen, Eliot had been encouraged by the aid of "a Society" in the old world, organized there, "for the propagation of the Gospel in New England"; and by Cromwell, by the Colonial government here, and otherwise. For in his pastorate at Roxbury, where he preached but once in two weeks generally, the remainder of his time being devoted to his books, and to the various tribes, as they gave him gospel gatherings, in the wilderness or near the sea-shore, he was sustained by a constant salary to the end of his life.

CONFERENCE OF SAGAMORES.

On the 10th of June, 1651, having called together, from all quarters, the many sachems and sagamores, and their attendants, of New England, he held a discourse with them, on the subject of religious worship, and of carrying his great undertaking into effect.

On that occasion, they were induced to subscribe to a general approval of his purpose, and among other things, they made choice of rulers, as follows: one ruler for an hundred men; two rulers of fifty each; ten rulers of ten men each.*

---

* Drake's American Indians, B. II, p. 113. Mather's Magnalia, B. III, p. 512. Memoirs of Eliot, p. 67. Life of Eliot, pp. 117, 118.

Before the adjournment, they signed Eliot's covenants, and endorsed their consent generally to the days of fasting and prayer, which, on that occasion, had been appointed.

THE COVENANT

which the Indians had signed, though somewhat long, was to the point. It began, and ended, thus:—

"We are the sons of Adam. We and our Fathers have a long time been lost in our sins; but now the mercy of the Lord begins to find us out again. . . . Oh! Jehovah, teach us wisdom in thy Scriptures! Let the grace of Christ help us, because Christ is the wisdom of God. Send thy spirit into our hearts, and let it teach us! Take us to be thy people—and let us take Thee to be our God!"*

CHURCH AT NATICK.

In the year 1661, Eliot's first Indian church was organized, it being a day of baptisms. At this date he had completed his translation of the New Testament. In 1663 he had also completed the printing of the Old Testament in the Indian language. At this, it is said, the commissioners of the four colonies were greatly pleased.

He then proceeded to the translation of the Psalter; and then to the "Practice of Piety," which, being printed in the Indian language, became popular among the tribes, who took several editions of it in the years 1665 and 1667, and up to 1687.

---

* Memoirs of Eliot, ch. 13, pp. 83, 84.

In 1666, Mr. Eliot had established a lecture station at Natick, his first Indian town; and about the same time, making proclamation, he called together a multitude of Indians at Marshpee. There he took from them confessions of their Christian knowledge, faith, and practice. Afterwards (Aug. 17, 1670), Mr. Bourne was ordained over the native church at Natick.

PEACE.

In the year 1671,* the settlers in Plymouth colony were threatening to make war against a neighboring tribe, the Missokonog Indians. Eliot hearing of this, and trembling for the safety of his Indian churches, at once dispatched a committee to proceed to that place of danger, as mediators, with instructions (from Eliot) as follows: —

We, the poor church at Natick, hearing that the honored Rulers, and good People of Plymouth, are pressing, and arming soldiers to go to war against the Mis-so-konog Indians, for what cause we know not. Though they pray not to God, we hope they will! And we do mourn, and pray for them, and desire greatly that they may not be destroyed. Especially because we have not heard that they have done anything worthy of death.

Therefore we do send these two brethren, Anthony and William, who were formerly our messengers to those parts; — and we request John Sassamon† to join them —

---

* Bacon's History of Natick, pp. 24–86.
† Sassamon was afterwards slain. — Drake, B. III, p. 9.

And this trust we commit unto you, our dear brethren and beloved —

First, to go to the misso-konog Indians, or who else may be concerned, in the quarrel; — tell them the poor churches in Natick, send them two Scriptures.

When thou comest nigh unto a city to fight against it, then proclaim peace unto it.

And it shall be, if it make thee answer of peace, and open unto thee, then it shall be, that all the people that is found therein shall be tributaries unto thee, and they shall serve thee.'

* Dare any of you, having a matter against another, go to law before the unjust, and not before the saints?

" 'Do ye not know that the saints shall judge the world? and if the world shall be judged by you, are ye unworthy to judge the smallest matters?

" 'Know ye not that we shall judge angels? How much more things that pertain to this life?

" 'If then ye have judgments of things pertaining to this life, set them to judge who are least esteemed in the church.

" 'I speak to your shame. Is it so, that there is not a wise man among you? no, not one that shall be able to judge between his brethren?

" 'But brother goeth to law with brother, and that before the unbelievers.' †

"If they of Missokonog accept this our exhortation, tell them, that the Church, also, have sent you to the Governor; — tell him that the Church hath sent you to be mediators of peace; — on behalf of the Missokonog Indians, or any other of their neighbors — . . .

---

* Deut. xx, 10, 11.   † 1 Cor. vi, 1-6.

"Nay, — beseech them all, to consider, what comfort it will be, to *kill*, or to *be* killed, — when no capital sin hath been committed, or defended by them —

"And we request you, our beloved brethren, to be speedy, in your motions. We shall endeavor to follow you in our prayers ; — and shall long to hear of a happy *peace*, — that may open a clear door for the passage of the gospel among the people.

"Thus, commending you to God, in prayer, — we do send you forth, upon this great service of peace-making, which is evidently the flower and glory of Christ's kingdom."

(Signed)   JOHN ELIOT,

with the consent $\}$

NATICK, *Aug.* 1, 1671.   *of the Church.*

INDIAN STATIONS.

About this time, the Apostle had towns of Christian Indians as follows : —

Natick, his first town, had in it some 29 families, and 145 inhabitants, occupying 6,000 acres of land. Here, as perhaps in other localities, the Indian people on the Lord's days, and on other lecture days, were called together at the sound of a drum.

Pakemit (Stoughton), then reckoned to be 14 miles south of Boston, contained 12 families, and 60 Indians, occupying 6,000 acres of land.

Has-sa-namesit (Grafton) had a church organized in 1671. About 30 of the natives had been baptized. It is said, in general, they all sustained the Sabbath, and church-worship, in a becoming manner.

Okom-ma-kemesit (Marlboro'), then 30 miles west of

Boston, had 10 native families, cultivated 6,000 acres of soil, with orchards planted by Indians. Solomon was their teacher.

Nashobah (Littleton), then 25 miles west-northwest from Boston, contained 10 Indian families and 50 souls, holding lands 4 miles square. John Thomas was their teacher.

Wagum-qua-cog, situated between Natick and Grafton, had 11 native families and 55 inhabitants, who, as appears, "worshipped God, kept the Sabbath, and adhered to the duties of civil order." Job was their teacher.

Pentucket (or Tewksbury), situated at the confluence of the Merrimac and Concord Rivers, contained 2,500 acres, had 15 Indian families, and 75 souls.*

Numphow lived here, as their ruler, and his son Samuel (named by the English) served his father here, as an assistant teacher. They had been educated at the expense of that society in England of which we have spoken.

This being a favorable fishing station, the tribes at certain seasons, from various quarters, often congregated here.

Eliot had sometimes preached at Pawtucket Falls during the long life-time of *Passaconaway.*† This venerable sachem was generally present to hear the sermon, to which he and his tribes usually listened attentively.

One day at the Falls, after the sermon, the Indians propounded to the Apostle many questions.

At one time (1648) the old chief, who probably had seen, upon these hill-sides, the frosts of an hundred

---

* Memoirs of Eliot, pp. 101, 102, 140.
† Drake's American Indians, B. III, pp. 93, 94.

winters, rose up at the close of the service, and publicly announced his belief in the Englishman's God. Among other things, Eliot himself speaks of him thus : —

" He said he never heard of God before as he now doth; that he would consider the matter, — and would persuade his two sons [then present] to do the same."

The Text

(Malachi i, 11), translated for the occasion, was as follows : " From the rising of the sun to the going down of the same, my name shall be great among the 'Indians'; and in every place, prayers shall be made unto my name; and a pure 'prayer';—for my name shall be great, among the 'Indians' (saith the Lord ' of hosts')." *

At Wamesit Again.

On the 5th of May, 1674, Eliot comes once again, to meet the assembled tribes, — Major-General Gookin attending the Apostle, — and holds a court here. They were together when they came, and when they went away.

Public notice had been given for the convention of the tribes, held at that time, where the Eliot Church, in Lowell, now stands. Gathering in, they filled up the space-way between the wigwams on that hill-side, to hear the Apostle, — all curious, all anxious.

At that time, the dark cloud, which had begun to overshadow New England, portending war, brought dread fear to all. This must have quickened the footstep of the Christian red-man, as he came in with his

---

* Francis' Life of Eliot, p. 107.

squaw and little ones, coming, as they did, from Amos-
keag and other places, that they might learn lessons, and
be encouraged by that great and good man, the Apostle!

Thus, now, the many tribes are here; Numphow is
here; Samuel and Wonalancet are here; and Gookin is
here. The sun has gone down beyond the Wachusette
hills; the shades of night are spread out in the skies;
the din of Pawtucket Falls is audible; and beneath the
stars of heaven, as they seem to gaze down approvingly,
the voice of the Evangelist, like the voice of a God, falls
in upon the assembled tribes, at Wamesit, for the last,
last time.*

WONALANCET.

He, then about fifty years of age, being present, was
seriously impressed among others; and rising up at the
close of the discourse, addressed Eliot and Gookin
thus : —

"Sirs, you have been pleased for four years, in your
abundant love, to apply yourselves particularly unto me
and my people; to exhort, press, and persuade us to
pray (to God). I am thankful to you for your pains. I
must acknowledge, have all my days been used to pass
in an old canoe; and you exhort me to change that old
canoe, to which I have hitherto been unwilling. But
now, I yield to your advice."†

He was a son of Passaconaway. The father, at the
age of more than a century (as recorded), had gone
hence. The son succeeding him, as chief sachem of the
Penacooks, including the Wamesits, had spread his

---

* Text, Matt. xxii, 1–14.   † Memoirs of Eliot, p. 102.

wigwam tent here, — and here, upon our beautiful Fort Hill, had erected his fortification, as we have seen. This was at about the beginning of dread hostilities, — during which, being a peace-maker, Wonalancet fled away with many of his men; but returned, when he had reason to believe the conflict had come to an end. At length (1677), disgusted with the repeated, unprovoked ill-treatment of some of the settlers towards him and his kindred race, he, after selling out all his lands, finally wandered away into Canada, leaving his native hills, — and never, never returned.*

Eliot's Progress.

In 1674, and up to that time, although terrible difficulties had intervened, yet Zion, even in a wilderness of many conflicts, as appears, had made progress. But now, through the threatenings of King Philip, under the many outrages of individual settlers, a terrible war is at hand.

The very elements are angry, and the muttering thunders of war are everywhere breaking in against Eliot's mission, and against the Christian civilization of the New England tribes.

The top of Zion's tree, so to speak, on which Eliot's Indian churches hang, is now beginning to be tossed by the tempest; the tornado gathers blackness, and the lightnings, followed by thunderbolts, are shooting down from the skies, chilling the blood of mortals, and, in spite of the Apostle and his peaceful Christians, distracting the populace, and turning their God-given love into mad-

* Drake's His., B. III, pp. 95–97.

9

ness, cruelty, and blood. Beneath its blackness are the fagot and the tomahawk, with all their nightly and morning horrors. Indeed, on the one side and on the other, it is known to be a war of extermination, — a war, not based upon the overwhelming power of Christian love, but upon the madness of brute force, wielding the blood-stained weapons of demons, — a war in which the peaceful Christian Indian will not be allowed to stand neutral; but is to be compelled to take up arms against his own kindred race, or be manacled, imprisoned, or slain by the white man ; and a war in which the Bible, the Psalter, and the Prayer-book are to be laid aside, giving place to the deadly carnal weapon.

To all this, Eliot, in the agonies of his heart, demurred.

CHAPTER IV.

The Alternative.

So it was; every neutral Indian, by the colonial government, was branded as an enemy, however pure in thought or deed, or circumspect in life, he might be.

Under this pressure, some of the natives, not being willing to allow their own kindred people to be destroyed, fled into the ranks of King Philip; some of them took up arms for the English; some of them, like Wonalancet, seeking peace, wandered away into the dense wilderness afar off; * while Eliot's non-resistant, Christian red-men were seized, as at Natick, manacled, and boated down Charles River, and were held at Deer Island as prisoners of war.†

James the Printer.

In sight of the dread alternative thus offered, in which Eliot's Indians were doomed to take sides, James, although always heretofore faithful to the white man, now turning, fled away, and joined his kindred nationality. He served under King Philip, and was found with Philip's forces in the invasion of Lancaster, which captured Mrs.

---

* Dearborn's Sketch of Eliot's Life, p. 15.
† Francis' Life of Eliot, pp. 277, 278.

Rowlandson, and held her for some months in captivity.* James had a desire, it seems, to save his race from the extermination then impending; yet remembering, as he must, the many good things which he had learned from the Apostle, redeemed himself in favoring the redemption of Mrs. Rowlandson from her captivity as follows. Long had this pious lady sought redemption, after extreme abuse, privation, and sorrow, but in vain. Being a clergyman's wife, a great price for her release was demanded.

One day, Mr. Hoar, with others from Boston, by permission entered King Philip's wigwam camp in the forest, to obtain this lady from captivity, and offering to Quinnopin, her master, an hundred dollars. He refused to give her up. The savage said it was not enough, and persisted in the refusal. It was all the money; and Mrs. Rowlandson is seen weeping, in a distracted, hopeless condition. James the Printer, seeing this, and his Christianized heart touched by the incident, approaching Mr. Hoar, said, "Go again to Quinnopin [her master]; offer him the hundred dollars again, and give him a pint of rum." His suggestion was obeyed; the money, *with the rum*, was accepted; and the oppressed captive was set free.

Soon afterwards this lady went forth with her revered husband, both as missionaries in New England preaching the gospel, until he was slain by the tribes; and then Mrs. Rowlandson prepared and published her popular book often found in our Sabbath schools, in which she gives many a startling incident of her captivity.

---

* Drake's American Indians, B. II, pp. 50, 51.

JOB NESUTAN.*

Nesutan, another of Eliot's disciples, when the dread alternative came, taking sides in the use of carnal weapons, elected to turn into the fight in behalf of the English. Job had been long with James the Printer in Eliot's service; was a good linguist in the English tongue, had worked on the Bible and other books as a printer in the Indian language. In war he proved a valiant soldier, and fell in the fight during the first expedition at Mount Hope.

OLD JETHRO.

This pious Indian preacher had labored in the vineyard under Eliot and Gookin at Lancaster and other places, and had been long in the service. But, sad for him, when the dread alternative of the contest offered itself, he was found on the side of his own kindred and countrymen. This was the extent of his crime; yet the last his Christian brethren saw of him, he was in the hands of desperadoes on the briery pathway to Boston, with a rope about his neck, to be hanged.† And the Christian "cry" of Old Jethro was heard no more "in the wilderness."

Thus it was that numerous desperadoes could have their own way, when carnal weapons had obtained the ascendency, encouraged, as they were, by the barbarous examples of cruelty and torture which had long lived to disgrace the government of England.

---

* Drake's American Indians, B. II, p. 51.
† Jethro. See Drake's American History, pp. 81, 83, 90.

DEATH OF KING PHILIP.

True it is, and it is but just to say it, when King Philip, in the fight for his country and nation, had been shot down in his native forest, his lifeless body torn asunder, and divided, was borne away in pieces as by brute beasts; and then the wife and the son were sold into slavery. Against all these, and other practices of the kind, Eliot, by his eloquence, by prayer and petition, constantly remonstrated. Philip is no more.*

> "He felt his life-blood freezing fast;
> He grasped his bow, his lance and steel;
> He was of Wampanoag's last,
> To die were easy — not to yield.
>
> "His eyes were fixed upon the sky;
> He gasped, as on the ground he fell;
> None but his foes to see him die;
> None but his foes his death to tell."

THE SHAM FIGHT.

As truth impels us, we turn next to the great Training. About a month after the death of King Philip, the war then being supposed to be ended, proclamation had been made by the English, that on the sixth day of September, 1676, there was to be a great training at Cocheco (Dover, N. H.), in which the red-man, from every part of New England, was invited to participate. That day arrived. The peaceful Wonalancet was there; four hundred other Indians were there; among whom were that scattered and bereaved remnant of Eliot's men, from

---

* Drake's Amer. Indians, Book III, pp. 42–44.

KING PHILIP, KILLED.

Wamesit, and from other places;—some of whom had
been pressed into the fight, as against a strong desire to
be neutral; some of them, peaceful, had fled away, but
had returned at the joyful news of peace;—and all,
willing to join the white man, bringing the Christian
olive-branch, had, as invited, come to the great training
at Cocheco. The brigade was formed, Major Waldron,
who four years afterwards was slain at midnight, was
the commanding-general of the day. In the order of
military exercises, there was to be a sham fight. In this,
the Indians, without weapons, were stationed to the
drag-ropes of the field-pieces of the artillery. The English, of course, had charge of the guns. All being ready
for the onset, a signal was given, by the discharge of a
field-piece; at which, by a preconcerted manœuvre, the
English infantry, closing in upon the Indians on all
sides, seized, manacled, and confined them all as prisoners of war.*

Thus, at Cocheco, were assembled the Wamesits, the
Penacooks, the Ossipees, Pequawkets, and others. all at
the pretended peace-making beck of the English; and
were under the benign protection, as they thought, of
the peaceful Wonalancet, and of Eliot's Christian civilization. But, alas! they were all prisoners.

Then and there, without a trial, they were separated,
the peaceable from the perfidious. About two hundred
of them with Wonalancet, then thought to be harmless,
were released. The other two hundred, being suspected
of evil intent, were marched or boated away to Boston.

---

* Hubbard, historian of that day, complacently says: "They were hand-
somely surprised, without the loss of any person's life, to the number of
400 Indians." Drake, B. III, pp. 96, 97.

Seven or eight of them were hanged as supposed murderers; some of them were sent to other parts; some of them sold into slavery.*

PETITION OF JOHN ELIOT AGAINST THE SALE OF INDIANS.

To the Hon. Gov. and Council, sitting at Boston, this 13th of the 6th, 1675.

THE HUMBLE PETITION OF JOHN ELIOT   SHEWETH:

That the terror of selling away such Indians unto the Islands for perpetual slaves, who shall yield up themselves to your mercy, is like to be an effectual prolongation of the war, and such an exasperation of them, as may produce we know not what evil consequences upon all the land.

Christ hath said, blessed are the merciful for they shall obtain mercy. This usage of them is worse than death. The design of Christ in these last days is not to extirpate nations, but to gospelize them. His sovreign hand and grace hath brought the gospel into these dark places of the earth. When we came we declared to the world (and it is recorded) yea, we are engaged by our Letters Patent from the King's Majesty, — that the endeavour of the Indians' conversion, *not their extirpation*, was one great end of our enterprise in coming to these ends of the earth. The Lord hath so succeeded that work as that, by his grace, they have the Holy Scriptures, and sundry of themselves able to teach their countrymen the good knowledge of God. And however some of them have refused to receive the gospel, and now are incensed in their spirits unto a *war against the English*, yet I doubt not that the meaning of Christ is to open a door for the free passage of the gospel among them.

My humble request is, that *you would* follow Christ's design in this matter, to promote the free passage of religion among them, and *not destroy them.*

To sell souls for money seemeth to me a dangerous merchandise. To sell them away from all means of grace, when Christ has provided means of grace for them, is *the* way for us to be active in the destroying their souls. Deut. xxiii, 15, 16, a fugitive servant from a pagan master might not be delivered to his master, but be kept in Israel *for the good of his soul;* — how much less lawful to sell away souls from under the light of the gospel into a condition where their souls will be utterly lost, so far as appeareth unto man.

All men of reading condemn the Spaniard for cruelty upon this point, in destroying men, and depopulating the land. The country is large enough;

---

* Drake's Amer. Indians, Book III, pp. 81–83.

The Squaw.

We, as well as Eliot, have reason also to lament the dealings of the desperadoes of our white race with the squaw sachem of Saconet.*

Prior to the death of Philip, a proclamation had been made, which called upon all his adherents to come in, giving them to understand, that they, in that case, should be dealt with mercifully. Thereupon, this squaw sachem, an ally of Philip, having first sent three messengers to the governor of Plymouth, suing for life, promising, under that proclamation, submission; and accordingly surrendered herself and tribes to Major Bradford.

But, sad to tell! they were slain, the entire one hundred and ten, that very day. Well might the Apostle expostulate.

> Great God, forgive our Saxon race,
> Blot from thy Book, no more to trace
> Fraternal wrath infernal!
> That taints the atmosphere we breathe,
> The sky above and earth beneath,
> With dearth and death eternal! †

—here is land enough for them and us too. Prov. xiv, 28. In the multitude of people is the King's honor.

It will be much to the glory of Christ to have many brought in to worship his great name.

I desire the Honored Council to pardon my boldness, and let the case of conscience *be discussed* orderly, before the King be asked. Cover my weakness, and weigh the reason and religion that laboreth in this great case of conscience.

JOHN ELIOT."

About three months subsequently, seven Indians were sold ["to be transported to any place out of this continent"], by the Treasurer of the Colony. See Genealogy of Eliot Family, pp. 133, 134.

* Drake's Amer. Indians, Book II, p. 40.
† From my Epics, etc., p. 167.

CHAPTER V.

EXTERMINATION.

THIS was avowed as well on the one side as on the other. And at the hands of desperadoes, the natives, in various ways, were constantly being crowded, to the end of their lives. Provoked variously, to madness and desperation, they fought, some against their own race, some against the English settlers; and, as Cowper hath, in truth, said, "the brands rusted in their bony hands."

In view of all this, it is much to be deplored that the unbiased historian, aside from Eliot's influence, has never been able to see any material difference between the so-called civilization of that day of trial, and native savage barbarism itself, as evinced by desperadoes on the one side and on the other.

So it was at

WAMESIT.

In 1675, the Indians (Oct. 27 and Nov. 4) had been provoked by English desperadoes, who had repeatedly fired upon them, at Chelmsford and elsewhere, upon suspicion that the Wamesits had been guilty of burning a barn, by and for which some of the natives had been killed.* Being thus indiscriminately accused and injured

---

* Francis' Life of Eliot, pp. 279, 280.

as barn-burners, it of course came to pass that the Wamesits, combining against the settlers in this locality, by reason of these aggressions long and often repeated, crossed the Merrimac in their canoes, and, falling in upon the English settlers on the north side of the river, near where the old garrison-house still stands (1880), — raising their fearful war-whoop cry, and burning down three dwelling-houses, one or more of which belonged to Edward Colburn and Samuel Varnum; said Colburn and others were shot at, and pursued by the Indians (forty in number); and while upon the river, in attempting to cross it, the two sons of Varnum in the conflict were slain. It was March 18, 1676. And on the 15th of April, then next, fourteen or fifteen English cottages in this vicinity were consumed.

MORAL.

From all this, we may clearly see how great a matter a little fire may kindle; indeed, how those, who unwisely take the sword, may perish by it; and above all, how wise it shall be to learn of Eliot, bearing, forbearing, and forgiving, advancing valiantly onward, following peace with the world under God's great golden rule, as he did.

OLD MEN AND WOMEN.

As Philip's war progressed, the Wamesits at one time went away, deserting the station, leaving only some few old men and women here, too old to get away.* Sad to relate, soon after the young Indians left, their wigwams at night were set fire to, and all those that remained

* Sketch of the Life of Eliot, pp. 15, 16.

perished. Their ashes, no doubt, are somewhere in this ground on which we tread.*

PHILIP'S FORCE.

For a considerable time he appeared to be strong and invincible. And yet that light and love, which by the Apostle had been diffused among the tribes, tended greatly to delay and dishearten a savage warfare.

But for this, the war would have been longer, and if possible more terrible; but for this, the general mass of natives would have gone over to King Philip. And in that event, the English settlers would have been most likely driven out, if not entirely exterminated. Eliot's mission to evangelize the Indian nations, although it fell short of his grand purpose, politically, as we have seen, it saved the white settler of New England,—serving, as it did, to concentrate a balance of power towards civilization and economical progress.

All the way, 'neath the war-cloud or otherwise, Eliot's constant prayer was for peace. So it was in the Missakonog troubles, which he so nobly averted and prevented. It was so in 1669, when the Massachusetts Indians made a six-years' war against the Mohawks. In that contest, along the borders of New York, seven hundred Indians, against the prayerful entreaties of Eliot, waged war in that wilderness, and more than half of them perished in the fight.† All this, and more, the Apostle had foreseen, and had raised his voice against it.

---

* Drake's American Indian Wars, B. II, p. 117.
† Drake, B. II, p. 45.

MALICIOUS MEN.

Conflicts with the natives were got up, not by the masses, on the one side or the other, but, through occasional depredations, the kindling embers of anger from time to time were fanned forth to furious flames. And although terrible scenes of war and blood had transpired, beclouding and hedging up the pathway of the Apostle, in the killing of his educated ministers and teachers, and in the distraction or destruction of his Christian churches and people of his care, Eliot still survived, — yet he mourned, bereaved, and what follows.

They thence, advance 'mid oft-recurring strife,
Through conflicts desperate kindled into life,
By hate implacable still lingering long,
Avenging Philip's death; and flagrant wrong,
Remembered well, encroachments rash, designed,
Repeated oft, as self had long inclined
The natives here. But through the lapse of time,
Whence wayward hearts to better faith incline,
Whence discord wanes away, — then *Truth* began
To shed with light the vagrant paths of man;
Distracted foes their errors soon discern,
And back to reason once again return.
Then Peace, that welcome harbinger of health,
Of generous thrift, foreshadowing weal and wealth,
Brings her glad-tidings down, and cheers the land,
With prompt good-will and noble deeds at hand,
To heal the broken heart, to make amends
For wilful waste, which from the past descends.

Thence this fair vale, from mountain to the main,
In vernal grandeur buds to bloom again;
And plenteous harvest, with her golden ears,
Crowning the prudence of progressive years,
Adorns the field, and grace triumphant gives

To honest toil.   Here Wonalancet lives,
Unscathed by war, a sachem wise and true,
Of fragment tribes still roving far and few,
Along these banks, where Penacook had stood
For countless years, through tempest, storm, and **flood;**
And further seaward where Wamesit lies,
Still well entrenched, a wigwam city thrives;
Rightly reserved, the home of hunters here,
A fort within and habitations dear
To friendly red-men.   While from dearth released,
From scourge of conflict, and in strength increased,
Through many a favored year the Pilgrim mind,
By faith and works religious freedom find:
Such as the fathers sought and had foretold
Should come, in grace abounding as of old.*

In that dread war, the Apostle had followed his
disciples, his ministers, his teachers, his printers, his interpreters, and other brethren to their places of imprisonment, at the pines on Charles River, as they were
boated away; and at Deer Island and other places, while
held imprisoned and in chains; and although powerless to
rescue them, his kind, discreet voice, everywhere and to
all, administered comfort, encouragement, and consolation.†

And when, at Philip's death, the rancor of war seemed
to subside, the Apostle again advanced, not as before, but
as well as he could.   On foot — in the forest, preaching,
and trying to re-establish his former missionary stations;
advancing, sometimes through torrents of rain, storms
of hail, or drifts of snow; and sometimes, for days together, without a dry thread in his garments.

---

* From my Epics, Lyrics, and Ballads, p. 346.
† Dearborn's Sketch of Eliot's Life, pp. 14–17.   Bigelow's Hist. of Natick,
p. 36.   Francis' Life of Eliot, pp. 277, 278.

PRISONERS OF WAR ON THE RIVER FOR DEER ISLAND.

Eliot at Nashua.

At one time, in the summer of 1652, he had started from Roxbury, to preach to the tribes at Nashua, some sixty miles away, as then reckoned. But while on the journey, a notice reached him of a conflict up there among the Indians, that might endanger his own life. Thereupon, for a day or two, he halted, turned aside, and waited.

The old chief at Nashua, hearing of this, at once organized an armed force of twenty Indian warriors, headed them himself, and bounding through the forest, surrounded their old Apostle, safely escorted him through, with gallant honors, to the place of his appointment,—thus they honored him, that he might preach to their waiting, assembled people.*

His Many Friends.

His Christians, those that had already been driven out from their native soil, those that had perished in the fight, or otherwise had been slain, or had died of disease or starvation during the conflicts, including those whom he, in his long life, had parted with at the common grave, had been thousands.

Yet he had consolation, that amid all the trials of earth, he had constantly borne to the breeze that gospel banner of righteousness, beautifully inscribed, " Love to God! Peace on earth, and good-will towards men."

---

* Drake's Hist. Amer. Indians, Book III, p. 85.

TESTIMONIALS.

Richard Baxter, the great author and scholar, in 1691, upon his death-bed in England, declared, among other sayings, "There was no man I honored above John Eliot. . . . I hope as he did ; it is for his evangelical succession that I plead."

Shepard, one of his cotemporaries, then minister at Cambridge, while the Puritan settlers were trembling (in the war) for the fate of New England, exhorting his people to take courage, declared, that "the country could never perish, so long as John Eliot lived."

Cotton Mather, speaking of Eliot's eloquence, says : "He would sound the trumpet of God against all vice, with a most penetrating liveliness, and make his pulpit another Mount Sinai, for the flashes of lightning therein displayed against the breaches of the law, given from that burning mountain." *

Edward Everett, in his oration at Bloody Brook, announced his belief, that "since the death of St. Paul, a nobler, a truer, a warmer spirit than John Eliot never lived." †

But what need have we for witnesses?

John Eliot is known of all New England ; and although his translations of the Bible and other books, into the Indian language, have become as a dead letter; and his Indian nations, whom he tried to save, were nearly destroyed, their descendants, being now unknown, and unheard of, save in some distant prairie or wilderness, still wandering afar off, few and far between.

---

* Life of John Eliot, p. 9.   † Hist. of Natick, ch. 2, p. 12.

'T is sad to tell how the Indian fell,
How the storm had swept the deck,
How the tribes of yore, all dashed ashore,
The craft became a wreck!

Bright stars shall burn, and seasons turn
Their sunny sides forever;
But ne'er to change, that mountain range
Again shall know them never.

True, true they say, there's a better day,
And *faith*, we ought to find it!
For the lights of love, that burn above,
Are lit for man to mind it.*

Eliot's Adherents.

Prior to the war, he had at his call many whom he had schooled for the Indian ministry, as teachers, as printers, as interpreters, proof-readers, etc., as we have seen; and who had aided him in his vast undertaking to civilize and evangelize the Indian nations. But first and last, and not least, among those who contributed to that great cause, there was a lady, diligent, circumspect, duteous.

Anna Mountfort Eliot.†

Their acquaintance had commenced in England; and after Eliot had been in Boston about a year, the cry, "Come over and help us," or some other cry, had reached the ear of Anna Mountfort. At once she made haste for the hazardous sea-voyage. Ah! how the gallant valor of that girl of the olden time looms up to our frail imagination!

---

* From my Epics, Lyrics, and Ballads, pp. 191–195.
† Genealogy of Eliot Family, pp. 44, 55.

Beyond the seas, I seem to see her there, at early morn, about to sever herself from the mates of her childhood and from kindred ties; there, at the dear old threshold of home; there, as she takes leave of a trembling, tearful old mother, the sister, or the brother, with that last sad good-by, which never on earth, orally, was to be repeated.

Thence, through her truth and love to John Eliot, she dares the dangers of the high seas; and three thousand miles away from all else dear to her, in 1632 lands in the New World, at Boston.

And such a girl! I 'll tell you true, — once here, it did not take her long to find her John's tenement, or the place of the parsonage. She had come here, bearing woman's olive-branch of peace and love. She had come, not to encumber, not to embarrass; not as a worthless, heartless image, embracing a bill of expense. No — she had come to *help John*, — had come to his field of honest labor. She had come to this wilderness, equipped and fortified with that force and power which no man on earth ever had, to wit, the transcendent power of woman's peaceful, faithful love! She had come to follow the leadership of the husband, and to advance to that sphere and vocation which the great God, in his wise economy, hath pointed out to all women.

Thus armed, thus endowed, with the power of woman's unfaltering, faithful love, that lady, just then married, was ready for duty, — ready, if need be, to enter the wild forest with her dear John, and to help him to fell the trees, and to gather together the bark and the boughs, and to build the wigwam.

HER FIRST WORK.

In the beginning, she busied herself, among other duties, in acquiring a knowledge of medicine and medical practice. But this, too, without hinderance, or interference with the cares of the household. So that, when disease, contagious or otherwise, came to the white-man or to the red-man, there she stood, by the side of John Eliot, a healing hand, holding an antidote for every languishing heart, a balm for every wound.

It was thus from the day of her marriage, that Anna Eliot became the leading exemplary spirit, in advance of those brave old New England mothers, who followed her in succession; the equals of whom, for valor, for frugal industry, for endurance, for truthfulness, and for a valiant faith in their God, the history of the world hath never known.

Thus this primeval leader of the wives of our fathers began; and thus she advanced, to the highest honors of life, and to a glorious immortality. All the way along, through a connubial life of more than half a century, — in the forest, in the field, in peace, and in dread war, — she had filled well her place, — a wife, a Christian pioneer, as well as a companion.

> With truth, and trust, and patient pride,
> At morn, at noon, or even-tide,
>   She calmed the cloudy hour;
> Her heart was full of love and song,
> She cheered her Eliot all along,
>   She brought him many a flower.†

---

* Life of Eliot, p. 269. Eliot Genealogy, pp. 44, 45, 48.
† From my Epics, Lyrics, and Ballads, p. 160.

Her Death.

We have seen how the girl had left the home of her childhood, and father and mother and friends, in the far-off England; and now that lady, after the lapse of more than fifty years, crowned with the plaudits of "well done," takes leave of earth itself, in presence of the Evangelist in tears; animated by that true faith in God which had led them onward together through the wilderness triumphantly, that exemplary heroic spirit fled away.

And when kind friends and neighbors had come to the threshold of a lonely home, the Apostle, rising, covered with the frosts of more than fourscore winters, and calling them to the casket, said, "Here lies my dear, faithful, pious, prudent, and prayerful wife."

O, what a God-given commentary!

And now the funeral obsequies are performed, "the long procession passes by," and the earth overshadows the mortal remains of Anna Eliot.

It was a new tomb, consecrated and reserved to her, as its first inhabitant, by the gallant people of old Roxbury.* It was a tribute to fervent faithfulness and to the insignia of truth. Yet cold, too cold, as best they could make it, was such a new tomb for so warm a heart.

Eliot's Charity.

Thereafterwards the Apostle, for the want of strength, could preach but little. He had arrived at the last three

---

* Eliot, Gen. History, p. 53.

years of his life. Knowing that Roxbury had been supporting two ministers, to make his own labors less, he appeared before its committee, and seeking permission to relinquish his salary, said, "I do here give up my salary to the Lord; and now, brethren, you may fix that upon any man that God shall make a pastor." *

But his confiding society said, no! They said it because they loved him, and because they knew that his venerable presence in their midst was by far of more value than any salary.

One day, the parish treasurer had paid him some money, and fearing he would give it away before he reached home, he tied it up in a handkerchief, closing it in with the hardest knots he could make.

The Apostle started homeward, and on the way he turned into the cottage of a good woman in poverty. Perceiving her penniless condition, he said, "Oh! I have brought some relief to you." And he tried to untie the knots, and could n't do it. At length, passing it to the poor woman, he said, "Take it; I believe the Lord designs it all for you." †

His Manners.

Hearing one of his ministry complaining of others, by reason of some unexpected coldness and ill-treatment, Eliot replied, "Brother, learn the meaning of these three little words : bear, forbear, and forgive!"

He had students; some of them, inclining to stupidity, did not rise early. "I pray you," said Eliot, "see to it that you be morning birds!"

---

* Sketch of Eliot's Life, pp. 20, 22, 24.   † Life of Eliot, p. 12.

Cotton Mather says, his manner of preaching was powerful, yet plain; that "his delivery was graceful; that at times his voice rose into great warmth and energy."

In his old age, while, of a Sabbath morning, an attendant was leading him up the hill to his church, "Ah!" said the Apostle, "this is very much like the road to heaven,—it is up-hill."

His Departure.

At length, on his long anticipated death-bed, while the sands of life were beginning to fall, a friend approaches him, in kindness making an inquiry. "Alas!" said Eliot, "I have lost everything,—my understanding leaves me, my memory leaves me; but, thank God, my charity holds out still."

Then, at a later hour, another of his ministry called, sympathetically. At the first sight of his friend, he whispered, "You are welcome to my very soul. Pray retire into my study for me, and give me leave to be gone." Of course the friend retired. Soon then, obtaining leave to be gone, the noble triumphant spirit of John Eliot vanished into thin air, beyond the clouds. Its last rays, like the rays of the beautiful sunset, shooting upward, thence beamed backward on this world of ours.

The very stars of heaven, at this moment, are typical, —just as if, bespeaking, they were still transfusing that evangelical light and love, which was first diffused here by the Evangelist, to the heathen nations of New England.

---

* Memoirs of Eliot, pp. 150, 151. Adams' Life of Eliot, p. 275.

The tones of his voice, audible everywhere, are still rising above the ordinary whispers of a sainted soul. In it there is no uncertain sound. It comes to us, like the voice of one crying in the wilderness, "prepare ye the way of the Lord," and make your paths straight.

From the very walls of your churches that same apostolic acclaim hath reverberated, for more than two hundred years. It is still here. The voice of the Evangelist still whispers to the young man, to the maiden, and to the little ones, — in the Sabbath school, at the fire-side, and at the family altar. Known of all men, the very name of the Apostle is glorious. Plainly it is known, at the distance of two centuries, as if it had forever been engraved upon the New England door-post, — known universally, as if from canvas it had swung upon the guide-post in all the highways of the land.

So it is, that New England still profits by the far-seeing leadership of John Eliot, by his apostolic plans, purposes, precepts, and examples, which have come down to us full of light, transfusing the primeval true lessons of life. Everywhere, spiritually, his Evangelical hand, far extended, is still writing upon the wall. It is an index, true, faithful, and profitable, serving to point the generations onward and upward, to that great

City Above Us,

Where the saints and the angels, with banners unfurled,
Chant holy hosannas to the God of the world;
Up there, where the fields, bright beaming, are proud,
Like the tints, 'mid the rain-drops, of the bow in the cloud;
Where the lakes and the rivers pure silver unfold,
And the rocks of the mountains are garnished of gold.

There, sweeter than morn, in the glory of spring,
The lily waves wide and the wild warblers sing;
From the farthest fixed star, as ye see it bright burning,
Around which the spheres, vast, eternal are turning;
Where did the great maker stand forth from his throne,
When he framed the creation, and called it his own; —*

There, there may you find the great New England evangelical pioneer, amid throngs of the blest, in robes of living light, and in the joys of his God.

EARTH'S CONFLICT.

This with the Evangelist was long and arduous. But now (1690) it hath come to an end. Not so with the Indian churches which he left living, of whom Cotton Mather says: "There were [then] six churches of baptized Indians in New England, and eighteen assemblies of catechumens professing the name of Christ. Of the Indians, there are four-and-twenty preachers; and besides these there are four English ministers, who preach the gospel in the Indian tongue."

It is sad to say that these, partly through the infirmity of membership, partly for want of constant ministerial support, and mostly by reason of depredations and ill-usage from many of the English settlers constantly crowding, were finally driven to distraction and to desperate ends.

Yet, as against all this, the Natick Indian church, after Eliot's demise, for many years maintained its town organization, until at length it became greatly diminished in population; and finally, by an Act of the legislature

* From my Epics, Lyrics, and Ballads, p. 18.

it yielded its entire organization to the English. So that, in 1792, there were in Natick but one Indian "family of five persons and two single women." *

And then, with all the rest of the New England enfeebled tribes disorganized, one after another, they wandered farther back into the wilderness, and thence vanished away to the ends of the earth.

During all these intervening years, from the death of the Apostle, murders and wars and conflicts of every description, with but brief interventions of peace, had ensued, many of which were terrible. For instance, as late as 1777, transpired the capture and murder of a young lady,

JANE McCREA (LUCINDA).

Thus it happened, that by reason of aggressions on the part of the English soldiery (the contest for the native soil not being then quite ended), a small tribe, skulking about the camp of Jones, a young English captain, where Jane, his betrothed, was briefly making a visit, seized her there and dragging her by the arms and hair, mounted her upon a horse, and hurried her back into the dense wilderness. The captain, missing the girl, at once dispatched two friendly Indians to pursue and obtain and bring back to him his dearest lost prize; then, hastening himself to another trail, he also pursued the tribe. Now, as appears, the Indians had obtained the young lady, but upon a dispute between themselves as to which should present her to the captain, and obtain a barrel of rum which had been offered for her return, they in the affray

---

* Memoirs of Eliot, p. 120.

struck her down with a tomahawk. The captain at that moment appearing in sight, and hearing the shriek of the dying girl, fell upon the two Indians, and they also were both slain at his hands. This was near the banks of the Hudson.

These are facts which tend to show how carnal weapons, even at that late day, were still used. How at the hands of desperadoes, seeking neither Christianity nor civilization, the earth was still being stained with the blood of mortals. This incident was long ago poetized by Barlow, and an extract is deemed appropriate.

" Lucinda's fate! The tale ye nations hear,
Eternal ages trace it with a tear.

" He hurries to his tent. Oh! rage! despair!
No glimpse, no tidings of the frantic fair,
Save that some car-men, as a-camp they drove,
Had seen her coursing for the western grove.
Faint with fatigue, and choked with burning thirst,
Forth from his friends with bounding leap he bursts;
Vaults o'er the palisade with eyes aflame,
And fills the welkin with Lucinda's name!

" The fair one, too, with every aid forlorn,
Had raved and wandered, till officious morn
Awaked the Mohawks from their short repose,
To glean the plunder ere their comrades rose.

" Two Mohawks met the maid, —historian, hold!
She starts, with eyes upturned, and fleeting breath, —
In their raised axes views her instant death.
Her hair, half lost along the shrubs she passed,
Rolls in loose tangle round her lovely waist;

. . . .

With calculating pause and demon grin,
They seize her hands, and through her face divine

> Drive the descending axe! the shriek she sent
> Attained her lover's ear!—he thither bent
> With all the speed his wearied limbs could yield,
> Whirled his keen blade, and stretched upon the field
> The yelling fiends; who there, disputing (stood)
> Her gory scalp, their horrid prize of blood!
> He sunk delirious on her lifeless clay,
> And passed, in starts of sense, the dreadful day." *

STILL, TRUE IT PROVED,

that after the Indian conflicts in New England, which had brought terror and dismay to our Pilgrim and Puritan settlers for more than half a century from the death of the Apostle, yet never forgetting him, the Indians, withdrawing from their rivers and ponds and from their hunting and trapping grounds, gradually disappeared. In their departure they left behind them, not the ruins of desolated cities nor lofty castles, but the same old wilderness, for the most part dense and dark as ever, and now and then on the banks of rivers and on the lake and ocean shores they accidentally left many a sample of their bows and arrows, their chisels, their tomahawks, and their mortars made of stone. Still, on the north, from the beautiful Lake Winnipesaugee in New Hampshire, one that may be called the last lone tribe, wandering, hunting, still lingered in that dense wilderness. Its great chief was the warlike, devil-daring

CHOCORUA.†

He was the last of the Pequawkets! Oh, what clusters of incidents, terrible in their impressions, seem to rally around that gallant but cruel historic name. Prior to the

---

* Drake's Amer. Ind., B. III, p. 101.   † Pronounced Cheh-corrua.

year 1766, and for years perhaps up to that time, this
great chief had hunted that old forest, of which the town
of Burton had become the centre, and in which that
lofty mountain which still bears Chocorua's name now
stands, as it hath stood from the Creation. This mountain historic hath ever been known and visited for its
tragical history, as well as for its scenery and the
beautiful landscapes that adorn it, near to it and in the
distance towards the great lake, towards the lofty white
mountain-peaks and far away to the high seas.

This old chief had a family. His squaw died, and
was buried (beneath a log structure, after the manner of
some of the tribes) by the brook-side where he had first
found her.

He had a small Indian boy, his son, who, after the death
of the mother, continued daily to tag after his father,
the chief, in his ramblings and huntings in the
wilderness.

At length, one day, as it happened, while at the
cottage of one Campbell, a white settler, the boy got
poisoned, and, returning home to the wigwam, soon died.*
Chocorua averred that the white-man poisoned the boy
purposely. Afterwards, one day, when the father of the
family had left home, returning at night, he found the
wife and children of his house all murdered. After
burying the dead, the white settlers followed Chocorua
to the same mountain which still bears his name, in Burton (now Albany, N. H.). They there discovered the
chief on the mountain cliff, at its highest pinnacle, and,
commanding him to jump off, "Ah," said he, "the great
Spirit gave Chocorua his life, and he'll not throw it

---

* See Legend by L. Maria Child.

away at the bidding of the white-man." At this, Campbell shot him; and, while dying, he, with doleful, husky exclamation, pronounced awful curses upon the English.

From that day to this, the want of vegetation in that mountain, all its deaths, and all the diseases upon the cattle and upon the inhabitants of that region, have been attributed to that "dread curse of Chocorua." *

Not many years since, on a hunting excursion to the New England mountains, we encamped beneath the brow of Chocorua over-night, and in a trance fell into the following

SOLILOQUY.

The tired hounds at length are sleeping,
And over our tent, wild night is weeping
   Dark dews in the Burton wood;
While from her distant radiant fountain,
The queenly moon lights up the mountain
   Where brave Chocorua stood.

To this the ills of earth had brought him,
'T was here the white-man sought and fought him,
   In daring, dashing numbers;
From whence despair had deigned to dwell,
Chocorua, wounded, faltering fell,
   And here in death he slumbers.

Entranced beneath thy craggéd peak,
Creation vast!—thy summit bleak,
   Thy varied vales I ponder;
I reverence Him who shaped the hills,
These silvery lakes, those glittering rills,
   Wild, in a world of wonder.

---

* Drake's Amer. Ind., B. III, p. 101.

Up 'neath the stars, yon glimmering slope,
Piled range on range, they fill the scope
    Of man's enchanted vision;
Bold there above a heaving sea,
For aye to vie in majesty,
    Earth's grandest, proud position!

Life and its joys Chocorua sought,
His tribe he trained, as nature taught,
    Mild in these magic mountains;
With bow and arrow known of yore,
Vast wood-lands, wild, he hunted o'er,
    Dame fed him at her fountains.

Of what wild waters yield in view,
Chocorua launched his light canoe
    On many a rapid river;
Fierce falcons faltered in the air,
And the wild-deer bounded from his lair
    At the rattle of his quiver.

From boyhood brave, a priest he roved;
Faithful at heart, he fervent loved
    Keoka, ne'er to sever;
No happier pair could earth produce,
Keoka true — and a proud pappoose
    Inspired that wigwam ever.

With truth and trust, and patient pride,
At morn, at noon, or eventide,
    She calmed the cloudy hour;
Her heart was full of love and song,
She cheered Chocorua's life along,
    She brought him many a flower.

Such was the life Chocorua sought,
Such were the charms Keoka brought,
    Unselfish, unpretending;
Kings of the earth, I 'd envy not,
Give me to know Chocorua's lot,
    Such faith, such favor blending!

Soon then, alas! sad fatal years,
That moved heroic hearts to tears,
　Fell heavy on Pequawket;
Dread death, that brought Keoka blind,
Had mazed Chocorua in his mind,
　The tribes began to talk it.

Of rushes rude they made her shroud,
In crooked form a casket proud,
　And laid her in the wild-wood,
Beside a rippling river shore,
Where many a song and dance of yore
　Had cheered her happy childhood.

Six logs laid high on either side,
Embraced they hold that sacred bride,
　With a rail-made roof around her;
Deep calm at rest, devoid of fears,
Of loves, of hopes, or tender tears,
　Where first Chocorua found her,

A white flag fluttered in the air,
Sweet stars from heaven glittered there,
　And the zephyrs came to love her;
Deep wood-lands whispered sighs unknown,
The plaintive pines their loss bemoan,
　And the wild rose creeps above her.

Ten times a day Chocorua wept;
Ten times a day his shadow swept
　In plumy form around her;
The partridge fluttered from his trail,
And the she-wolf nightly heard his wail,
　To a troubled trance it bound her.

Where'er he turned, where'er he roamed,
Or when around the grave he mourned,
　There prompt and true to mind him,
His little lad with lifted eye,
As if to hail that mother nigh,
　Tripped on, and stood behind him.

'T was thus Chocorua's heart was pressed;
Long months moved on, but gave no rest;
   Sad thus, dread fate had made it;
Still there is grief as yet unknown,
" One trouble never comes alone,"
   Our dear old mothers said it.

Next then indeed, how true it proved!
Another fate as fortune moved
   Came cruel quite as t'other;
By hidden drugs, in malice made,
Alas! the boy hath fallen dead,
   To moulder with his mother.

Then wailed Chocorua wilder still,
Without a heart, without a will,
   A ghost-like, lurking wonder;
Yet in his flesh there's native fire,
Though earth and hell in crime conspire,
   To drive the soul asunder.

True, true the story oft is told,
Chocorua hateful here of old
   Brought maledictions many; —
" Curse on yr white-man's soul!" he prayed;
" Curse on yr living and yr dead,
   Nor give him gospel any!

" Yr war-path let it lay in snares,
Yr fields laid low of frost and tares,
   Yr pestilence supernal;
Of crime accursed, for aye to know
Prompt penalties of pain and woe
   On all yr heads infernal.

" Vile, heartless knaves! ye killed my boy,
My own Keoka's darling joy; —
   E'er in the grave she rested;
By deadly drugs laid low, he died,
Me too, ye 've slain! — let devils deride
   Ye, tortured, damned, detested.

"Ho! let the war-whoop lead the fight,
The torch, the tomahawk, at night,
   Yr habitations storming!
Drive deep the axe, the scalping blade,
Spare never a white-man, child or maid,
   Give carnage to the morning!

"Great Spirit, let thy lightnings flash!
Thy fiery vengeance, let it dash
   Down where the pale-face prowls;
On Campbell's head, on all he owns,
Let panthers perch upon his bones
   While hot in h—l he howls!"

Thus prayed Chocorua, bleeding, slain;
Vengeance from thence eternal came
   To a devastation certain;
Nay, ever since, from then to this,
Not a breath of hope nor breeze of bliss
   Hath moved these woods of Burton.

Veiled now in shadows stands the sun,
The Indian hunter's day is done
   In these New England borders;
A baleful shaft his heart hath broken,
Out from the cloud the fates betoken
   Unwonted strange disorders.

Dread on that night and hitherto
The heavens let fall malarious dew
   Far down these murky mountains;
Of all the flowers, not one is known;
The maple leaf is dry, half grown,
   And death is in the fountains.

The moping owl hath ceased to hoot,
The scrub-oak falters at the root,
   And the snail is lank and weary.
The fated fawn hath found his bed;
Huge hawks, high-flying, drop down dead
   Above that apex dreary.

Faded, the vales no fruits adorn;
The hills are pale with poisoned corn;
   The flocks are lean, repining;
No growth the panting pastures yield,
And the staggering cattle roam the field
   Forlorn, in death declining.

'T is thus we 're made the slaves of earth,
Mope in miasmas, deep in dearth,
   Sad, from some bad beginning;
From cruelty to friend or foes,
Our morbid pains or mental woes
   Prove but the pangs of sinning.

High now a voice is in the air,
As if Chocorua still were there
   With wood-nymphs wild attending.
'T is heard far up the mountain-side,
That plaint of earth's down-trodden tribe,
   Bleak with the zephyrs blending.

Great God, forgive our Saxon race!
Blot from Thy book, no more to trace
   Fraternal wrath infernal,
That taints the atmosphere we breathe,
The sky above, and earth beneath,
   With dearth and death eternal!

.   .   .   .   .

Come, boys! we 'll take our tents away
To better vales.   'T is break of day;
   And the hounds are awake for duty.
Blow, blow the horn!   A gracious sun
Hath brought a brotherhood begun
   In life, in love, in beauty!

THE BOODEYS.

"Ah! what is life? At best a brief delight!
A sun scarce brightening ere it sinks in night;
A flower at morning fresh, at noon decayed;
A still, swift river, gliding into shade."

"Catch, then! oh, catch the transient hour;
Improve each moment as it flies."

ILLUSTRATIONS.

बुद्ध

TABLE OF CONTENTS.

RETROSPECTIVE.

ANNALS OF THE BOODEYS.

In the foregoing account of the Eliots in England, and of the Apostle on these shores, we have endeavored to present to the reader many of life's best lessons. From the date of the Apostle's death in 1690, down to the present period, we now propose, through the lineage of the Boodey race in New England, to present, illustrate, and perpetuate whatever comes to us from familiar life, which may be amusing and profitable to the incoming generations of men.

Early to the New England settlements was the advent of our ancestor from France, whose remote progenitors doubtless originated in Eastern Asia; and in coming here, it is no wonder that this boy, then in his eighteenth year, full of manly aspirations, standing upon the deck of a French ship, became elated at the sight of a New World.

He had brought with him a biblical Christian name, "Zechariah," and a surname spelled in the original Sanscrit language, Buddha; in the Hungarian or German, Budae; in the French, Boudé (pronounced Boo-day'), and in English, spelled in all the old records and by all our best scholars, Boodey. The original word Buddha signified, as used in Asia, "divinity," or "divine knowledge."

From this comes the denominational word Boodism, out of, or under which name, has come forth the most extensive multitude of religionists in all the earth. It prevails in "China, Japan, Siam, Assam, Ceylon, Tartary, and is the state religion of Thibet and Burmah." They now number about three or four hundred millions. Their grounds of belief, as lately given by the Rev. James Freeman Clarke, are these : "The doctrines of Boodism are that all men are equal; that there should be no distinction of caste; that all events are governed by universal and unchanging laws ; that whoever obeys those laws, ascends in the scale of being to something better ; that whoever disobeys them, descends to something worse; that the highest condition is that in which men escape from vicissitudes and change, and that conduct determines destiny."

It is said to be a part of the pride of that vast, numerous class of religionists to extend the growth of shade-trees in and all about their towns, and in and along all the highways, to overspread and cool the heads of way-worn travellers; and that, in all instances, the most decrepit and dejected personages, as they come staggering along, must be treated to the best parlor of the neighborhood ; and that the most forlorn, ragged subject must, by the populace, be adorned with the best suit of clothes. These are some of the religious observances of a genuine Boodh in the Asiatic world.

"Boodism" is defined by Webster, the lexicographer, to be, "A system of religion in Eastern Asia, embraced by more than one third of the human race. It teaches that, at distant intervals, a Buddha, or deity, appears to restore the world from a state of ignorance and decay, and then sinks into entire non-existence, or rather, perhaps, of bare existence, without attributes, action, or consciousness. This state, called 'Nirvana,' is considered as the ultimate *supreme good* and the highest reward of virtue on earth. Four 'Buddhas' have thus appeared in this world, and have passed into *Nirvana*, the last of whom, 'Gaudama,' became incarnate about 500 years before Christ. From his death, 543 B. C., many thousand years will elapse before the appearance of another." This likewise appears to be a part of their belief.

The name *Buddha*, as found in the original Sanscrit, and as now spelled in English, Boodey, is undoubtedly one and the same. The leaving out of the *e* from the last syllable of it, as has often been done, is delusive, as it tends to change the sound of the name by throwing the entire accent on the first syllable, which appears to be contrary to the original intent, both of the French and English. Hence it seems our name should be pronounced, not *Boo*-dee, but Boo-day'.

The Advent of Zechariah.

From an invariable tradition, this adventurer has, at all times, been reported and known as having deserted from a French ship which had landed in Boston. The penalty to the deserter was death ; yet, with several others, desiring to remain in the New World, this lad, taking his chance, deserted the ship. Being advertised, some of his comrade-deserters, on an offer of a reward, were arrested, carried back to Boston, and there were executed. Our Boodey boy escaping uncaught, found his way through the wilderness to the Parish of Madbury, in a remote corner of Cocheco (Dover, N. H.),

and sought rest for his weary limbs in a secluded hovel.
Some two or three cows were fed there, and beneath
the hay-mow he crawled at night, hiding himself away
from detectives who, for the reward offered in Boston,
were on the alert, seeking his life. Knowing the day
when the ship was to take its departure back to
France, the boy, feeding himself for days, as he did, on
the milk of cows, took courage, kept concealed, and
patiently awaited the welcome day, when the ship, its
officers and crew, would leave these shores, and leave
him to himself and to the care of Nature's God. Here
he was, single and alone, in a wilderness, in the midst of
savages, a stranger in a strange land. The days were
chill and cheerless ; the nights dark, lonely, and dreary.
The fear of the detective in the search, constantly
haunting his senses, kept him mindful of the terrible death-warrant. Easy it is to imagine how every
bleak gale that rattled the loose bark on the hovel, cau-
tioned concealment ; easy to imagine how every sound
admonished the daring and valiant boy adventurer to
the most vigilant care.

The Red-man.

Strange indeed, to our adventurer, must have been
the first sight of the American Indian, then green, as
he was, from the Old World. The Indian's fashion
of dress, his wild, rude manners and habits, his plume,
his painted form and unbearded visage, must have
seemed quaint and curious. The Indian's creation, or
advent to this wilderness world, has ever been to the
European a subject of speculation, as it must have been
then to the boy Boodey himself.

THE TWO NATIONALITIES.

We have heretofore discoursed, in measured language,
of the nativity and habits of the

First Indian.

Out, then, from a curious germ beneath the sod,
Inspired through needful care of Nature's God,
Whose eye, all-seeing, here began to scan
The strange invention of mysterious man;
By vigorous thrift, as fell the beaming rays
Of Phebus, fitly felt on vernal days,
Came forth an Indian's infant form divine,
First spawn of manhood on the stream of time;
Basking in valleys wild, earth formed, earth fed
For ripened age, by native reason led;
And chief o'er beast and bird in power became
A fitful terror to the timid game.

Increased at length by nature's selfsame laws,
To numerous tribes prolific, men and squaws,
From artful wigwams now spread o'er the land,
First skill evinced in architecture grand,
He wanders wild, belted with arrows keen
And blest with knowledge, right and wrong between,
A stately priest at peace, — provoked to strife,
He wields a hatchet and a scalping-knife
With dire revenge; e'er true to self and squaw,
He knows no faith, no code, but nature's law.

His footsteps fondly dwell where now we trace
Primeval heirlooms of the human race;
The chisel smooth and tomahawk first made
Of stone, ere art had formed the iron blade;
Where, from a narrow dock with native crew,
He launched in naval pride the first canoe,
And plowed the floating wave; his dripping oar
Ripples the waters, never pressed before;
Bestirs the scaly tribes to nervous fear,
For rights most sacred thus invaded here.

As if by instinct they the chieftain knew
To be a tyrant and a glutton, too;
Intent on native beast, on bird, or fish,
By slaughter dire to fill a dainty dish;
Whose webs are nets from bark of trees alone,
And mills that grind are mortars made of stone;
Who clothed his tribes, if clad they e'er appear,
In raiment plundered from the bounding deer;
Who maketh treacherous hooks from guiltless bones,
And drags a deadly net o'er sacred homes.

Wild, thus o'er land and sea for ages long,
A race of red-men vagrant plod along,
With language taught from nature's rustic throne,
And habits, each, peculiarly their own;
On growth spontaneous fed, content with prey,
What serves the purpose of a single day.

Their god is seen afar at rise of sun,
Their life in heaven is hunting, here begun;
By laws unwritten, sachems rule the tribes,
And lead the hosts wherever ill betides,
To fatal war; by force of arrows hurled,
They reigned sole monarchs in this western world.*

Most plainly may we see how closely our ancestor
must have adhered to his hiding-place by day, and to
the coverts of the frail, clattering old barn by night;
how uneasily he slept; and when rest he had, how wild·
must have been his dreams, — dreams of the father, the
brother, the lovely sister, or of that dear old mother,
who had cradled him, and who had given him her last,
long farewell salutations, away, three thousand miles
away, beyond the high seas; — nay, how oft noises of
footsteps of the milkman at eve, coming to feed the
fold, or of his cruel curse at the cows for not giving

---

* From my Epics, Lyrics, and Ballads, p. 333.

down their usual supply of milk; and now and then, how oft a war-whoop cry at night, of savages still lurking about, here in the wilderness, seeking English blood, came to caution our hero, thus hidden beneath the hay-mow of a hovel.

This was about the year 1695, while the continued conflicts of war between England and France, and the natives, were in progress, all at the time claiming to have dominion over this, our New England soil; yet, our hero, being of French descent, and, according to tradition, meek in his manner, the Indians would not harm him. It seems that, although they sometimes delighted in the murder of an Englishman, they would scorn to injure an honest, isolated French boy. Hence, it is no wonder the red men rallied around him, with kindly hearts; no wonder that they should yield to him these lands; no wonder that they should often build their camp-fires roundabout his habitations; and no wonder they engraved the mortar in that granite rock, which of late has been erected to mark his resting place. Upon this soil obviously they were at times wont to assemble to grind their corn in the rock, and to extend a generous heart and hand to their honest friend, our ancestor.

It was here, at Madbury, in this westerly corner of Cocheco, that this boy, in western phrase, "squat," as if by consent of the tribes, enclosing an excellent farm (one hundred and seventy-five acres) of wild lands, built his cabin, cleared up some of the acres, soon turning them into fair fields and green pastures; and, within five rods in front of this, our Madbury Town-house, reared up a family of eight duteous daughters: Eliza-

beth Boodey (Pitman,) Hannah Boodey (Huckins),
Charity Boodey (Leathers), Sarah Boodey (Jenkins),
Abigail Boodey (Drew), Kesiah Boodey, Betty Boodey
(Rowe), one infant daughter, and one son, *Azariah
Boodey*, of Madbury, and latterly of Canaan, in Bar-
rington, from whom all of the race, who bear the name
of Boodey in New England, have descended.

DEEDS.

No title-deeds to or from the said ancestor, or other
record directly concerning him, have as yet been found;
but on the Strafford county registry there is recorded
(Book I, p. 17) a deed, bearing date November 18, 1758,
and in the 31st year of His Majesty's reign, George II,
King of Great Britain, France, and Ireland, a deed of
quit-claim, from his five daughters first named, to his
only son, *Azariah*, in which deed they refer to the lands
therein described, as having descended from their "*Honored Father*, Zechariah Boodey, deceased."

Zechariah had died about the year 1755. Other old
deeds have been found, but these are on the records of
the Rockingham registry, one of which, dated June 29,
1759, is from Azariah (the son) to Ebenezer Demeritt,
of the Parish of Madbury, in the Province of New
Hampshire. It conveyed to said Demeritt a certain
parcel of said estate, including the old homestead,
"dwelling-house, barn, and trees on ye same," together
with "ye ten acres of common right, which was given
to [his] my Honored Father, Zechariah Boodey, deceased, by the town of Dover."

It was at this time that the entire Boodey estate had,
by purchase, fallen into the possession of *Ebenezer De-*

meritt, partly disposed of, as appears by the ancestor in his last years, and partly by the son after his decease, obviously for the purpose of raising the means of purchasing farms in Canaan, at Barrington, New Durham, Limington, and elsewhere, where the heirs, including the son, and grandsons Robert, Zechariah, Joseph, John, and others, at first severally settled.

Thus it was that Ebenezer Demeritt succeeded to the ownership of the Boodey estate, which he and his descendants have honorably honored down to this day.

The generous Ezra E. Demeritt is still here, with a gallant, enterprising family, faithful and buoyant, making progress onward, upward. Here, too, is his neat, commodious, modern mansion. Here, as ever, the lofty shade-tree looms up to adorn the highway; and in a summer day waves its branches, casting a grateful shade to the weary traveller. Here, too, the stately "Mahorrimet" (Hicks' hill), verdant and cone-like, in its grandeur, still lifting its green forest high towards the clouds, overlooks the landscape.

This historic elevation, during the New England wars, stood, undoubtedly, at times as a fortress to the wandering tribes, overshadowing, as it did, the then wild wilderness around it. Behold it now! It portends in prospect the fair, fertile field, and the flowery lawn, bearing up to the breeze, each in its season, the lily, the rose in its perfume, and last, but not least, the spiky, autumnal harvest.

The Highway.

The original road, which ran in front of this mansion-cellar, and on the westerly side of it, has, since we first

15

saw it, sixty years ago, changed its place. Now, it is
found located easterly of it, on the back side of the
cellar, much farther from the grave of the ancestor than
it was then ; and yet, its large shade-trees give to the
new road the appearance of being an old one, and its
more modern walls are touched by the marks of time.

CEMETERY.

Now, directly east, and opposite to the cellar, and
within a stone's throw of it, is the Madbury Town-house ;
and in front of which, in the field, westerly, is the grave,
now marked by the rude monument of the ancestor, and
of his dear Yankee wife, whose history, and whose
maiden name, oblivion, in its gloomy shadows, has
buried deep beneath the dread, silent scenery, which
now beclouds her memory! Still, she rests in peace ;
but her first name, her parentage, and her first childhood
home, now are unknown. Yet, as ever do the sweet
sunbeams of earth come and go, tenderly painting the
sacred turf that conceals the image, the name, the fame,
the frugality, and the duteous examples of that old, ven-
erated common mother of us all, who constitute this
great family.

In November, 1879, and after the lapse of more than
half a century, as appears, we a second time visited this
burial-ground ; the old elm-tree, that had stood there,
worn of age, dying, had crumbled to dust, and another
elm, young and thrifty, as if by a divine impulse, was
now gradually growing, advancing upward at the very
headstone of the ancestor. There, at noonday and at
night, it waves, extending its lofty boughs and its vernal honors to the consecrated urn of the ancestor and

his dear lady, and some of their daughters, the first Boodeys in New England. Now, as ever, a rough, rude stone marks the resting-place of each.

THE MONUMENT.

On this farm, as we perceived, there was a large, oblong, round rock, perhaps of eight or ten tons' weight, in which the wild Indian had chiseled in the stone a large mortar, obviously in which to grind his corn. We at once sought for it as a monument to our ancestor, and our generous young friend, *John Demeritt,* presented it to us. With us, he entered at once into our scheme, of erecting it as the red-man's rock, to mark the resting-place of the first ancestor, and to adorn his time-worn grave. From this hour, leaving the matter with him, I sojourned for a few days among kindred in the country, and on returning to Massachusetts, obtained by mail information that Madbury, moving in the matter of the monument, had yoked up the lowing herds, and under the drive of nine gallant teamsters, to wit, *Ivory H. Kelley, Charles H. Cockins, A. N. Jackson, James H. Daly, Charles E. Tebetts, Asa Young, John C. Hanson, Henry Stiles,* and *E. E. Demeritt,* the red-man's rock had advanced from its original bed, on the Boodey landscape, and upon a heavy drag, on the first heavy snow of November, had found its way to the grave of him who, so long, long ago, had cared for it, a monument to the ancestor, as well as to the native tribes.

Now, after the frosts of winter had vanished, and a mild May day (1880) having come, we again visited the place, caused "the red-man's rock" to be set upon its solid foundation, which had been previously laid for it by our

generous Demeritts, and which now stands four feet
north of the rude old moss-covered headstone.

We then caused this monument to be engraved, as the
stand-point where two races — the white man and the
red-man — had met; and in this instance, in mutual
kindness, unstained of blood.

We have graven it in large, deep-cut letters and figures,
according to the cut below inserted.

King Philip.
1675.

N.

Cavarly.
1880.

W.

E.

Demeritt.
1758.

S.

Boodey.
1695.

Zechariah Boodey, the honored father of his race in
·New England, fell upon these shores, as we have seen,
in his youth, and in troublesome times. Then it was
that the dense old wilderness waved its ancient tree-tops
at every breeze. Then it was that the wild wolf still
howled at night; angry savages roamed the forest, the
river, and the sea-shore, rampant at times, seeking conflagration and blood. Then it was that English garrison-
houses, in the hamlets, stood numerously throughout the
New England settlements, into which the English set-

tlers gathered for safety, whenever the tribes from the neighboring forests, and from Canada, instigated by the hostile French, lurking about at morn or at midnight, with fagots, with tomahawks, and battle-axes, to break in upon, murder, and destroy them. So it was at Salmon Falls, at Exeter, at old York, and at other neighboring settlements, as well as at Cocheco.

In the midst of all such tragical Indian conflicts, our meek ancestor, who, of tradition, is said to have been a pattern of uprightness, had, as we have seen, little or nothing to fear from the native tribes. He was not here quite early enough to witness at Cocheco the great training of 1676, under Major Waldron, nor of its disgraceful sham fight, wherein four hundred Indians upon the river bank were by stratagem seized and made prisoners. Nor could he have witnessed, in 1680, as an opposite, that cruel murder of Major Waldron, by an angry Indian tribe, within the gates. He was here too late for that, yet he landed on these shores quite in season to witness many a sad incident in savage warfare in his life-long pioneer experience, which, for at least half a century of his days, continued its ravages.

INCIDENTS.

Among the many dread, startling events of his time were those at Lovewell's Pond in Wakefield, not far away from his parish of Madbury, the conflagrations and many murders at Haverhill, and the slaughter of savages on the Contoocook, from which Hannah Duston became the world's renowned heroine.

Oh, how the news from Haverhill and from that tragic event, as it came down the Merrimac and out through

the wild woods of Madbury, must have startled the
senses of our young adventurer then and there, single
and alone, as he stood at his rude hut of logs, at Cocheco.

This story, then told, and since then a thousand times
repeated, was, that the Indians having set fire to Haverhill, and having kidnapped Mrs. Duston and others, and
murdered many of its inhabitants, had escaped, and far
away having encamped on an island of the Contoocook,
Mrs. Duston, Mrs. Neff, and Leonardson, the boy, had
risen up at night, while the tribe was yet asleep, and with
tomahawks had killed ten of them — had scalped them;
and, with scalps, tomahawk, and gun, these captives
escaping, had all three found their way through the
forest back to Haverhill. Many incidents, and also an
account of the taking of the thirteen captives, and of
the murdering by the Indians of twenty-seven of the
inhabitants of Haverhill, including Mrs. Duston's infant,
March 15, 1697, we had given in measured lines years
ago; and, as an incident of our ancestor's early days,
we give place to the story of Mrs. Duston here.

THE CAPTIVITY.

The angry French with England disagree,
Which next portends what carnage hence shall be,
What man's estate must prove, — a varied life;
From quiet peace proceeds terrific strife;
.From plenty, dearth; from faith and virtue, sin;
From health, disease, that wages war within.

Thus strangely intermixed are good and ill;
True to the purpose of a sovereign will,
Nature but thrives by fire that burns within;
From planets broken, other worlds begin.
Yet bloody conflicts, such the world abhor

As mark the advent of avenging war;
And such the crime that now involves the race,
Fraught with its cruel curse and deep disgrace,
That through successive years again devours
The vital substance of contending powers.

From war-whoops wild, and earth in crimson glow,
A wail goes up, — a note of woman's woe!
Fierce vengeance tempts her singleness of heart,
Her heroism true, her guileless art,
Her purity, her own maternal care,
Her faith in God, that never knows despair,
Her love indeed, that triumphs most and best
In trial sad, when most by danger pressed;
Whose truth endures, when fails our vital breath,
Inspires fond hope, and smooths the bed of death.

Such were the hearts whose wails went up afar,
That brooked the fury of King Philip's War;
Whose just protection savages defied,
And dearest hopes of house and home denied;
Around her hearth from hidden ambush springs
The lurking foe, and death, with horror, brings.

And this is war! —and such in wrath makes haste
To lay the white man's cot and village waste;
That deals in daggers poisoned, coated o'er,
The fagot torch, and gluts on human gore.

Against such crime the settlers strong unite;
In various ways they rally for the fight;
Some seek defence by force of gun and dogs;
Some take to garrison, strong built of logs;
And some in squads with weapons rude assail
The foe, and fierce pursue the hidden trail.
'T was so at Newbury and at Bradford Town,
Far farther north and seaward farther down,
Along the vale where'er the white man dwelt,
Still unprovoked the selfsame scourge was felt.

And at old Haverhill, as Mather tells,
The flaring fagot burns where Duston dwells.
The faithful father, frenzied to dismay,
Hastens the flight of children far away,
But not the infant; that in wrath is slain.
Its mother, captured, trudges in the train
Of savages; while in the clouds are shown
The crackling ruins of an English home.
The tribes evade pursuit; they skirt the glen,
Fast hastening through the fields away, and then
Dense woods and sable night conceal the foe; —
There, couched on broken boughs in beds of snow,
Repose they seek.   Still mindful of the past,
Her heart depressed, by sleep benumbed at last,
There dreams that mother, weary, sick, at rest,
Of happy home, — of father, children blest, —
Of life's sweet joys profusely, kindly given, —
Of angel visits from the throne of Heaven, —
Of that true bliss religious life inspires,
That wafts the soul above earth's frail desires.

Thus moved congenial thought her dreamy mind;
As moved that mighty forest in the wind,
Thus, on, till twilight gray with breaking beam
Now turns the tenor of a fleeting dream;
When half aroused, before her vision gaze
Appear grim visages and fagot blaze; —
Tall spectres, gaunt, whose garments drip with gore
From that infanticide the day before,
Wrought strange convulsions.   Whence that fearful wail?
'T was Hannah Duston, waking for the trail.

Her dark-brown hair back on her shoulders spread,
The frosts of night still on her garments laid.
At sight of death, at sound of war-whoop cry,
Avenging justice flashes in her eye;
Still, far beyond the cloud-capt tree-tops, shown,
There gleamed in prospect yet another home;

Light paints a tinge upon her pallid brow,
And up to God above she made a vow;
For on the trees are marks of kindred blood,
And vengeance just is whispered in the wood.
Firm as the granite hills that brave the storm,
That mother's will is fixed, and waxes warm.
Yet held to follow through the rugged way,
Kept equal step for many a weary day
('T was death to falter 'mid a savage throng)
With Mary Neff and boy; all move along
Through winding paths and tangled wildwood fens,
Where prowled the wolf, and where the serpent dens;
Declivities they wind, and ford the brooks
That leap the mountain-pass from granite rocks;
Thence in dark thicket, then in sunlight gleam,
And then in boats of birch on spacious stream,
Up where old Contoocook unites in pride
With Merrimac, profound in rolling tide;
There, on an island wild, are captives shown
The wigwam rude, an Indian's favored home.

And there on mats, around the camp-fire flame,
Seated in group, they glut the slaughtered game,
Which hunger sought; and night, now gathering in,
Spreads her dark mantle o'er the woods within;
While from afar, a gentle zephyr breeze
Plays grateful music on the waving trees,
Inviting rest from th' rambling drudge of day,
That lulls the spirit from the world away.

Still does that zephyr omens strange portend,
A baleful bickering, some tragic end;
Yet ne'er more safe, ne'er less by danger pressed,
Than felt the drowsy foe reclined at rest; —
And sleep sonorous, which fatigue inspires,
Drowns deep the tribe in front of midnight fires.

Then rose that mother, noiseless, moving near
To Neff, breathes mandates startling to her ear;

16

To Samuel, too, her vent of vengeance went
That fired his heart.   They move with joint intent
And signal stealth.   Around the foe they felt,
And drew a tomahawk each, from the belt,
That touched his loins; and then erect they stand,
Lifting that bloody blade with heedful hand; —
Down on his guilty head, three times they strike,
And three times three death follows, each alike.

No groan nor sigh is heard, nor sign of woe;
But stiff and cold there lies the bloody foe
'Neath clouds of night; the wigwam embers fade,
And phantom-shadows stalk along the glade
In depth of woods.   The hills are hushed aloof, —
No voice, save from the owl or hungry wolf,
That clamors for his prey.
                         Yet as these three,
Once captive bound, now turn away, thus free,
Bright beaming stars, through parted clouds between,
True guides intent from Heaven's arch serene,
Look down; while truth, still valiant to prevail
O'er wrong, and justice stern with even scale,
Approve the deed; and from that crimson glade,
That dark, lone wigwam with unburied dead,
Relieved, yet sad, they board a light canoe
To dip the oar in hope of home, pursue
Adown bright Merrimac in generous tide,
That bears the craft on high through borders wide;
Thence paddling east, they gain a favored shore
Above the fall, where troubled waters roar
Below, — all safe at land.
                         The day-star rose;
Nature anon awakes from night's repose;
Wild birds, from far thick gathered in the trees,
Warble sweet welcome on the morning breeze
To strange adventurers; while all that day
Along the winding shore that leads the way
To Haverhill, they thoughtful trudge and talk,

STATUE TO THE MOTHER.

What each had seen in life's bewildered walk, —
Of childhood years beguiled with favorite toys, —
Of love, — of home delights, — of buried joys.

This tragical incident of the olden time, with scores
, of others that transpired in the days of our ancestor,
startling as they came, shall last forever. One of the
results from this act of heroism is a monument on the
Merrimac upon an island of the Contoocook in New
Hampshire, as a tribute to our New England mothers,
from whom we — the most of us — descend. It was
erected in 1874, — stands twenty-five feet in height,
and bears the image, larger than life, of Mrs. Duston,
that heroine of 1697, bearing away in her right hand the
Indian tomahawk, and in her left the ten scalps of the
slaughtered tribe, the murderers of her infant, Martha.

A likeness of that statue, which relates back to the
early days of Zechariah, we here include.

Household of Zechariah Boodey,

Born in France. His wife, a Yankee lady, unknown to
the records. They resided in the parish of Madbury,
Cocheco. Each lived to an advanced age. He died
about the year 1755. Children :—

1 ELIZABETH, b. in Madbury; m. Ebenezer Pitman.
2 HANNAH, b. in Madbury; m. Robert Huckins.
3 CHARITY, b. in Madbury; m. Abednego Leathers.
4 SARAH, b. in Madbury; m. Benjamin Jenkins.
5 ABIGAIL, b. in Madbury; m. David Drew.
6 BETTY, b. in Madbury; m. James Rowe.
7 Dau., name unknown, b. in Madbury; d. in early life.

⁸ KESIAH, b. in Madbury; unmarried in 1758.
⁹ AZARIAH, b. Aug. 15, 1720 ; m. a Bushbie.   1

Second Generation.

¹ **II.** **Azariah**⁹ Boodey, son of Zechariah, our ancestor, born Aug. 15, 1720 ; married Bridget Bushbie, whose
parents are said to have lived at the Bermudas and at
Boston, and whose remote ancestor emigrated to this
country in the ship "True Love," of whom we have the
following from the records in England :* "April 8, 1637.
The examinaction of Nich : Bushbie of Norvich, in Norff,
weauer, aged 50 years and Bridgett his wife aged 53 yeares
with four children, Nicho : John : Abraham : and Sarath :
are desirous to goe to boston in New England to inhabit."†
Bridget Bushbie Boodey, wife of Azariah, reared five
children, and died in Barrington, July 30, 1785, aged
about 70 years. Two years after her decease, it not being
meet that man should live alone, the venerable Azariah,
having concluded a second marriage contract with a
gallant lady at Berwick, Me., started off on horseback to
be married to her. This being done, he brought homeward his bride some twenty miles on horseback, as she, according to the necessity and fashion of that day, clung to
the horse and to him on a pillion. They were quite corpulent, the two weighing not less than four hundred pounds.

"How quaint to be seen, the two coming together,
   On the steady old nag, enjoying one mind;
Unheeding the pathway, the wind, and the weather,
   While closely she sticks to the pillion behind."

---

* See Samuel Drake's Founders of New England, p. 45.
† The writer of this book has a round table, curious in its workmanship,
which was brought over by, and has descended from, this same family.

Azariah was born in the Parish of Madbury, N. H., in that part of Cocheco which in 1755 was incorporated as the town of Madbury, and resided there up to about the year 1760(?), when he purchased his farm in Canaan, at Barrington, where he finally settled, reared a large family, and through his long, useful, and exemplary life, witnessed many of the startling conflicts which moved the hearts of pioneer life. He helped to hew down that old ancient forest which never before had heard the sound of busy industry, nor of the deadly axe of the gallant white man leading the way to a fruitful, progressive civilization.

From his early youth he had witnessed the conflicts of his time, unstained of blood, and in undeviating moral rectitude, unscarred by the cruelties of an ungodly, cruel warfare. At the age of five years he must have received his first impressions of its bloody deeds, when Lovewell and his men came down from "the Pond," bearing the startling news of the death of an entire little tribe, of which Belknap says: "This brave company, on Feb. 24, 1725, with ten scalps stretched on hoops and elevated on poles, entered Dover (Cocheco) in triumph, and proceeded thence to Boston; there they received the bounty of one hundred pounds for each scalp, out of the public treasury." But sad for Lovewell, on the 16th of the following April, he, with forty-six men, went again to the ponds, and in that famous battle with Paugus, both leaders were slain, and out of Lovewell's forty-six, fourteen only returned.

Immediately afterwards, Colonel Tyng, of Dunstable, visited that battle-ground, found and buried the bodies of twelve of the company, carved their names upon the

trees, and then again left them alone in the dark, deep
forest to a silent repose.*   Belknap says: "The names of
the dead on the trees, and the holes where the balls had
entered and had been cut out, were plainly visible when
I was on the spot in 1784.   The trees bore the appearance of being very old; one of them had fallen down."

The following is a part of the song which doubtless
was often sung in Azariah's lifetime: —

"Up then the tribes to battle rose,
    Who'd hid themselves in ambush dread;
Their knives they shook, their guns they aimed,
    The famous Paugus at their head.
Thus Paugus led the Pequawket tribe;
    As runs the fox would Paugus run,
As howls the wild wolf would he howl,
    A huge bear-skin had Paugus on.
But Chamberlin of Dunstable,
    He whom a savage ne'er could slay,
Met Paugus by the water-side,
    And shot him dead upon that day.
Then did the crimson streams that flowed
    Seem like the waters of the brook
That brightly shine, that loudly dash
    Far down the cliffs of Agio-chook.
Ah! many a wife shall rend her hair,
    And many a child cry, 'Woe be me,'
When messengers the news shall bear
    Of Lovewell's dear-bought victory."

It was during these and similar conflicts of many years
of his own experiences, that had been continued through
and from his father's lifetime, that Azariah Boodey lived,
cleared away the lofty forest, and made progress in
husbandry, to an improved civilization and to an abund-

---

* See Indian Wars. by Caverly, p. 346.

"AGIOCHOOK."

ant success in pioneer life. He died Feb. 26, 1803, leaving eight children: —

10 ROBERT, b. April 3, 1743; m. Margery Hill. He
        d. April 21, 1814.   2
11 ZECHARIAH, b. Aug. 12, 1745; m. Mary Demeritt.   3
12 JOHN, b. June 23, 1749; m. Susana Langley.   4
13 MOLLY, b. June 23, 1749; m. Peter Hodgdon.   5
14 JOSEPH, b. May 16, 1752; m. Olive Drew.   6
15 SARAH, b. March 8, 1755; m. Isaac Waldron.   7
16 HANNAH, b. March 29, 1758; m. Aaron Waldron.   8
17 AZARIAH, b. Nov. 29, 1761; d.
18 BETSEY, b. Nov. 2, 1763; m. John Caverly.   9

Third Generation.

2 **III. Robert**[10] Boodey, Rev.; married, 4th month, 13th day, 1763, Margery Hill, born April 23, 1744. He was born in Madbury (a parish up to 1755), April 13, 1743; settled first in New Durham, N. H., in 1770, holding many places of trust; in 1772 he removed to Limington, Me., where, from his stern integrity and prompt faithfulness in duty, he was chosen one of the first officers of that town, then new and progressive, of which he was selectman and treasurer alternately up to the end of his life. Such was the faith of his townsmen in this pioneer, as well for his sound judgment as for his faith and truth as a man, that he, though dead at least three-score years, is still remembered by the elder inhabitants of Limington; and many of the great and good things which he in his lifetime said and did, are still repeated of

him there as household incidents. We well remember, in that neighborhood, of hearing kind and quaint sayings of him forty years ago.

At one time, as they say, he having, while residing in New Durham, been a town officer, was now, after many years, sent for on a question at law depending on the correctness of one of its town lines. At the call away he went, some fifty miles, in search of the boundary of the disputed line at New Durham, called for a spade, and digging down soon came to a pile of solid pitch knots. "There," said he, "twenty years ago, when the old line-tree at the end of its life fell, I deep planted, precisely where it lived, this pile of pitch-knots"; and turning to a young man, then present, said, "Thee will please remember this." It was thus a long lawsuit was prevented, and indeed it hath been remembered.

Forty years ago we sometimes heard his faith and force and manhood talked over among the then old men, who in their early life had seen him. Among other things, at one time, when there was a complaint against an unequal taxation, an old veteran in town-meeting advanced an opinion as a fact, that they "never had had any equal taxes in Limington since the old Minister Boodey used to guess them out."

This Robert Boodey, the first, was a clergyman of the denomination of Quakers, and in his long lifetime quakerized many of the inhabitants of Limington and its neighboring towns; and in fact in his ministry he was the leading spirit of that denomination, both in New Hampshire and in Maine. On the 30th of June, 1780, he and his brother, Joseph Boodey, had united with the Rev. Benjamin Randall in the organization of that denomination of worshippers known as Freewill Baptists, now large and progressive. They, with Nathaniel Buzzell, Judith Cartel, Margery Boodey (Robert's wife), Mary Buzzell, and Rev. Benjamin Randall, eight members in all, constituted its first church; and soon afterwards the said Robert, on Sept. 2, 1780, was ordained to preach and to serve as its first deacon, and Joseph, his brother, and Nathaniel Buzzell were sent forth as ruling elders. Robert Boodey long lived a faithful minister and exemplary townsman, — an honest man. He died in Limington on the 21st of the 4th month, 1814. His faithful Margery died there also at an advanced age. Children of Robert: —

19 AZARIAH, b. Feb. 6, 1764, in Barrington, N. H.; m. Betsey Chick; d.   10

20 MOLLY, b. May 26, 1766, in Barrington; m. Robert Hastings.   11

21 ROBERT, b. Aug. 27, 1768, in New Durham, N. H.; m. Mary Storer; d.   11½

22 ABIGAIL, b. Nov. 2, 1770, in Barrington; d. Nov. 17, 1770.

28 SARAH, b. Aug. 28, 1771, in New Durham; m. David Storer; d.   12

24 JOHN H., b. Sept. 18, 1773, in New Durham; m.; d.   13

25 BETSEY, b. Jan. 15, 1777, in New Durham; m. Ebenezer Morton, Aug. 5, 1798; d. Feb. 4, 1846.   14

26 RUTH, b. June 13, 1779, in New Durham; m. a Greene, and went west; d.; she at 30 weighed 330 pounds.

17

[27] JOSEPH, b. Jan. 31, 1782, in New Durham; m.
        Soloma Clark; d.
[28] ISRAEL, b. Feb. 12, 1784, in New Durham; m.
        Hannah Strout; d.   He died Dec. 1, 1855.   [15]
[29] BENJAMIN, b. April 11, 1786, in Limington; m.
        Jane C. Winslow; d.   [16]
[30] EDMUND, b. Aug. 15, 1788, in Limington; m.
        Lydia Jones; d.   [17]
[31] HENRY H., b. Aug. 15, 1788, in Limington; m.
        Mary Pond; d.   [18]

III. Zechariah[2] Boodey, son of Azariah[1], born
in Madbury, Aug. 12, 1745; married Mary Demeritt,
born Nov. 28, 1743; settled in New Durham in Nov. 1768.
New Durham had been incorporated only four years
previously. Zechariah[2] felled the wild native forest,
cleared up his lands, and built his barn and dwelling-
house thereon, and there settled, — a valiant pioneer of
the wilderness, cultivating the soil, sustaining his government, and with an undeviating, sterling integrity,
through a long life he acted well his part to the shaping
of morals and to the advancing of a better civilization.
During the late Southern rebellion, on a lecture tour in
the raising of troops for the Union army, we turned
aside, on a Saturday, taking shelter overnight and during
the Sabbath beneath the roof of that same old mansion,
whose posts and cross-beams had been hewed down from
that lofty forest of a previous century, which from the
beginning of the world, up to our uncle's time, had been
known only to the red-man. The same permanent structure, with heavy timbers, was still standing, apparently
untouched of time or tempest, in form precisely as it

had stood through the storm and tempest of an hundred years; the same ceiling was overhead; the same old floors, deep-worn, yet firmly fastened down with hardwood pegs, as in the beginning; and the same old wooden door — handles and latches made of hickory — were still there, and were held sacred and cherished by Joseph, the son of the settler, who then still lived, and by Joseph the grandson, now still there. That same old mansion still remains, a quaint, primeval New England monument, to this day.

Zechariah[2], during his seventy-six years from his birth, had made the most of all the vicissitudes of youth, of manhood, and old age; had witnessed the departure of the native wilderness and of the ferocious wild beast; had contributed to the defence of his country in the days of Revolution, which most of all tried the souls of men in his day and generation; and to the overthrow of an offensive dynasty on this American soil, he nobly had contributed his mite, to the establishment of this republican government, under which he afterwards lived, rejoiced, and made progress, for nearly half a century, up to the date of his death, by cancer, June 14, 1821. Mary, his widow, surviving him fourteen years, died Oct. 3, 1835. Children of Zechariah[2]: —

[32] BRIDGET, b. 1769; m. Thomas Ransom, of Vermont; d.

[33] BETSEY, m. Joseph Gilman, of New Durham. He owned what is called the old fulling mill; d.

[34] JOHN, d.

[35] DANIEL, d. in 1805.

[36] JOSEPH, b. April 12, 1773; m.; d. May 12, 1867. [19]

4 III. 𝔍oɦn[12] Boodey, Capt., son of Azariah[1], of Barrington, N. H., born June 23, 1749; married Susannah Langley, b. March 6, about the year 1750. He was a frugal, enterprising husbandman; inherited the homestead of his father; was a captain in the militia, and was sometimes honored by his townsmen by offices of trust. After the make of the Boodey descendants generally, he was a man large and heavy in stature, of portly presence, of sound common-sense, and of prepossessing good manners. He died April 23, 1815; his widow, Susannah, survived but a few years; they rest at the old homestead of his father, at their own favored Canaan, in his native town of Barrington. Children of Capt. John : —

37 AZARIAH, b. Sept. 11, 1772; d.

38 AARON, b. Dec. 30, 1773; d. April 7, 1815.   **20**

39 JOHN, b. Jan. 1, 1777; d. April 18, 1815.   **21**

40 ZECHARIAH, b. Feb. 2, 1779; d.

41 ROBERT, b. Dec. 10, 1780; d. June 18, 1804; drowned.   **22**

42 ELIZABETH, b. March 24, 1782; m. Obadiah Langley, of Durham, N. H.; d.   **23**

48 MOLLY, b. April 11, 1785; m. Joseph Boodey, Jr.; d.   **24**

5 III. 𝔐olly[13] Boodey, daughter of Azariah[1], born June 23, 1749, a twin sister; married Peter Hodgdon, of Madbury. Uncle Peter was a nervous, marvellous old gentleman. When a lad I saw him once, but can just remember his outlines. His dear Molly had then gone beyond the river, — we had never seen her. He always travelled horseback on his old nag, fleet as the

"OLD BRIGHT" LET LOOSE.

wind. Time then had in its toil and trial appeared to
hang heavily upon him. His aged face had been seamed
all over with its cares, his voice appeared cracked and
broken, and his wintry locks lay loosely upon his
shoulders. We can just remember how his veiny hand
trembled as he sat at our mother's table feeding himself.
We remember he spoke of his infirmities as painful to
him, saying he used at home a wooden plate, with which
to steady his fork. But, oh! it would have been music
to you, to see the old hero come and go.

Tradition in and about Madbury, among many other
things, says old Peter's horse, old Bright (by that name
he called him), was a wonder among men and colts. The
common highway was no sort of guide to old Bright;
his end and aim was always onward through the shortest
way in the shortest time. Once given the point of compass, Bright needed no other direction; his course was
always in a direct line, straight forward through quag-
mires, over hedges, fences, brooks, walls, and ditches.
As this venerable charger leaped up and down, old Peter
would occasionally be seen in the distance, leaning
towards his journey's end, both hands fastened to the
mane, his long gray locks tossed by the tempest, and the
skirts of his garments at an angle of forty-five degrees,
carried back and fluttered by the breeze. The octage-
narians of Madbury still remember old Bright, as well
as that venerable horseman, and have given us a very
kind word of him. Peter passed away in advance of
the advent of the daguerreotype art, hence no genuine
likeness of him can be found; otherwise as to old Bright,
let loose in his prime, whose likeness we insert. Peter
died April 19, 1827, and he and his Molly rest in peace,

the wife in Canaan, and the husband at the old homestead in Madbury, now owned and occupied by Stephen
Jenkins, Esq., who, as I believe, is also a descendant of
our first ancestor in New England. Children: —

44 PETER HODGDON, b. in Madbury; d. in Massachusetts.

45 JOHN HODGDON, b. in Madbury; d. by accident,
young.

46 STEPHEN HODGDON, b. in Madbury; lived and
d. in Massachusetts.

47 PATIENCE HODGDON, b. in Madbury; m. Jonathan Jenkins.

48 —— HODGDON, b. in Madbury; m. Joseph
Burnham.

49 ABIGAIL HODGDON, b. in Madbury; m. Elijah
Tuttle.

6 **III. Joseph**14 Boodey, Rev., son of Azariah
and Bridget (Bushbie) Boodey, born in Dover, Parish of
Madbury, May 16, 1752; married Olive Drew, born June
3, 1752; resided first in Barrington, at Canaan, and
thence in Strafford, N. H., the remainder of his days.
His homestead was on the Province road on the north,
from Bow Lake. He died in 1824, and his ashes still rest
there.

This eloquent clergyman was endowed with a sound
judgment, a far-seeing mind, quick wit, and great force
of character. His education was from the family; from
the common school, whenever one was kept; and from
everybody he met in life, in youth or in manhood. The
Bible was his rule of action, and in every part it was
familiar to him. On his visits to the homestead of our

boyhood, he often amused us. We would open the New Testament to any of its texts, read to him a verse of it, and invariably he would repeat from memory the contents of the text that followed it. It appears that on June 30, 1780, he had united with Benjamin Randall in the organization of the First Freewill Baptist Church. Eight members only constituted its first formation. His brother, the Rev. Robert, as we have seen, served and was at that organization its first ordained deacon, the said Joseph Boodey and Nathaniel Buzzell being thereafterwards made its first ordained ministers.

After this, the Rev. Joseph had charge of the churches in Barrington and its neighboring towns. Among the historic events of the year 1800, it is of record that the "Rev. Joseph Boodey, Sen., made a tour into northern Vermont, in the autumn, and preached with great effect. He baptized eighteen in Sheffield ; and on the same day, a branch church of fifty-six members was formed, in connection with his own church in New Hampshire, more than one hundred miles distant."

Joseph, as well as his brother Robert, being independent in his opinions, would not agree with the religious extremists of his time. He could not believe in the final loss of the infant under a general decree of a just God. Nor did he believe with them that it had become the duty of saints of the church to exchange the washing of feet, nor even with the immortal Watts, that " God, the Mighty Maker," had died. In truth, he believed that, man upon earth, as if by a divine decree, being born free and independent, should and would forever be dealt with, and adjudged of, as a free moral agent. Outspoken, in his ministry and otherwise, as against such apparent absurdities, he at times became a target to the shafts of private resentment, and sometimes subject to secret slanders. But such was his honest, straightforward purpose, force of character, and power of eloquence, that no defamer dared at any time to assail him publicly.

Randall, his cotemporary and brother in the ministry, died early (1808), leaving the gospel field of his denomination to the leadership of Joseph Boodey, the senior, and other faithful ministers, comparatively, at that time, few in numbers, yet honest at heart and valiant for the truth.

His Manners.

Many an anecdote of this old pioneer minister was told of him sixty years ago, in his native neighborhood, two or three of which, for example, we here tell.

The Chain.

A certain man, in an adjoining town, had been directly charged of stealing a trace-chain, which belonged to a man by the name of Berry. A month afterwards this same man, for some slight cause, became offended with our Rev. Joseph, and charged him of assuming too much authority, and called him "Governor." "Governor!" says the old man, "if you don't like your governor, perhaps you may as well take George Berry's chain and try to chain him."

Profanity.

At one time this old clergyman had admitted to the church a teamster by the name of John Hall. Hall afterwards, with a team loaded with boards, in endeavor-

ing to ascend a hard hill south of Bow Lake, in common
phrase, got "stuck in the mud." Soon his old minister
riding along, Hall calls out to him and says, " Before I
joined the church, I used to make my oxen draw by
swearing at them; but now, having reformed, I am unable
to do it, — they refuse to obey. I wish you would assist
me up the hill." At this our minister came from his
horse, and placing his shoulder firmly to the wheel,
" Now," says he, " *swear at um a little easy, brother
John.*" The wheel of course turned, and the load went
up the hill.

THE BAPTISM.

At one time, this clergyman having been away to a
neighboring protracted meeting, where he had baptized
and admitted several persons to the church, among
whom there was a man by the name of Noah. On his
return homeward, he met a snob, who reproached him
thus: "Why," said he, "that Noah is as big a *thief*
as ever lived in Barnstead." " Well," said the old man,
"thief or no thief, I have baptized him, and we have
taken Noah into the church; but *if he don't behave well,
you may have him back again.*"

Rev. Joseph Boodey, from 1780 up to his decease,
Jan. 17, 1824 (44 years), was the senior leading clergyman of his denomination in Barrington, Strafford, and
neighboring towns, although in his later years old age
had somewhat diminished the extensive labors of his
more active, progressive, useful life. Sometimes, as
appears of record, he had served Barrington in its
State legislature; had preached the funeral sermons
of many hundreds; and at one time, by request, had

18

preached a like sermon prospectively, while the man himself was yet alive, at the chimney-corner, still hearing the solemn news of his death, and of that resurrection which seemed as if it were wafting his spirit away to that world above, whence no traveller returns.

On the records of Barrington, among other things, under the head of Marriages by Rev. Joseph Boodey, as found and furnished by J. Colby Caverly, Esq., are the following, which may be of interest to the many descendants of the parties married.

"1787, Dec. 6, married John Woodman and Sarah Foye; both of Barrington.

1788, Oct. 17, married Wm. Peavey, Jr., and Sarah Neal; both of Barrington.

1789, Sept. 13, married Nicholas Roberts and Molly Furnald; both of Barrington.

1791, Feb. 12, married Samuel Bunker, of Pittsfield, and Betty Hill, of Barrington.

1791, June 5, married Wm. Young and Charity Howe; both of Barrington.

1791, July 12, married Ebenezer Spencer, of Nottingham, and Mehitable Buzzell, of Barrington.

1791, Oct. 20, married John Howe and Lydia Swain; both of Barrington."

Rev. Joseph and Olive Boodey left children: —

50 MOLLY, b. Dec. 23, 1773; m. James Howe; d.   25
51 JONATHAN, b. June 24, 1776; m.; d. July, 1847.   26
52 AZARIAH, b. Dec. 3, 1779; d.   26½
58 JOSEPH, b. March 16, 1782; m. Molly Boodey; d.   27
54 OLIVE, b. Sept. 10, 1788; m. George Foss.   28
55 COMFORT, b. Feb. 10, 1791; m. Charles Caverly;
    d. March 30, 1876.   29
56 JOHN, b. April 16, 1795; m.; d.   30

⁷ **III. Sarah¹⁵** Boodey, born March 8, 1755, daughter of Azariah; married Isaac Waldron, of Barrington, N. H., born in 1746, who afterwards for several years was colonel of the 25th Regiment of N. H. Militia, raised a company, and served at Portsmouth as a colonel in the war of 1812, and served his own adopted town of Barrington as its representative to the legislature of New Hampshire seventeen years in succession, twenty-one years in all. He was a gentleman of the old-fashioned type, and was endowed with sound common-sense, force of character, honesty, and practical good manners. She died March 6, 1805. He lived to the advanced age of ninety-five years, and died in the year 1841. He and his wife, and some of their children (now all translated), are at rest at the old homestead, which still stands there in his favored Barrington, very near the place where stood the old garrison-house of early days. Children of Sarah : —

⁵⁷ ISAAC WALDRON; m. a Wallace of Rye; d.   81
⁵⁸ JOHN WALDRON; m. Comfort Haynes; d.   82
⁵⁹ SALLY WALDRON; m. T. Wright Hale; d.
⁶⁰ POLLY WALDRON; m. a Shannon; d.
⁶¹ ABRAHAM WALDRON; d. at sea.
⁶² AZARIAH WALDRON; d.
⁶³ AARON C. WALDRON, b. Oct. 6, 1792; m. a Goodwin; d. Oct. 26, 1878, at Limington, Me.   82½
⁶⁴ DANIEL WALDRON; m.; d. Oct. 7, 1842.   83
⁶⁵ HANNAH WALDRON; m. —— Batchelder, of Northwood; 2d, Elisha Tasker, of Strafford, N. H.; d.

⁸ III. 𝕳annah[16] Boodey, daughter of Azariah[1], born March 29, 1758; married Aaron Waldron, of Strafford, born Aug. 1, 1749. Aaron was a thrifty husbandman, who, in offices of trust and otherwise, held the confidence of his townsmen. His homestead was in the north part of the town. He reared a large, progressive family, — nine sons and three daughters, — only one of whom (1880), the amiable Sarah, still survives. Aaron Waldron, commencing life in the middle of the last century, enjoyed the valuable experiences of a pioneer; had helped to clear away the forest; had witnessed the commencement of dread hostilities, leading to the wars of the Revolution; had faithfully contributed his share in establishing, on these shores, the form of a republican government. He had lived long to see much of the conflicts between the contending nations. He, at the outset, with others, had seen the portentous clouds of conflict gathering; had felt the alarm at the unprovoked aggressions of England's power.

WAR.

Then self-control began to seek solution,
A thirst for freedom threatens revolution.
At first provoked by Britain's indiscretion,
Her power assumed, her flagrant legislation,
And other wrongs, invasion comes at length,
Resistance follows, — then a tug at strength
Full seven years. On hostile fields engaged,
The armies gathered, and the battle raged.

John Bull, in strength of scientific drill,
Inflamed the ardor of untutored skill; —
The Yankee's firelock belched terrific flame,
Against whose vengeance science was but vain; —
And scythe and pitchfork wielded for the right,

The better weapons proved, in such a fight.
True valor thus from pilgrim hearts of yore,
Drove the brave Britons from Columbia's shore.

Then through the vale, the Veteran we trace,
Firm in deportment, faithful to his race,
Down from the fields of conquest and renown,
Observed of all the host, the heroes of the town; —
Ben. Pierce is there, far seen amid the throng,
With laurels crowned, they wind the way along;
And there's old John, who, when the field was dark,
Would risk his life at risk of "Molly Stark."
These were our fathers, manly in their might,
From whom descended liberty and right.

Where now they rest shall fragrant flowers grow;
Their valiant deeds shall coming ages know;
And filial care shall cherish evermore,
That noble tree they planted at our door.*

Aaron and Hannah (B.) Waldron had children : —

66 AZARIAH WALDRON, b. Aug. 5, 1775; d. Nov. 11,
1825.   34

67 AARON WALDRON, b. Feb. 6, 1779; m. Mary ·
Huckins, of Barrington, N. H.; d. Jan. 25,
1825.

68 ISAAC WALDRON, b. Aug. 21, 1780; d. Oct. 19,
1856.   35

69 JOHN WALDRON, b. Aug. 20, 1782; d. June 1,
1848.   86

70 ABRAM WALDRON, b. April 6, 1784; d. Oct. 10,
1787.

71 ROBERT WALDRON, b. April 3, 1786; d. May 11,
1826.   87

---

* From my Epics, Lyrics, and Ballads, p. 366.

[72] ABRAHAM WALDRON, b. April 17, 1788; d. May 4, 1793.

[73] WILLIAM WALDRON, b. Feb. 23, 1790; d. Oct. 26, 1866. 39

[74] HANNAH WALDRON, b. May 22, 1792; m.; d. Dec. 13, 1825. 39½

[75] RICHARD WALDRON, b. March 6, 1795; d. Oct. 17, 1839. 40

[76] LOVEY WALDRON, b. May 14, 1797; d. June 13, 1860. 41

[77] ZECHARIAH WALDRON, b. July 19, 1799; d. Oct. 27, 1827. 42

[78] SARAH WALDRON, b. Jan. 14, 1802; m. James B. Foss, Esq., of Strafford, N. H. 43

The father was killed accidentally by the fall of a tree, Dec. 9, 1820. His widow Hannah died Feb. 7, 1830; and they repose at their old homestead in Strafford, having left the New World improved and much the better than when they found it. '

[9] **III. Betsey**[18] Boodey, daughter of Azariah[1], born Nov. 2, 1763; married John Caverly, of Portsmouth, N. H., born May 11, 1752. They settled in Barrington (afterwards Strafford) about the year 1777. He prostrated the native forest, burned and cleared away the fallen trees, built walls of the granite rocks, lined his highways with thrifty fruit-trees, fenced his fair fields permanently; and as the result of a gallant, industrious husbandry, soon, very soon, the green pastures became vocal with the bleating flock and the lowing herds, and his productive plow-lands gave him, annually, grateful returns, and so continued all the days of his long life.

Active during the Revolution, this husbandman stood firmly on behalf of the colonies, contributing, as a patriot, his humble means to the victories of the Revolution ; and his record is thus still to be found upon the test-lists at the capital of New Hampshire. Thus did John (Lieut.) live, an honest, industrious, frugal life ; faithful to his God, to man, to law, and to the freedom of his country. He left the world on the twenty-seventh day of April, 1842, at the venerable age of 90 years. His generous, frugal wife died Nov. 17, 1832, at the age of 69. They rest at their old homestead, with several sons, daughters, and others of their descendants, who are also within the same sacred enclosure. Children : —

79 BRIDGET CAVERLY, b. Aug. 21, 1779; m. Samuel Caverly ; d. July 20, 1826.
80 HANNAH CAVERLY, b. Oct. 22, 1781 ; m. ; d.   44
81 BETSEY CAVERLY, b. Oct. 30, 1784 ; m. ; d.   45
82 SARAH CAVERLY, b. Sept. 4, 1787 ; m. ; d.   46
83 JOHN CAVERLY, b. Aug. 23, 1789 ; m. ; d.   47
84 AZARIAH CAVERLY, b. Dec. 28, 1792 ; m.; d.   48
85 JOSEPH CAVERLY, b. April 15, 1795 ; m.; d.   49
86 DANIEL CAVERLY, b. Jan. 23, 1798 ; m.   50
87 MARY CAVERLY, b. May 4, 1800 ; m.; d.   51
88 IRA CAVERLY, b. April 9, 1804 ; m. ; d.   52
89 ROBERT BOODEY CAVERLY, b. July 19, 1806; m.   53
90 ASA CAVERLY, b. Oct. 5, 1812 ; m.   54

Fourth Generation.

10 **IV. Azariah**[19] Boodey, a son of Rev. Robert, born Feb. 6, 1764; married Betsey Chick, of Falmouth, Me., born June 7, 1765; married March 30, 1789. He

was born in Barrington, N. H., and lived an industrious farmer in Limington, Me., and died there Nov. 16, 1836. His worthy wife, surviving him, died May 10, 1843. These, all born in Limington, were their nine children: —

91 DANIEL, b. July 26, 1789; m. April 1, 1819; d. Oct. 4, 1855. **55**

92 STEPHEN, b. Aug. 30, 1791; d. May 8, 1793.

93 BETSEY, b. March 20, 1794; m. Caleb Cole, April 28, 1839; d. March 20, 1874. No children.

94 GEORGE, b. July 19, 1796;·d. Dec. 28, 1797.

95 ABIGAIL, b. Dec. 4, 1798; m. Nathan Chadburn, Feb. 12, 1818; d. Nov. 1875. **56**

, 96 THANKFUL, b. Dec. 12, 1801; d. Oct. 30, 1803.

97 ASENATH, b. Feb. 15, 1804; d. Oct. 24, 1808.

98 MARY, b. Dec. 9, 1806; m. Pelatiah Carl, Oct. 20, 1827. **57**

99 ASENATH, 2d, b. April 26, 1809; d. Nov. 9, 1818.

11 **IV. Molly**[20] Boodey, daughter of Rev. Robert, of Limington, born May 26, 1766; m. Robert Hasty, of Parsonsfield, Me. The wife died in October, 1833; the husband, surviving her, died March, 1856, leaving children: —

100 WILLIAM HASTY, b. Feb. 15, 1788; m. —— Strout. **58**

101 SALOMA HASTY, b. Dec. 10, 1792; m. Charles Kimball; d. May 3, 1871. **59**

102 MARY ANN HASTY, m. Stephen Fenderson; d. March, 1871. **60**

103 COMFORT HASTY, m. —— Edgcomb; 2d, —— Drew; d. Sept. 1876. **61**

[104] JOHN W. HASTY, m. —— Pease; d. March, 1839. **62**
[105] GEORGE B. HASTY, m. —— Pease. **63**

11½ IV. Robert²¹ Boodey, son of Rev. Robert and Margery (Hill) Boodey, of Limington, born Sept. 27, 1768; married Mercy Stover, of Limerick, in 1795, born 1770. He died in April, 1836, and his wife Mercy in the year 1834. They had children: —

[106] MARGERY H., b. 1795; d. 1799.
[107] MARY H., b. July 16, 1797; d. Sept. 3, 1875.
[108] HANNAH H., b. March 12, 1799; d. 1839.
[109] RUTH W., b. April 13, 1801; m.; d. July 7, 1836.
[110] SIMEON S., b. March 8, 1807; d. 1839.
[111] JOSEPH B., b. May 25, 1811; m. Oct. 14, 1833. **64**

12 IV. Sarah²² Boodey, daughter of Rev. Robert and Margery (Hill) Boodey, born Aug. 28, 1771; married David Stover, born March, 1769. Children: —

[112] JOHN STOVER, m.; d.
[113] WILLIAM STOVER, d.
[114] ISRAEL STOVER, m.; d.
[115] DAVID STOVER, m.; d.
[116] GEORGE STOVER, d.
[117] ROBERT STOVER, m.; d.
[117½] MARY STOVER, m. —— Warren. **65**
[117½] HENRY STOVER, m.*
[117½] DANIEL STOVER, m.
[117½] GEORGE STOVER, 2d, m.; d.
[117½] WILLIAM STOVER, m.
[117½] SALLY STOVER, d.

---

* Henry Stover, above named, in early life enlisted on board a war-ship, served his country there about sixteen years, visited many parts of the world, and then returning settled in the midst of the granite rocks of Limerick, on what then was called the old Charles Bean farm.

19

[13] **IV.   John 弦.**[24] Boodey, son of Rev. Robert,
born 9th month, 18th day, 1773; married Patience Red-
man, of Scarborough, Me.   He was from Limington;
was a house-carpenter and farmer, a good citizen, and
settled in Jackson, Waldo Co., Me.   They died at their
homestead in Jackson, Me., the husband, July 15, 1848;
the widow in August, 1854.   Children:—

[118]   JOHN, b. in Scarborough, Sept. 18, 1796; d. at
        sea.
[119]   ISABELLA, b. April 10, 1799; m. Edward Murch,
        of Portland; 2d, m. Charles Bradford; 3d,
        m. —— Gallop.   66
[120]   SALLY, b. June 16, 1801; m. John Emery.   67
[121]   LUCINDA, b. Aug. 7, 1803; m. Moses Saunders.   68
[122]   DAVID, b. Nov. 9, 1806; d. of cancer, August,
        1879; was a man of extraordinary force of
        character.
[123]   REDMAN, b. April 4, 1811; m. 1834.   69
[124]   HARRIET, b. Oct. 31, 1812.   70
[125]   HENRY H., b. Nov. 10, 1816; m. Sept. 3, 1846.   71
[126]   ALVIN, b. July 12, 1819; d. Oct. 23, 1858.   71½

[14] **IV. Betty**[25] Boodey, daughter of Rev. Robert
and Margery (Hill) Boodey, of Limington, born in New
Durham, Jan. 15, 1777; married Aug. 4, 1798, Ebenezer
Morton, of Gorham, Me., born July 19, 1773.   He was
killed by the falling of a tree upon him July 17, 1813;
Mrs. Morton died Feb. 4, 1846.   Children:—

[127]   MATTHIAS MORTON, b. in Limington, Nov. 1,
        1798; m.; d. 1877.
[128]   MARY MORTON, b. in Limington, June 15, 1800;
        m. —— Cook.

¹²⁹ MARGERY MORTON,* b. in Jackson, April 28, 1802; m. Michael Sawyer. 71½

¹³⁰ SALOME MORTON, b. in Jackson, Dec. 29, 1803; m. —— Douglass; d. 1875.

¹³¹ ROBERT MORTON, b. in Jackson, Feb. 28, 1805; m. —— Boodey.

¹³² SARAH MORTON, b. Jan. 9, 1807; m. —— Skilinger.

¹³³ RANSON MORTON, b. January 8, 1809; m. —— Rand; d. 1877.

¹³⁴ ELIZA MORTON, b. June 1, 1811; m. April 14, 1850, —— Pingree, of Standish, Me.

¹⁵ **IV. Israel**²⁶ Boodey, son of Rev. Robert and Margery (Hill) Boodey, born Feb. 12, 1784, in New Durham, N. H.; married Dec. 12, 1800, Hannah Strout, of Gorham, born Oct. 26, 1783; died March, 1825. He died Dec. 1, 1854. They resided on the old homestead of his father, and still rest there. His lady was from a notable family. He was a faithful husbandman, an honest man. We knew him well. Children of Israel: —

¹⁸⁵ WILLIAM E., b. Feb. 2, 1802; d. Oct. 3, 1852.

¹⁸⁶ TAMZON L., b. Sept. 2, 1807; d. Jan. 30, 1810.

¹⁸⁷ LORAINE, b. Jan. 20, 1809; d. May 17, 1841.

¹³³ TAMZON L., 2d, b. Aug. 6, 1810; d. Nov. 12, 1817.

¹³⁹ ISRAEL, b. July 18, 1812; d. July 28, 1867. 72

¹⁴⁰ ROBERT, b. April 1, 1814; d. April 2, 1814.

¹⁴¹ EUNICE S., b. May 2, 1815; d. May 29, 1857. 73

¹⁴² ROBERT, b. April 8, 1818; d. Aug. 7, 1836.

¹⁴³ ZECHARIAH, b. Aug. 9, 1819; m. Abby Wentworth. 74

---

* Margery was the first child born in Jackson.

¹⁴⁴ HENRY H., b. April 10, 1821; m.   **75**
¹⁴⁵ EDMUND T., b. April 4, 1823; m.   **76**
¹⁴⁶ ALBION K. P., b. Jan. 29, 1825; m.   **77**
¹⁴⁷ HANNAH P., b. May, 1829.
¹⁴⁸ LYDIA S., b. May 6, 1831; m. Phineas Hanscom.   **78**

¹⁶ **IV. 𝔅𝔢𝔫𝔧𝔞𝔪𝔦𝔫**²⁹ Boodey, son of Rev. Robert
and Margery (Hill) Boodey, born April 12, 1786, at Limington; married Jane Crane, in 1806, born June 24,
1785; settled in Westbrook; Jane died April 22, 1826;
2d, married Sarah Winslow, April 21, 1830. He died
Dec. 16, 1844.   Children of Benjamin: —

¹⁴⁹ ANN J., b. Oct. 22, 1807; m. Henry Adams,
        May, 1831.   **79**
¹⁵⁰ JANE C., b. Aug. 22, 1809; m. May 6, 1830; 2d,
        m. John Maxcy, 1842.   **80**
¹⁵¹ NATHAN W., b. April 12, 1811; m. May 4, 1843. **81**
¹⁵² ELLEN M., b. May 22, 1813; m. Feb. 1837; d.
        Oct. 14, 1845.   **82**
¹⁵³ MARTHA F., b. July 2, 1815.
¹⁵⁴ HENRY H., b. March 22, 1817; m. July 2, 1840.
¹⁵⁵ CHARLES E., b. June 23, 1819; m. May 10, 1849.
¹⁵⁶ FREDERIC W., b. July 2, 1821; m. Sept. 1847;
        d. Jan. 7, 1856.   **83**
¹⁵⁷ GEORGE W., b. Aug. 15, 1824.   **84**
¹⁵⁸ HARRIET S., b. Aug. 15, 1824; d. Nov. 20, 1875.

    Children by second marriage: —

¹⁵⁹ BENJAMIN F.
¹⁶⁰ ALFRED A.
¹⁶¹ ELIZABETH W., m. Daniel H. Walker, Dec. 2,
        1861.   **85**

[17] **IV. Edmund**[30] Boodey, son of Rev. Robert and Margery (Hill) Boodey, born Aug. 15, 1788, at Limington; married Lydia Jones, of Windham; settled as inn-keeper at Windham, Me., and living there a useful, profitable life; died Dec. 1853. Children: —

[162] SEWALL, b. Sept. 6, 1808; m. March 11, 1832; d. April 25, 1873.   86

[163] LOVINA, m. Jason Webb; d.

[164] EMMA, m. Robert Morton; 2d, Thos. McDonald.

[165] MARTHA, m. Ephraim Nason.

[166] MARY J., m. Ezra Towle; d.

[167] LYDIA, d.

[18] **IV. Henry H.**[31] Boodey, son of Rev. Robert, born Aug. 15, 1788 (a twin with Edmund); married Mary Bond, and during all of his industrious, economical business life resided in Portland, Me. Coming down, as he did, from a noble stock, he needed no introduction to the confidence of all who knew from whence he came to commence for a livelihood the business of life. Yet he had the gallant boy's misgivings and discouragements to grapple with; still, knowing that but one life was allotted to him upon the earth, and resolving to make himself an independent man, and with the noble intent to stand uprightly, and to live to help others to live, he took leave of the old homestead in Limington. The father, the old minister, gave him encouragement, good advice, and the needful loose change which the economy of that day could afford; and that, with a kind blessing of his dear old mother Margery, Henry, with a buoyant heart, pack in hand, started off upon his life-journey, on foot for the then town of Portland.* The distance, thirty

---

* Portland, taken from Falmouth, was incorporated in 1786, but was not chartered as a city until 1832.

miles, bearing the pack, was a full day's journey, long
and weary for a boy of Henry's age. It was late that
night when he neared the town. The lights had nearly
all gone out, so that the stranger boy, not knowing at
what house he might obtain a cheap resting-place, tired,
turned in, and took lodgings in a barn. In the morning he commenced his first day's work in making the
acquaintance of some of the noblest hearts of Portland,
especially those who knew the old Quaker, the father of
Limington. Without any recommendation other than
his honest father's fame, his own honest bearing, and his
own apparent force of character and good manners, this·
boy advanced to a favorable position among men, and as
a merchant to a fortune honestly earned, and to a good
name and fame worth living to obtain. He was concerned largely as a merchant in navigation; his services
for some years were sought and obtained at the Portland
custom-house as a weigher and gauger, and for nearly
forty years he held the office of treasurer of the Ancient
Landmark Lodge of Freemasons of that town and city.
He died in the year 1852, and his lady in 1855. Of her,
as of him, we may speak. She favored the poor, yea,
"she stretched forth her hands to the needy; she opened
her mouth with wisdom; and in her tongue was the law
of kindness." No children. They rest in peace.

[19] **IV. Joseph**[36] Boodey, Rev., 3d, son of Zechariah, 2d, of New Durham, N. H., born in a log-cabin,
April 12, 1773; married Nov. 13, 1800, Marcy Pike, born
Oct. 16, 1777, who died Aug. 23, 1856, much mourned.
He, as a member of "the Church of Christ," afterwards
known as a denomination of Freewill Baptists, was
ordained to the gospel ministry, Oct. 18, 1799, together

with the Rev. Micajah Otis, of Strafford, Simon Pottle, of Middleton, and James Jackson, of Eaton, N. H. His ordination was on the nineteenth year of the existence of that denomination, who now in New England have become quite strong and numerous. Probably no two men did more in the establishing and organizing its original churches in Vermont and New Hampshire than this clergyman and his uncle, the Rev. Joseph Boodey, of Barrington, named on page 134, both of whom were contemporaries, coadjutors, and companions of Benjamin Randall. At this ordination Randall preached the sermon.* Of Joseph Boodey, Jr.'s, eloquence and influence, the history of that day favors him. His energies as a minister of the gospel, as well in common business as in the duties of life, were always effective and on the right side. All the way through his laborious, useful journey, he was honored with high positions of trust and confidence. Politically, he was generally as steadfast in a minority as in a majority, and yet his integrity and ability, natural and acquired, often gave him success in whatever of good works he undertook. Many a time he had been called upon to serve as an officer of the town or county. Oftentimes, though a minister, he was a representative in the State legislature. While there at one of its sessions, a bill being introduced, the effect of which was to exempt clergymen from taxation, he most eloquently assailed it, and in an elaborate, well-timed, and eloquent speech, prevented its passage. This position against self-interest proves not less honorable to his constituents than to himself, as a man or as a clergyman.

He was a good prose-writer, and often indulged him-

---

* History of Freewill Baptists, pp. 161-170.

self in the art of poetry. Here we give place to a few
lines extracted from the pen of his old age.

PAINE THE PEDLER.

It was on a cold and cloudy day,
Paine took his trunk and went away;
Tired, to a house he turned aside,
And asked to stay, but was denied.

They said, 'twas early in the day;
He'd better go ahead and stay;
Farther he wandered on, and tried,
And there poor Paine was still denied.

To every house he made a call,
But each refused him, one and all;
Night coming on, he did not know
What he could do, nor where to go.

Sad, Pedler Paine was at a loss,
But came at length to Solon Foss;
Solon, with heart and soul within,
Rose from his bed and let him in.

Foss made a fire to warm his guest,
As quick the wife was up and drest;
And soon indeed the table was ready
With tea and victuals for the needy.

They soon conducted him to bed,
Well clothed, and pillows for his head;
Next morn they welcomed him to stay,
But thankfully Paine went away.

All this was generous, wise, humane;
This kindness shown to brother Paine!
Please write it on thy record rolls:
A just rebuke to narrow souls.

Inscribed to Robert B. Caverly, Esq.,

NEW DURHAM, *Jan.* 9, 1862.   JOSEPH BOODEY.

RANDALL'S MONUMENT.

This marble block marks the clay
Where do the bones of Randall lay;
The leader of a noble band
Of travellers to another land.

He had no polish to assume,
No vain ambition, pride, or plume;
The Bible was his constant chart,
God's gracious spirit moved his heart.

Cleanly in person, neat in dress,
His soul was fed of righteousness;
In faith and tears he taught the Word,
And sinners turned to worship God.

Not for the sake of worldly gain,
Nor filthy lucre to obtain,
Both eastward, westward he unfurled
God's royal ensign to the world.

Thus bravely on, through heat and cold,
The glorious gospel to unfold,
In highway, lane, or night or day,
Wherever duty led the way, —

Through drifting snows, the rattling hail,
The constant care that made him pale,
For aye obedient to his Lord,
He preached, persuaded, and adored.

This monument of earth's renown,
Grown old of time, shall crumble down;
Its solid base shall loose its bed,
And mingle with its honored dead.

Still, there's another high above
In golden letters, lined with love:
Eternal there, in that blest land,
Engraved by an Almighty hand.

In the great coronation day,
When sin and death are done away,
I'll hail my Randall on that shore
Of sainted souls, the hosts of yore.

NEW DURHAM, *Sept.* 14, 1859.   JOSEPH BOODEY.

Over and around his photograph likeness, his son, late deceased, printed, with the square and compass on either side, the following record of his father, thus:—

"God our Father." "Christ our Example."

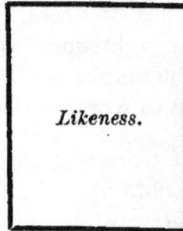

Likeness.

ELDER JOSEPH BOODEY,
Born in New Durham, N. H., April 12, 1773.
Commenced preaching Dec. 1797. Ordained Oct.
18, 1799. Preached his last sermon July 10, 1866.
Died May 12, 1867, aged 94 years 1 month. Bur-
ied in due and ancient form by the Masonic Frater-
nity of which he had been a member over fifty years.
Sermon by Rev. Moses Howe, of New Bedford, Mass.
Text, Acts 20: 24–25.

Children of Joseph:—

168 ZECHARIAH, b. Sept. 7, 1801; d. Oct. 17, 1801.
169 ARTEMAS, b. Aug. 29, 1802; d. March 22, 1803.
170 ALMIRA H., b. Dec. 3, 1805; d. July 21, 1826.
171 DANIEL, b. April 1, 1808; d. Sept. 7, 1858. He
    was in his time a major in the militia, a sur-
    veyor of public lands in Maine, and a teacher
    of youth in Kentucky.

[172] JACOB P., b. Sept. 15, 1810; m.; d. Feb. 28,
    1880.   87
[173] ZECHARIAH, b. June 20, 1813; m.   88
[174] SOCRATES H., b. May 2, 1816; m.   89
[175] BETSEY P., b. Jan. 9, 1819.
[176] JOSEPH M., b. Sept. 10, 1821.

20. **IV. Aaron**[38] Boodey, son of Capt. John, born
Dec. 30, 1873; settled in New Durham or Brookfield;
married Polly Haynes. He was an industrious farmer.
Children : —

[177] JOHN SULLIVAN BOODEY; was a very intelligent
    husbandman; he settled on an island in Lake
    Winnipiseogee; he died recently at about
    the age of sixty years.
[178] SUSAN, d.
[179] AARON, d.
[180] ROBERT, d.
[181] LUCY, d.
[182] MARY, b. about the year 1805; was adopted at
    the age of ten by her great-aunt, Betsey
    Boodey Caverly. She lived unmarried; was
    an intelligent lady, and proved a worthy
    example of truthful industry and usefulness.
    She rests in the cemetery at Dover, N. H., in
    the lot of her friends, Messrs. Robinson (inn-
    keeper) and Wadleigh, formerly of the Dover
    Inquirer.

Aaron Boodey's widow survived him several years.
He died April 7, 1815. They rest at the family homestead.

[21] **IV. 𝔍𝔬𝔥𝔫**[39] Boodey, 2d, son of Capt. John,
born Jan. 1, 1777; married Susanna Hayes, of Nottingham, born Nov. 25, 1775. He, a worthy husbandman,
resided on the homestead of his father, and now, with
his immediate kindred, rests there. He died April 18,
1815. His excellent wife survived him. At her decease,
her death was announced in a public journal, from which
we copy: "Died, April 6, 1844, Susanna Boodey. She
had been a valuable member of the F. Baptist Church
some twenty-six years. Leaves nine children and many
friends to mourn the departure of one highly esteemed
by all who knew her." Children: —

[183] AZARIAH, b. June 27, 1799; d. Sept. 23, 1800.
[184] IRA, b. April 26, 1801; m.   [90]
[185] ZECHARIAH, b. Sept. 4, 1802; m.; d. Sept. 5,
    1869.   [91]
[186] LUCINDA, b. March 26, 1804; m.   [92]
[187] AARON, b. Sept. 28, 1805; m.   [93]
[188] JOAN, b. Nov. 29, 1807; m.; d. Dec. 19, 1865.   [94]
[189] DANIEL, b. April 14, 1809; m. Sarah Wiggin.   [95]
[190] SUSANNA, b. Jan. 31, 1811; m. Israel Huckins; d.
    March 11, 1850.   [96]
[191] JOHN H., b. Nov. 28, 1812; m.   [97]
[192] ROBERT W., b. March 7, 1815; m.   [98]

[22] **IV. 𝔕𝔬𝔟𝔢𝔯𝔱**[41] Boodey, son of Capt. John, born
Dec. 10, 1780; married Abigail Watson, of Barrington;
died in Newburyport, Mass. (drowned), June 18, 1804.
Child: —

[193] ROBERT.

[23] **IV. Elizabeth**[42] Boodey, daughter of Capt. John and Susanna (Langley) Boodey; born March 24, 1782; married Obadiah Langley. Children: —

[194] JEDADIAH LANGLEY. [198] ALFRED LANGLEY.
[195] JONATHAN LANGLEY. [199] JOHN LANGLEY.
[196] ROBERT LANGLEY. [200] SUSAN LANGLEY.
[197] OBADIAH LANGLEY. [201] ELIZA LANGLEY.

Eliza married Josiah S. Howe, of Lowell, Mass. They had one son, who bears the name Charles L. Howe.

[24] **IV. Molly**[43] Boodey, daughter of Capt. John, born April 11, 1785; married Joseph Boodey, Jr., son of Rev. Joseph, of Strafford, born March 16, 1782. Children: —

[202] HIRAM, b. about the year 1818.
[203] MARY, b. about the year 1820.
[204] SUSAN, b. about the year 1822.
[205] ELIZA, b. about the year 1824.
[206] HARRIET, b. in 1826; m. —— Clough; they had five children; the eldest, Samuel F. Boodey, who was secretary of the corporation called the Pacific Stock Exchange.
[207] HANNAH, b. in 1832; m. H. G. Wilson, of San Francisco, Cal., where in prosperity they now reside in the midst of all the glories of the Golden State. They live at No. 1722 Hyde Street, where the string of the door-latch is never found pulled in.

[24½] **IV. Stephen**[46] Hodgdon, son of Peter and Molly (Boodey) Hodgdon, born in the Parish of Mad-

bury, N. H., and settled somewhere in Massachusetts.
Children : —

²⁰⁸ ELIZABETH HODGDON; m. Mial Parker; they
resided in Lowell, Mass. He died, leaving
one son, who lived to be a Union soldier, and
served in the late rebellion. Elizabeth (again)
married, March 15, 1847, Nathaniel Paine, of
Centre Harbor, N. II., at which place they
lived and prospered, and died at advanced
ages. Elizabeth was a lady of the old-fashioned good manners, and of praiseworthy
enterprise.

²⁵ IV. **Molly**⁵⁰ Boodey, daughter of Rev. Joseph,
born Dec. 23, 1773; married, Jan. 23, 1793, James Howe,
of Strafford, born Oct. 28, 1771. They removed from N.
H., and settled in Lowell, Mass. He died Oct. 15, 1847.
Mrs. Howe died Feb. 27, 1864. Children : —

²⁰⁹ OLIVE HOWE, b. April 4, 1795; m. John Russ;
d. March 14, 1867.
²¹⁰ NANCY HOWE, b. Dec. 5, 1797; m. Samuel M.
Foss; d. Dec. 23, 1827.
²¹¹ JOSEPH HOWE, b. March 4, 1799; m. Sept. 1,
1820; d. Aug. 29, 1849.
²¹² HEZEKIAH D. HOWE, b. Jan. 30, 1801; m. Sept.
30, 1834; d. May 19, 1865.
²¹³ COMFORT HOWE, b. Feb. 3, 1803; d. April, 1880.
²¹⁴ SARAH B. HOWE, b. March 18, 1805; d. May 27,
1864.
²¹⁵ POLLY HOWE, b. Sept. 13, 1807; m. Dec. 18,
1828; d. Dec. 28, 1859.

²¹⁶ DANIEL B. HOWE, b. May 17, 1810; d. Nov. 15, 1866.

²¹⁷ MEHALA HOWE, b. Dec. 27, 1812; m. May 29, 1842. 98½

²¹⁸ CYRENE HOWE, b. Nov. 15, 1815; m. Dec. 2, 1842. 99

²⁶ **IV. Jonathan**[51] Boodey, son of Rev. Joseph and Olive (Drew) Boodey, born June 24, 1776; married Nancy Evans, born in 1781; settled and resided for several years at Stanstead, P. Q., latterly at Lowell, Mass. He died in July, 1847; his wife had died in July, 1842. Children: —

²¹⁹ LOT, b. 1799; m. Oct. 7, 1847; d. July 8, 1854. 100

²²⁰ JOSEPH WARREN, b. 1800; d. June 4, 1867. 101

²²¹ MARY, b. Dec. 14, 1804; d. May, 1876. 102

²²² DANIEL, b. 1806; d. Oct. 26, 1876.

²²³ THOMAS J., b. 1809; d. Aug. 1832. 103

²²⁴ NANCY, b. April 11, 1812; m. Nov. 27, 1839. 104

²²⁵ AZARIAH, b. 1815. 104½

²²⁶ ELIZA A., b. Nov. 25, 1822; m. Jona. Nelson, March 17, 1842. 105

²²⁷ OLIVE, b. 1824; d. 1837.

^{26½} **IV. Azariah**[52] Boodey, son of Rev. Joseph and Olive (Drew) Boodey, born Dec. 3, 1789; married Betsey Bartlett, of Newburyport, Mass. Child: —

²²⁸ JOHN J.

²⁷ **IV. Joseph**[53] Boodey, Jr., son of Rev. Joseph and Olive (Drew) Boodey, born March 16, 1782; married Molly Boodey (see No. 24, p. 157).

[28] **IV. Olive**[54] Boodey, daughter of Rev. Joseph and Olive (Drew) Boodey, born Sept. 10, 1788; married George Foss, b. Feb. 4, 1790. They resided for several years in Strafford, N. H.; moved westward. Children:—

[229] FRANCIS E. Foss, b. Jan. 3, 1811; d. Oct. 30, 1827.
[230] JOSEPH B. Foss, b. July 13, 1814.
[281] JOHN D. Foss, b. Dec. 23, 1817.
[282] ZECHARIAH B. Foss, b. Feb. 15, 1822.
[283] CLARISA A. Foss, b. Nov. 26, 1823; m. Nath. E. Hanson.   **106**
[234] GEORGE F. Foss, b. Sept. 30, 1838.

[29] **IV. Comfort**[55] Boodey, daughter of Rev. Joseph and Olive (Drew) Boodey, born Feb. 10, 1791; married, Aug. 12, 1812, Charles Caverly, of Strafford, N. H., born Sept. 27, 1784; he was a respectable farmer; lived on the homestead of his father, Philip Caverly; filled some important offices. He died June 6, 1872; she followed him March 3, 1876, aged 85 years. Children:—

[235] ELIZA J., b. Nov. 1, 1813; d. March 3, 1826.
[236] JOSEPH B., b. April 21, 1815.   **107**
[238] LEONARD W., b. Nov. 7, 1818.   **108**
[239] CHARLES H., b. May 26, 1823.   **109**
[240] CYRUS G., b. Nov. 15, 1825; d. in the war.   **110**
[241] ISAAC L., b. May 31, 1835; d. Jan. 31, 1864.

[30] **IV. John**[56] Boodey, son of Rev. Joseph and Olive (Drew) Boodey, born April 16, 1795; married Sally Hall. He died in Lowell, Mass., May 22, 1874. Children:—

[242] JOSEPH B., b. June, 1821; m.; now of California, near Stockton, Oneil Township, San Joaquin Co.; a husbandman, wealthy, independent, and progressive.   **110½**

[243] LOT, b. Jan. 17, 1824; m. Oct. 1825, Aldana
    Newbert; 2d, Sarah Heath.
[244] JOHN W., b. July 20, 1828; m. Harriet Cheney,
    and resides in Nottingham, N. H.   110¾
[245] EMILY S., b. May 14, 1831; m. Geo. W. Foss.   111

[31] **IV. Isaac**[57] Waldron (B.), 2d, son of Sarah
(B.) and Isaac Waldron, of Barrington, born in Barrington; married —— Wallace, of Rye, N. H.; settled in
Portsmouth, N. H.; became a distinguished, prosperous
merchant there. He died many years ago. About the
year 1831, we, in quest of a school, visited Portsmouth,
and with pleasure shared for a day and night Isaac's
fraternal, commodious hospitalities. Peace to the ashes
of one of nature's generous, native noblemen.

[32] **IV. John**[58] Waldron, of B., son of Sarah (B.)
and Col. Isaac, of B., born about the year 1788; married
Comfort Haynes; settled in Barrington; was often
chosen a selectman, and otherwise shared the confidence of his fellow-men in the fulfilment of other
places of trust. He died several years since, leaving
children: —

[246] ISAAC WALDRON, b. in 1800.
[248] SARAH B. WALDRON, m. John Harriman.
[249] MARY ANN WALDRON; resided at Lowell; d.
[250] WELLS WALDRON, m. —— Pierce, of Dover.
[251] JOHN H. WALDRON, m. Salome Wallingford.
[252] CAROLINE WALDRON, m. Harry Thompson, of
    Limington.
[253] HORATIO G. WALDRON, of Charlestown, Mass.;
    died.

²⁵⁴ MARTHA WALDRON, m. Bradstreet Plummer, of
    Newburyport.

²⁵⁵ ELIZA WALDRON, d. young.

^{32½} **IV. Aaron C.**⁶³ Waldron, son of Col. Isaac,
of B., and of Sarah (B.), born Oct. 6, 1792; married
Eleanor Goodwin, of Berwick, and settled at Limington,
Me. He died Aug. 26, 1878, aged 86 years. Children:—

²⁵⁶ CAROLINE M. WALDRON, b. Sept. 15, 1813; m.
    I. H. Libbey.

²⁵⁷ JULIA A. WALDRON, b. 1815; d. 1855.

²⁵⁸ HENRY P. WALDRON, b. 1817; m., 1st, Sally
    Small; d.; 2d, —— Sanborn, of Standish.

²⁵⁹ ISAAC WALDRON, b. 1819; m., 1st, Julia Marr, of
    Standish; 2d, Margaret Woodman.

²⁶⁰ ALPHONZO H. WALDRON, d.

²⁶¹ LEONARD F. WALDRON, m. Martha Ward, of
    Standish, Me.

³³ **IV. Daniel**⁶⁴ Waldron, son of Col. Isaac and
of Sarah (B.), of Barrington; married: 1st, Eliza K.
Woodbury, of B., born Nov. 4, 1796, daughter of the
celebrated Dr. Robert Woodbury, and sister to the wife
of the late Gov. Noah Martin, born Nov. 4, 1806. She
was married Sept. 22, 1819; died June 27, 1821. Children:—

²⁶² ROBERT W. WALDRON, b. Oct. 26, 1820; m.
    July 13, 1845, and resides in Maine.

Daniel married, 2d, Feb. 17, 1822, Lois Glass, born in
1797, who died March 20, 1827. Child:—

²⁶³ JOHN C. WALDRON, b. Feb. 13, 1823; m.   **112**

The said Daniel married, 3d, Oct. 15, 1827, Irene Dearborn, who died Aug. 15, 1870. Children:—

[264] ASA D. WALDRON, b. Dec. 13, 1829; d. Dec. 11, 1879.

[265] DANIEL G. WALDRON, b. April 16, 1833.

[266] SARAH F. WALDRON, b. June 20, 1839.

Daniel Waldron, whose genealogy is given above, was a progressive, practical farmer, a man of sound sense and sterling integrity; was held in high estimation, and was often appointed by his fellow-citizens to important offices of responsibility and trust. He died at Acton, Me., Oct. 7, 1843, and there rests at the homestead.

[34] **IV. Azariah[66]** Waldron, Col., son of Aaron, of Strafford, and Hannah (B.) Waldron, born Aug. 5, 1775; married Deborah Brown, of Northwood; kept a store of dry and English goods; carried on an extensive trade in Barrington, and in Strafford after it was severed in 1820 and incorporated by itself as a town. In the military he was a captain, major, and colonel, and in the civil service he was often a selectman and representative to the halls of legislation in New Hampshire, from the votes of his native Barrington, as well as from the recently organized town of Strafford. He died Nov. 11, 1825; his good lady, whom we well remember, survived him but a few years. They rest at their old homestead. His old store-house, in front of his mansion, worn somewhat of time (1880), still stands there. Children:—

[267] RHODA, d.   [268] SAMUEL, d.   [269] MARY, d.

[35] **IV. Isaac[68]** Waldron, 2d, son of Aaron and Hannah (B.) Waldron, born Aug. 21, 1780; married

Mary Whitcher, of Northfield. He settled on a farm near Bow Lake in Strafford. Their lives were successful. His son William W. inherited the homestead, and still resides there. The father died Oct. 19, 1856, aged 76, and the mother May 5, 1861. Children:—

270   SARAH WALDRON, b. Dec. 1, 1800; d. Aug. 16, 1878.

271   WILLIAM WALDRON, b. Feb. 3, 1803; d. 1803.

272   JONA. WHITCHER WALDRON, b. Feb. 5, 1804; d. May 28, 1859.

273   DANIEL B. WALDRON, b. March 19, 1806.

274   MARY JANE WALDRON, b. Nov. 12, 1808.

275   GILBERT A. WALDRON, b. June 12, 1811.

276   HORACE WALDRON, b. Dec. 23, 1813.

277   LOVEY WALDRON, b. Dec. 10, 1817; m.; d. Nov. 20, 1851.

278   WILLIAM W. WALDRON, b. March 10, 1822; m.   113

279   PAMELIA WALDRON, b. Oct. 24, 1824; d. Feb. 22, 1858.

36   **IV. John[69]** Waldron, son of Aaron and Hannah (B.) Waldron, born Aug. 20, 1782; married Elizabeth Paul, of Dover, N. H. He died June 1, 1848, leaving children: —

280   ELIZABETH ANN WALDRON.   283   BENJAMIN.

281   OLIVER.   284   CHARLES.

282   CLARA.   285   ADALINE.

37   **IV. Robert[71]** Waldron, son of Aaron and Hannah (B.) Waldron, born April 3, 1786; married Mary Abbott, of Barrington, N. H. He died May 11, 1826. He left children: —

286   CHARLES WALDRON.   287   MARY.   289   ANN.

[39] **IV. William**[73] Waldron, son of Aaron and Hannah (B.), born Feb. 23, 1790; married Mercy Felker, of Barrington, born Oct. 20, 1794; died Dec. 18, 1878. He was a husbandman highly respected; he died Oct. 26, 1866, aged 76. Children:—

290   JONA. C. WALDRON, b. Jan. 18, 1815.
291   ROBERT B. WALDRON, b. Aug. 7, 1818.
292   AARON WALDRON, b. Oct. 26, 1822.
293   AZARIAH WALDRON, b. Sept. 8, 1826.
294   HANNAH WALDRON, b. Dec. 14, 1829.

[39½] **IV. Hannah**[74] Waldron, daughter of Aaron and Hannah Boodey Waldron, born May 22, 1792; married, Jan. 2, 1812, Joseph Huckins, of Strafford, N. H., born July 28, 1789, a thrifty, enterprising farmer. Mrs. H. died Dec. 13, 1825. Joseph died Feb. 5, 1845. Children:—

MARTHA A. HUCKINS, b. Nov. 18, 1812; m.
    Joshua Woodman, Esq.   [113¼]
JOHN HUCKINS, b. March 12, 1815; m. Miss
    Hannah Abbie Hill, born April 21, 1818.   [113½]
ABRAM W. HUCKINS, b. May 25, 1817; d. Jan.
    19, 1844.
HANNAH E. HUCKINS, b. Oct. 5, 1819; d. March
    10, 1821.
AARON W. HUCKINS, b. Feb. 16, 1822; d. Jan.
    19, 1844.
RHODA W. HUCKINS, b. Sept. 17, 1824; d. March
    12, 1826.

. Joseph Huckins married, 2d, Sarah Waldron, Dec. 12, 1826, born Dec. 1, 1800, daughter of Isaac and Mary

(Whitcher) Waldron. Sarah died Aug. 1878. Children: —

DANIEL W. HUCKINS, b. Aug. 19, 1828.
JOSEPH HUCKINS, b. Dec. 28, 1830; d. June 22, 1880.

40 IV. Richard[75] Waldron, son of Aaron and Hannah (B.), born March 6, 1795; married Rhoda Keniston, of Barnstead, N. H., and resided, a farmer, in Strafford. They had one child: —

295 AARON WALDRON.

41 IV. Lovey[76] Waldron, daughter of Aaron and Hannah (B.) Waldron, born May 14, 1797; married Richard Leighton in 1817, born Feb. 19, 1787. He died May 9, 1834. She surviving him, died June 13, 1860, at their homestead in Epsom, N. H. Children: —

296   ZECHARIAH LEIGHTON, b. March 9, 1818; m. Mishel Bartlett, April 13, 1812.   **114**
297   HANNAH E. LEIGHTON, b. July 14, 1822; m. 1842, William Meader.   **114½**
298   ABRAM LEIGHTON, b. March 2, 1826; d. July 2, 1827.
299   JOSEPH E. LEIGHTON, b. Jan. 18, 1829; husbandman, residing in Northwood, N. H.
300   ALMIRA LEIGHTON, b. May 8, 1833; m. 1856, Oliver J. Gray.   **115**

42 IV. Zechariah[77] Waldron, son of Aaron and Hannah (B.) Waldron, born July 19, 1799; married Polly Willey, of Barrington. He died Oct. 27, 1827, leaving two children: —

301   ALMIRA WALDRON, m. Smith George, Esq., of Barnstead, N. H.
302   OLIVER WALDRON.

[43] **IV. Sarah**[78] Waldron, daughter of Aaron and Hannah (Boodey) Waldron, born Jan. 14, 1802; married James B. Foss, Esq., of Strafford, N. H. He in life has been, and still (1880) is, active at a venerable age, and is an independent husbandman. His frugal, intelligent lady, now at the advanced age of 78 years, still takes pride in the charge of her own household, and in doing old-fashioned kindnesses to the neighbor, to the weary-worn traveller, or to the healing up of the broken heart. She, like the last leaf upon the tree in a bleak autumn, still clings to the tossing branch; is the last child of a numerous family, and the last daughter of a noble parentage. Long, long, may she still live, a memorial of a generous ancestry; and a bright example of faith, industry, economy, and usefulness to the advancing generations of her kindred, as they hence shall come and go. Children: —

[303] AARON W Foss, b. July 20, 1824.   [116]
[304] HANNAH Foss, b. Oct. 25, 1825.
[305] RICHARD W. Foss, b. Aug. 7, 1827.
[306] ADALINE Foss, b. Aug. 2, 1830; d. Aug. 6, 1878.
[307] JAMES H. Foss, b. Aug. 3, 1835; d. Aug. 20, 1837.
[308] MARY A. Foss, b. July 6, 1840.

[44] **IV. Hannah**[80] Caverly, daughter of John (Lieut.) and Betsey (Boodey) Caverly, born Oct. 22, 1781; married, March 15, 1804, Robert Huckins, a son of Israel, who was a son of Robert and Hannah (Boodey) Huckins, the first. He was a progressive farmer, born June 2, 1783. They resided first in Strafford, and afterwards in Madbury, N. H. He owned and cultivated two farms. He died Oct. 17, 1832, and his faithful wife

March 7, 1833. They peacefully rest at their first old homestead, on a beautiful hill, which from the east overlooks Bow Lake. Children : —

309   JOHN C. HUCKINS, b. March 29, 1805; a bachelor, residing at the old homestead.

310   ASA HUCKINS, b. Dec. 21, 1807; m.; d.   117

311   JONATHAN HUCKINS, b. Sept. 28, 1813; a bachelor, also residing at the old place in Strafford.

312   ROBERT HUCKINS, b. July 8, 1821; m.   118

313   ELIZABETH LYDIA HUCKINS, b. May 20, 1829; m. 119

45   IV. Betsey[81] Caverly, daughter of John (Lieut.) and Betsey (Boodey) Caverly, born Oct. 30, 1794; married to George Foss by Rev. Joseph Boodey; was a thrifty farmer; inherited the homestead of his father on Strafford Ridge. He died Nov. 11, 1841, and the farm was inherited by his industrious son Azariah, who, with the aid of an amiable, frugal wife, still holds and improves it. The mother died Jan. 13, 1871, at the advanced age of 87 years. Children : —

314   LOUISA FOSS, b. Nov. 17, 1815; m.   120

315   JOHN C. FOSS, b. Jan. 12, 1819; m.   121

316   AZARIAH FOSS, b. Jan. 24, 1821; m.   122

317   HANNAH P. FOSS, b. June 2, 1823; d. June 21, 1837.

318   BETSEY C. FOSS, b. March 2, 1825; d. May 3, 1857.   122½

46   IV. Sarah[82] Caverly, daughter of John (Lieut.) and Betsey Boodey Caverly, born Sept. 4, 1787; married Joseph Hill, of Strafford, born May 3, 1781. He was a farmer, honest, and in all things true and faithful. His

wife, from an industrious parentage, proved worthy of her calling. She died Dec. 11, 1855; he in March, 1868, aged 88 years. They rest at the old farm, which had been cleared up from the wilderness by her father. Children: —

315 HANNAH HILL, b. Feb. 8, 1806; d. Oct. 20, 1828.

320 ELIZA HILL, b. Dec. 11, 1809; d. March 5, 1867. 123

321 SUSAN HILL, b. Feb. 12, 1811; d. July 14, 1861. 124

322 MEHALA C. HILL, b. March 20, 1814; m. 125

323 AZARIAH B. HILL, b. Dec. 26, 1817; m. 126

324 SARAH HILL, b. April 20, 1819; m. 127

325 NANCY HILL, b. May 22, 1821; m. 128

326 ALMIRA HILL, b. April 12, 1830; m. Seth T. Hill, Esq. 129

327 LOVINA HILL, b. Sept. 12, 1832. 130

47 **IV. John** [83] Caverly, Rev., son of (Lieut.) John and Betsey (Boodey) Caverly, sister of the Rev. Robert and Joseph, was born Aug. 23, 1789. Beyond the common schools of his time, he obtained an academical education at Gilmanton, N. H., and for a considerable time was employed as teacher of youth; and then, in 1812, when and after the war was declared (June 18) by the United States against Great Britain, he enlisted as a volunteer, and served in the U. S. Army at Portsmouth. The war coming to an end, he settled in Strafford on his large farm, near Canaan, N. H., which supported numerous flocks and herds, yielding to him a profitable income. He took a leading interest in the academy of his native town. In 1827, being ordained to the gospel ministry, he was installed the pastor of a church there, and thus continued to the end of his life,

22

most of the time, by exchanges and otherwise, supplying
the pulpits of other towns occasionally in that vicinity.
He was a man of much force of character, of good manners, and to a great and good purpose exerted an extensive influence.   His excellent lady was Nancy French,
born Sept. 9, 1795, with whom he had united in marriage
in 1819.   She died Jan. 22, 1855; he, surviving her
about eight years, died at his homestead, March 23, 1863.
His funeral discourse was preached by his long-revered
friend and associate in the ministry (and of much renown),
the Rev. Enoch Place, assisted by other clergymen of
that neighborhood.   His last resting-place, with his dear
wife and others of his family, was preferred at the old
homestead of his father.   Children: —

328   JOSEPH F. CAVERLY, b. May 27, 1820; m. Eliza-
          beth Boodey (p. 92).
328½ ZECHARIAH CAVERLY, b. March 20, 1822; m.
          Rebecca M. Crosby.   131
329   DARIUS CAVERLY, b. 1825; d. Jan. 24, 1828.
330   ROBERT B. CAVERLY, b. 1827; d. Aug. 12, 1846.
331   J. COLBY CAVERLY, b. 1829; d. June 10, 1834.
332   ELIZABETH O. CAVERLY, b. Dec. 5, 1832; m.
          Aaron W. Foss, Esq. (p. 87).   131½
333   JOHN B. CAVERLY, b. June 16, 1836; m.   132
334   LUTHER M. CAVERLY, b. Dec. 15, 1839; m.   132½

48   **IV. Azariah**[84] Caverly, son of (Lieut.) John
Caverly and Betsey Boodey, born Dec. 28, 1792; died
Dec. 14, 1843, at his residence in Strafford.   His death
in middle life was caused by an injury received in the
overturning of his carriage by a frightened horse.   He had
high aspirations, and was industrious and enterprising.

He took an interest in the militia; filled several offices; for a considerable time he served as commander of a company called the Strafford Light Infantry. May 12, 1816, he married Sally Adams, daughter of Ebenezer, who built the first dwelling-house in Barnstead, N. H. She was born June 18, 1792; died May 28, 1830. Children: —

335 NANCY CAVERLY, b. Nov. 6, 1817; d. June 19, 1830.

336 BETSEY CAVERLY, b. Aug. 22, 1820; m.; d. Aug. 29, 1849. **133**

337 EBENEZER A. CAVERLY, b. Sept. 10, 1822; d. Dec. 13, 1827.

338 EVERITT F. CAVERLY, b. Oct. 31, 1825; d. Jan. 11, 1858.

339 JOHN H. CAVERLY, b. Oct. 17, 1828. **134**

. Again, Azariah was married to Eliza Tasker, born June 4, 1812; married Jan. 23, 1832. She died May 30, 1870. Children : —

340 GEORGE A. CAVERLY, b. Jan. 28, 1833. **135**

341 SARAH J. CAVERLY, b. Dec. 15, 1835; d. Sept. 16, 1865.

342 HIRAM P. CAVERLY, b. May 20, 1839; m. **136**

343 ELIZABETH A. CAVERLY, b. April 29, 1843; m. **137**

49 **IV. Joseph**[85] Caverly, Col., son of (Lieut.) John and Betsey (Boodey) Caverly, born April 15, 1795; inherited the old homestead of his father, and with success cultivated it, making himself profitable and agreeable to his kindred, and to the neighborhood and town in which he lived. He favored the military, and from time

to time officiated as a captain, a major, and a colonel,
ever holding and enjoying the confidence of all who
knew him. He married, Feb. 28, 1832, Lovina French,
sister of the late Joseph French, Esq., of Concord, N.
H., and daughter of the late Joseph French, Sr., of New
Durham, N. H. Col. Joseph died Jan. 23, 1853. His
Lovina, at the age of 74 years, still (1880) lives, a praiseworthy example to her day and generation. Children: —

344 SETH W. CAVERLY, b. Oct. 22, 1834; m.   138
345 MARY LIZZIE CAVERLY, b. Oct. 4, 1836; d. May
    16, 1856, much lamented.
346 SARAH JOSEPHINE CAVERLY, b. Sept. 12, 1840;
    still lives at the old homestead.

50 IV. Daniel[86] Caverly, son of John (Lieut.)
and Betsey (Boodey) Caverly, born Jan. 23, 1798, and
now (1880), in his eighty-third year, a highly respectable,
successful husbandman, remains still in good health and
strength. He stands erect, the senior (or at least among
the seniors) of his kindred race in New England. He
has lived to see much of the old native red-man's forest
fall creaking down at the stroke of the white man's axe.
His early birth gave him a sight of many of the first old
fathers and mothers of New England, who in infancy
had been protected, as was Moses in the rushes, within
the rude walls of the garrison-house. He had seen the
veterans of the Revolution, who in the time of England's
conflict with us, had on the battle-field fought for and
secured the political liberties of this great nation, and
has seen the vanguard of the generations that then
followed and are still following the fathers downward in
succession, unnumbered, in their constant onward prog-

ress. He has seen the fashions of the first fathers of
New England, and their devout, economical habits, their
generous, warm-hearted manners, and their customs
among men. He has seen their simple, frugal, whole-
some style of living, their fashions of dress, their houses
constructed of logs and poles united at their ends by
joints made by the rude old axe, and the crevices
between the logs filled or plastered by a mixture of mud
and clay or of straw, the roof being covered with the
bark of trees, or of thin timbers split or hewn out, and
made thin like boards. The oven, built of stone and
covered over with clay, was sometimes outside; the
fireplaces of the cot being constructed of stones rudely
piled up, between which the fire, kindled upon the earth
beneath, blazed forth, while through a hole made in the
roof of the cot, the smoke rolled upward, escaping to the
clouds. Both by day and night he has seen at dreary
winter, the crackling, brisk old fire that ceased not to
burn. And further onward our veteran had seen those
rude old cots, under the march of industry and improve-
ments, pass away as did the garrison-house which had
shielded his immediate fathers and their households in
their infancy. He had seen how, by honest, economical
labor, frugality, and abstinence, the forefathers had made
themselves independent freeholders, and became wise
and happy in the dignity and pride of a progressive,
useful life; how, with the consciousness of having
acquired their own fortunes, not through the labor of
others, but with their own hardy hands, their lives
had been blest. Such men our veteran had seen,
and such men conserved the noble example which he
himself hath cherished and followed. Thus, from the

fortitude, sufferings, strivings, and success of the ancestor, the descendant catches the glow of ambitious life, truthfulness, and patriotism, and follows onward and upward in the faith of the fathers. By such examples the young heart becomes prepared, with patience and self-reliance, to encounter the hardships of the desert, and, if need be, to face an enemy in defence of his lands, his life, or of the freedom of his country.

All these things, and more, our senior has lived to see, as they came to pass, and thereby has been much profited. In early manhood (Oct. 26, 1820) he had married Nancy Hill, an amiable lady, daughter of Henry Hill, of Barrington. She died Oct. 27, 1829. Children:—

347   ELIZA H. CAVERLY, b. July 21, 1821; d. March
        31, 1840.
348   MARY A. CAVERLY, b. May 13, 1823; m. John
        C. Peavey, Esq.   138
349   JOHN HENRY CAVERLY, b. June 2, 1826; m. Miss
        Susan A. Quimby.   139
350   DARIUS E. CAVERLY, b. May 21, 1828; m.;
        killed in battle, July 19, 1863.   140

Second marriage, Jan. 27, 1831, with Isabel Morrison, sister of Gen. Nehemiah Morrison, late of Alton, N. H., born Feb. 7, 1791. She died June 24, 1870, aged 79 years. Children:—

351   NANCY I. CAVERLY, b. Aug. 25, 1831; m.   141
352   JANE E. CAVERLY, b. April 17, 1833; m.   142

51   **IV. Mary**[87] Caverly, daughter of John (Lieut.) and Betsey (Boodey) Caverly, born May 4, 1800; mar-

ried John Peavey, Esq., of Strafford, born July 8, 1790,
who was prominent in life for industry and usefulness;
was a captain in the militia, and more than once served
his town as a representative in the legislature of New
Hampshire. The honored wife died Feb. 20, 1857, and
the husband Dec. 6, 1865. They rest at the homestead
on Strafford Ridge, now (1880) held as inherited by his
son, Robert Boodey Peavey. The location is pleasant.
Children : —

353   John C. Peavey, b. Sept. 9, 1819; m.   143
354   Robert B. Peavey, b. Jan. 17, 1824; m. Emily
     P. Montgomery.   144
355   Mary E. Peavey, b. May 5, 1828; m.   145

52   **IV.**   Ira88 Caverly (Dea.), son of (Lieut.) John,
born April 9, 1804; married Lydia Libby, May, 1825,
born in June, 1804. For some years he was in trade;
was a citizen of Lowell, highly respected, in life constantly to be depended on. In every good work re-
quiring aid, and in the various activities of life, he was
always to be found on the right side. He was a kind
neighbor, a faithful friend. His good wife died August,
1839. Children : —

356   Daniel D. Caverly, b. at Strafford, 1825; m.   146
357   Susie E. Caverly, b. at Strafford, Dec. 4, 1828;
     married.   147

Second marriage with Sarah Colcord, of Nottingham,
N. H., Sept. 8, 1840. Children : —

358   Sarah Caverly, d. in infancy.
359   J. Henry Caverly, b. July 7, 1844; m.   148

Dea. Caverly died Dec. 6, 1877, and reposes beneath an aged oak on Washington Avenue, Lowell Cemetery.

[53] **IV. Robert**[89] Boodey Caverly, son of John (Lieut.), was born at Barrington, N. H., now Strafford, July 19, 1806; was a lawyer, poet, and author of books. When quite young, he held the office of colonel in the major-general's staff, an inspector in the New Hampshire Militia. He graduated at the Harvard Law School; practised law at first six years in Maine, Limerick Village, and thence at Lowell, Mass., and to the end of his life. A mention of his early progress may be found in the History of Limerick, in the Annals of York County, page 60, as follows: "Many eminent men have resided in Limerick in connection with the academy or in the practice of their professions. Among others may be mentioned President Smith of Dartmouth College, President Harris of Bowdoin, and Robert B. Caverly, the poet and author."

The record of his life as a lawyer may be found in the published reports of the highest courts in Maine, in New Hampshire, in Massachusetts, in the supreme court of the District of Columbia, in the high court of claims in the capitol at Washington City, and in the supreme court of the United States. His poetry or authorship may be found in his volumes of Epics, Lyrics, and Ballads, and in his several Orations; in his History of the Indian Wars of New England; in his Lessons of Law and Life from John Eliot the Apostle; in his Legends and Dramas, entitled Battle of the Bush, and other works.

His first wife was Clara W. Carr, daughter of Andrew, and granddaughter of Col. James Carr, of the Revolution; his last was Emily Parker, daughter of Benjamin, formerly of Boston, latterly of San Francisco, Cal.; married Oct. 15, 1853. Children: —

360   ADELAIDE CAVERLY, b. July 7, 1838; d. June 10, 1841.
361   CLARA W. CAVERLY, b. April 23, 1841; d. Aug. 10, 1842.
362   EDWARD CAVERLY, b. Oct. 4, 1844; m.   149
363   FRANK CAVERLY, b. Feb. 15, 1846; d. Nov. 16, 1850.
364   CARRIE CAVERLY, b. Sept. 4, 1854.
365   MARY CAVERLY, b. July 29, 1857; m.   150

54   **IV.**   **Asa**[90] Caverly, son of John (Lieut.) and Betsey Boodey (C.), born Oct. 5, 1812; now (1880) still living in Strafford, pursuing the honest and productive occupation of a husbandman, and in this he does all things well. On Oct. 28, 1833, he married Susan Bunker, of Strafford, born Aug. 14, 1807, who is also still living. His farm-house is on the hill upon the same road, near the old parental homestead.

Fifth Generation.

55   **V.**   **Daniel**[91] Boodey, son of Azariah[2] (B.) and Betsey Chick, of Limington, born July 26, 1789; married, April 1, 1819, Abigail Varney. Child: —

366   MARY ELIZABETH.

Married, 2d, Mary Ann Cole. Children: —

367   CYNTHIA.   368   DANIEL.

56 **V. Abigail**[95] Boodey, daughter of Azariah[2], of Limington; married Nathan Chadburne. Children:—

369 AZARIAH CHADBURNE.   372 NATHAN CHADBURNE.
370 LUCY CHADBURNE.   373 ABIGAIL CHADBURNE.
371 LYDIA CHADBURNE.   374 MARSHALL CHADBURNE.
                    375 ELIZABETH CHADBURNE.

57 **V. Mary**[98] Boodey, daughter of Azariah (B.), of Limington; married Pelatiah Carle. Mary died Dec. 1, 1879. Children:—

376 GEORGE W. CARLE, b. Feb. 20, 1825; m. Almira
      Blodgett.
377 BETSEY JANE CARLE, b. Dec. 17, 1825; m. An-
      drew Anderson.
378 COMFORT ANN CARLE, b. April 11, 1830; d.
379 ASENATH CARLE, b. March 17, 1832; m. Ivory
      Wentworth.
380 MARY M. CARLE, b. Oct. 26, 1834; m. Charles
      Anderson.   150½
381 GARDNER P. CARLE, b. March 4, 1836; m.
      Almira Hasty.   151
382 LUCY ELLEN CARLE, b. 1838; d.
383 HENRY LEE CARLE, b. 1846; m. Ellen Plummer. 152

58 **V. William**[100] Hasty, son of Robert (II.) and Molly Boodey, late of Limerick, Me., born Feb. 15, 1788; married Polly G. Strout, Feb. 13, 1809, born June 17, 1792; was a farmer and an industrious citizen. She died June 6, 1868; he, surviving her, died March 3, 1872. Children:—

384 EMMA HASTY, b. Sept. 25, 1809; d.
385 SIMEON S. HASTY, b. July 23, 1812; m. Sarah
      Watson; d.; eight children.   153

[386] MARY ANN HASTY, b. Sept. 13, 1814; m.; five children.   **154**

[387] ESTHER S. HASTY, b. Aug. 29, 1818; m.; ten children.   **154½**

[388] ROBERT HASTY, b. Dec. 12, 1823; m.   **155**

[389] SALOMA HASTY, b. Dec. 13, 1828; m.; settled in South America.

[390] JOHN W. HASTY, b. Dec. 15, 1829; m.; d. Feb. 4, 1854.

[391] WILLIAM G. HASTY, b. June 26, 1832; m. Feb. 7, 1856; d. Sept. 4, 1874.   **156**

[392] CAROLINE HASTY, b. June 17, 1835; d.

[59] **V. Saloma**[101] Hasty, daughter of Robert (H.) and Molly Boodey, born Dec. 10, 1792; married Charles Kimball, of Exeter, N. H., Sept. 17, 1817. She died May 30, 1870. Two years later, Jan. 10, 1872, he died, leaving children: —

[393] ROBERT H. KIMBALL, b. Sept. 22, 1819; married —— Boothby, Nov. 19, 1843, now of Boston.

[394] MARY E. KIMBALL, b. Oct. 7, 1824.

[395] EMELINE A. KIMBALL, b. Jan. 10, 1827.

[396] HARRIET J. KIMBALL, b. Aug. 9, 1830.

[397] ABBA A. KIMBALL, b. Feb. 19, 1834; married Sept. 26, 1854, Noah Barker, now of Portland, Me.

[60] **V. Mary**[102] Hasty (B.), daughter of Robert (H.) and Molly (Boodey) Hasty; married Stephen Fenderson, of Parsonsfield, Me. Children: —

[398] COMFORT A. FENDERSON, m. —— Moulton.

[399] JULIA A. FENDERSON, m. —— Sanborn.

61 V. Comfort[103] **(B.)** Hasty, daughter of Robert (II.) and Molly Boodey; married William Edgcomb. Children:—

400 BENJ. M. EDGCOMB, d.
401 SARAH M. EDGCOMB, m. —— Drew.
402 OLIVE T. EDGCOMB, m. —— Hatch, of Mass.
403 MARY E. EDGCOMB, m. —— Philpot; d.

62 V. John W.[104] Hasty (B.) son of Robert (II.) and Molly Boodey; married Mary A. Pease, of Parsonsfield. Children:—

404 LOVINA P. HASTY, m. George Lord, of Parsonsfield.
405 ALONZO P. HASTY, m. Mary Ann Wolf, of San Francisco.
406 JOHN W. HASTY, m. —— Cooper, of Parsonsfield.

63 V. George B.[105] Hasty, son of Robert (II.) and Molly Boodey, of Limington; m. Children:—

407 ADDIE S. HASTY, m. —— Tarbox.
408 EMELINE K. HASTY, m. Wm. Jones, of San Francisco.

64 V. Joseph B.[111] Boodey, son of Robert, Jr., grandson of Rev. Robert, b. May 25, 1811; married Oct. 14, 1833, Abigail Nason, born Sept. 4, 1805. Children:—

409 SYLVESTER O., m. Ruth Bean. **157**
410 SUSAN A., m. Asa Morse, of Massachusetts; no issue.
411 ROBERT M., m. Mary W. Osgood. **158**

Second marriage with Rebecca W. Chamberlain, born March 12, 1823, of Randolph, Vt. Child: —

[412] CHARLES S., b. Feb. 16, 1855.

[65] **V. Mary**[117½] Stover, daughter of David and Sarah (Boodey) Stover, and granddaughter of Rev. Robert Boodey; married Sabina A. Warren. Second marriage with Zechariah Durgin. Children: —

[413] ELIZABETH DURGIN.   [415] ORRIN DURGIN.
[414] MELISSA DURGIN.   [416] JOHN DURGIN.

[66] **V. Isabella**[119] Boodey, daughter of John H. Boodey and Patience Redman (B.), of Jackson, born April 10, 1798; married, 1st, Edward March, of Portland. After his decease, she married Charles Bradford, of Bangor. They had one son ([417]), now residing in Waldo County, and after Mr. Bradford's death, she married a Mr. Gollof. She is now (1880) believed to be still living at Bangor.

[67] **V. Sally**[120] Boodey, daughter of John H. and Patience (Redman) Boodey, born June 16, 1804; married John Emery, of Ripley, Feb. 17, 1842, and is now (1880) residing at Corinna, Me. Mr. Emery died June 26, 1860. Children: —

[418] Carrie P. Emery, b. May 31, 1843; long a teacher in Wisconsin.
[419] Alvin Boodey Emery, b. July 3, 1845; m.   **159**
[420] Prucia Emery, b. Dec. 25, 1846; m.   **160**

[68] **V. Lucinda**[121] Boodey, daughter of John H. and Patience (Redman) Boodey, b. Aug. 7, 1803; married Moses Saunders, of Bangor.   Child:—

[421]   HELEN SAUNDERS, who became the wife of J. Currier, a gentleman of wealth and worth, who has of late died, leaving her a widow, still residing at Bangor.

[68½]   **David**[122] Boodey, son of John H. and Patience (Redman) Boodey, b. Nov. 9, 1807; married Lucretia Mudget, of Prospect, Me.   He died in August, 1879. Children:—

[422]   FITZ HENRY A., m. April 27, 1832, Hannah Jane Ames, of Stockton, Me.   [161]
[423]   DAVID A., b. Aug. 13, 1837; m. Abbie Treat.   [162]
[424]   JOHN H., m. Miss Nora Seely.   [163]
[425]   LAURA JANE, m. Dr. Samuel Johnson, of Dixmont.
[426]   NAPOLEON B., clerk, 58 Broadway, N. Y.; active in business.
[427]   JOSEPHINE, m. Drew Fogg, of Jackson.

David Boodey, Sr., is said to have been a man of strong mental faculties and of sterling integrity. He died of cancer at his native Jackson, in 1879.

[69]   **V. Redman**[123] Boodey, son of John H. and Patience (R.) Boodey, of Jackson, Me., born April 4, 1811; married in 1833, Mary Twitchell, of Dixmont, born in 1811.   They reside in Jackson.   Children:—

[428]   PERSIS T., b. 1835; m. Coleman Hall in 1856.   [164]
[428½] JOHN A., b. 1837; d.

429 ANN MARY, b. March 27, 1838; m. 1858, S. S.
Roberts. 165
430 HENRIETTA, b. 1840; m. 1859, Darius Drake. 166
431 CLARANDON, b. 1842; m. 1866, Rosa A. Roberts. 167
432 GEORGIANA, b. 1845; m. 1863, Robert Plummer. 168
433 CAROLINE, b. 1850; m. William T. Putnam. 169
434 EDWIN C., b. 1847; m. Dora F. Roberts, 1871. 170
435 WELLINGTON R., b. 1853; m. 1877, Cora Jewell. 171
436 CARRIE E., b. 1856; m. 1878.

70 V. 𝕳arriet[124] Boodey, daughter of John H.
and Patience (Redman) Boodey, b. Oct. 31, 1812; married, Dec. 5, 1839, Samuel Eastman, born at Falmouth,
N. H., Sept. 2, 1802, of Bangor, now residing at Six
Mile Falls, Penobscot Co., Me. Children : —

437 FRANK HENRY EASTMAN, b. at Bangor, June 23,
1842; d. at Jacksonville, Ill., Dec. 30, 1870.
438 ELLA FRANCENA EASTMAN, b. at Bangor, July
9, 1844.
438½ JOHN ALVIN EASTMAN, b. at Bangor, June 6,
1849; m. Mary E. Wattom. 171½

71 V. 𝕳enry 𝕳.[125] Boodey (Hon.), son of John
H. and Patience (Redman) Boodey, late of Jackson,
Me., born Nov. 10, 1816; married, Sept. 3, 1846, the
amiable Charlotte Mellen Newman, of Berwick, daughter of Professor Newman, born July 23, 1823. She died
at Brunswick, Feb. 5, 1876. Two children.

This Henry H., through industry, economy, and extraordinary abilities, both natural and acquired, has made
himself prominent in wealth, influence, and affluence
among the lords of New York; and although the loss of

an entire cheerful and interesting family brings grief, yet, though alone, he falters not, but manfully continues to make progress, maintaining a lofty ambition, and a noble, generous independence.

In 1842, graduating from Bowdoin College, he became a tutor in that institution, holding also, commencing in the year 1845, and continuing nine years, up to 1854, a professorship in the department of rhetoric at the same college. Then, at the end of his term, resigning his professorship, he was elected to the State senate of Maine, and served for that year. Thence by his fellow-citizens of Brunswick, he was thrice elected to the house of representatives, and served the additional sessions of three years in the Maine legislature.

In 1859 he established himself in business in New York City. There, actively concerned, he has had much to do, among other employments, in carrying forward railroad enterprises, some of them the largest in the country. Of the Illinois railroad companies he for a long time was treasurer.

Much has this our kindred friend done in furtherance of the publication of these annals of our noble race. May his days be prolonged. Children: —

439 HENRY PHILIP, b. Nov. 28, 1847; d. April 19, 1871.

440 CAROLINE KENT, b. July 4, 1850; d. Sept. 27, 1861.

71½ V. Alvin[126] Boodey, son of John H. and Patience (Redman) Boodey, graduated at Bowdoin College in 1847; married Sarah Ellen Sewall, of Auburn, Me. He held the place of preceptor of the academy at

Auburn for several years, and then became principal of the academy at Fryeburg, and in each place proved successful. In 1856 he commenced business in the town of Hudson, Wis., in connection with his brother, Hon. Henry H. Boodey, of New York, and there industriously and faithfully brought to himself and brother an abundant, profitable income. Alvin was a man of sound sagacity, of honest purpose, and good judgment. He died at Hudson in October, 1855, much lamented. They had one child, who died in infancy.

72 V. Israel[139] Boodey, 2d, son of Israel and Hannah (Strout) Boodey, born July 18, 1812; married Harriet Cilley; was a shoe-dealer in Portland, Me., and lived and died there. Children: —

.441 HANNAH L.; a dressmaker; m.
442 MARTHA A.; d.
443 SARAH F.; m. —— Lamb.
444 ELLA M.; m. —— Anderson.

73 V. Eunice S.[141] Boodey, daughter of Israel and Hannah (Strout) Boodey, born May 2, 1815; married, in 1850, Edmund Douglass, of Limington, born in 1818. Children: —

445 LUELLA DOUGLASS, b. 1855; m. —— Ayer; two children.
446 EDMUND DOUGLASS,
447 HENRY H. DOUGLASS, } Twins, b. May 29, 1857.

74 V. Zechariah[143] Boodey, 4th, son of Israel and Hannah (Strout) Boodey, born Aug. 9, 1819; married in 1848, Abby Wentworth, of Limington. He is a hus-

24

bandman and shoe-manufacturer.   She died in 1856.
Children : —

448   CYRUS W., m. Martha Whitton.
449   HENRY LEE, d. 1865.

Second marriage with Fanny Black, of Limington.
Child : —

450   JOHN F., b. Jan. 1859; m. Mary E. Gilman.

75   V.   𝕳enry 𝕳.¹⁴⁴ Boodey, 3d, son of Israel and
Hannah (Strout) Boodey, born April 8, 1822; married,
Nov. 30, 1845, Elizabeth L. Lombard, of Standish, born
Aug. 31, 1825. He died May 29, 1877, leaving his home-
stead in Windham, Me., to his son Frank.   Children : —

451   LORANA, b. Sept. 1, 1847; m. Fred Legrow.   172
452   ELLA, b. March 18, 1849.
453   FRANK H., b. March 13, 1853.   Has been a town
        officer and legislator.
454   HARRIET L., b. July 16, 1845; d. Dec. 8, 1855.
455   FREDERICK, b. Oct. 30, 1856; d. Dec. 18, 1856.
456   CHARLES L., b. Feb. 5, 1858; d. Aug. 5, 1859.
457   ANGIE, b. Dec. 27, 1859.
458   HOWARD, b. Dec. 16, 1862.
459   LOUISE L., b. April 9, 1865; d. Aug. 8, 1865.

Henry H. Boodey, last above named, had made himself prominent in business at Windham, first in the
smith business, then in the trade of goods, then in the
lumber traffic and in the manufacturing business; always
reliable, firm in his integrity, — living to help others
to live, and always successful. That he left to himself
and family an enduring good name and fame is no
wonder.

[76] **V. Edmund T.**[145] Boodey, son of Israel and
Hannah (Strout) Boodey, born April 4, 1823, in Limington, Me.; married, June 18, 1844, Lucinda Emery, of
Great Falls, N. H., born May 10, 1819, and hitherto has
occupied the old homestead of his father and of his
grandfather, Rev. Robert, the Quaker. Edmund T. cher-
ishes the memories of the fathers. He, in good taste
and example, clings to what they left to him as heirlooms,
with tenacity and reverence. Accordingly, the same
old garments preserved, are still kept at the old homestead, which had been cast off by the revered grandfather, when in the faith of his God, for the last time
he laid them off, taking his departure to the realities
of another world.

The same old arm-chair of his choice, in which he was
accustomed to rest him in wearied life, is still sacredly
adhered to and cherished as a god-send of the olden
time. The same old vest that he wore, with its numerous buttons and vast dimensions, in that far-gone
day, and which had been fitted to his corpulent, stately
proportions of nearly three hundred pounds, is still there.
Edmund favors us with the following description of it:
"It covers a circumference of four and a half feet; its
lower corners are rounded at the bottom; it has an
eight-inch opening on either side of it to make room
for the hips; its buttons, two and a half inches apart,
are eleven in number, and large in size."

In the old bureau are many an ancient letter of the last
century, soiled by the touch of time as it hath moved
onward. Many of these ancient epistles, some of which,
being from correspondents in England, are novelties,
and would be useful to be printed, read, and studied.

Edmund T. still keeps, and, as we have seen, sacredly maintains the old mansion of the Rev. Robert, and since of Israel his father, in all of its ancient form and quaintness. Near by it is the old apple-tree of that primitive day, still yearly yielding its fruit, grafted to baldwins by our revered ancestor Robert, the Reverend, seventy years ago. And near to the mansion is the grave of the ancestor himself, by the side of his dear Margery, who, on the 30th of June, 1780, had knelt by his side in the old Boodey mansion in New Durham, N. H., when on that day together they united at the altar in the formation of the Free Baptist church at its origin, and assisted in the writing out of its first covenants.

This grandson of Robert the first has of late done much for his race by his praiseworthy endeavors in the obtaining of genealogical information for the enlargement and publication of these annals.   Children: —

460   FRANK E., b. April 11, 1845; d. Dec. 1, 1855.
461   EVERETT W., b. April 17, 1848; m.   173
462   SYLVANA A., b. Aug. 17, 1850; m. Oct. 22, 1870.   173½
463   An infant son, b. May, 1852; d. May 16, 1852.
464   CALESTA, b. Oct. 10, 1859.

77   V. Albion K. P.[146] Boodey, son of Israel and Hannah (Strout) Boodey, born Jan. 29, 1825; married, Oct. 21, 1853, Julia A. Staples, born March 6, 1853; died March 14, 1878, at Limington.   Children: —

465   IDA E., b. Sept. 1, 1855; m. Oct. 17, 1855; d. March 8, 1873.
466   CHARLES H., b. Feb. 4, 1858.
467   MILLARD F., b. March 16, 1860.
468   HATTIE B., b. June 27, 1861.
469   JENNIE M., b. Jan. 21, 1866; d. Dec. 18, 1870.

[78] **V. Lydia S.**[148] Boodey, daughter of Israel and Hannah (Strout) Boodey, born May 6, 1831; married Phineas Hanscomb, of Platt Valley, Wis. Children:—

[470] CHARLES HANSCOMB. [471] EVA HANSCOMB.

[79] **V. Ann J.**[149] Boodey, daughter of Benjamin and Jane (Cram) Boodey, born Oct. 22, 1807; married, May, 1831, Henry Adams, d. Child:—

[472] MARTHA ELLEN ADAMS.

Married, 2d, —— Maxy. Children:—

[473] EMILY MAXY. [475] JANE MAXY.
[474] BENJAMIN B. MAXY. [476] SARAH B. MAXY.

[80] **V. Jane C.**[150] Boodey, daughter of Benjamin and Jane (Cram) Boodey, born Aug. 22, 1809; married Henry M. Minot in Feb. 1837. She died in 1868. Children:—

[477] MARY F. MINOT. [479] WILLIAM MINOT.
[478] JOHN H. MINOT. [480] ALBERT F. MINOT.

[81] **V. Nathan W.**[151] Boodey, son of Benjamin and Jane (Cram) Boodey, born April 12, 1811; married —— Proctor; resides in Westbrook. Children:—

[481] JANE. [483] NATHANIEL. [485] FREDERICK F.
[482] HATTY. [484] FRANK H. [486] CHARLIE.

[82] **V. Ellen M.**[152] Boodey, daughter of Benjamin and Jane (Cram) Boodey, born May 22, 1813; married William Pride. Children:—

[467] ELLEN M. PRIDE. [468] JENNY PRIDE.

By second marriage with Joseph Hoes. Children:—

[489] CHARLES B. HOES.   [490] HENRY B. HOES, } Twins.
                          [491] MARY B. HOES, } Twins.

[83] **V. Frederick W.**[156] Boodey, son of Benjamin and Jane (Cram) Boodey; married —— Roberts. Child:—

[492] FREDERICK MAY, d.

[84] **V. George W.**[157] Boodey, son of Benjamin and Jane (Cram) Boodey, born Aug. 15, 1824, a twin with Harriet S.; married. Children:—

[493] SARAH.   [494] CHARLES.

[85] **V. Elizabeth W.**[161] Boodey, daughter of Benjamin and Sarah (Winslow) Boodey; married Daniel H. Walker, of Casco, Dec. 2, 1861. Children:—

[495] ALFRED A. WALKER.   [496] SARAH WALKER.

[86] **V. Sewall**[162] Boodey, son of Edmund and Lydia (Jones) Boodey, of Windham, Me., born Sept. 6, 1808; married, March 11, 1832, Cornelia Ann Greene, born May 24, 1811, at Portland, Me. He died April 25, 1873. Children:—

[497] ELIZABETH JONES, b. Feb. 6, 1833; m. June 6,
       1859.   [174]
[498] FRANCIS GRANVILLE, b. Aug. 31, 1834; m. May
       29, 1856.   [175]
[499] EMMA CAROLINE, b. Oct. 18, 1836; m. Dec. 4,
       1856.   [176]
[500] EDMUND, b. Oct. 28, 1838; d. Sept. 17, 1859.
[501] MARTHA JANE, b. Sept. 18, 1841; d. Oct. 6, 1843.

[502] LEONARD GREENE, b. Dec. 6, 1843; m. May 3, 1869. [177]

[503] CHARLES SEWALL, b. Dec. 7, 1846; d. Feb. 22, 1856.

[504] MARTHA JANE, b. Feb. 28, 1849. Has favored our annals.

[505] CORNELIA ADELAIDE, b. July 28, 1852; m. Dec. 21, 1870. [178]

[506] JOHN GREENE, b. Sept. 21, 1855; m. Jan. 8, 1879, Deborah G. Gowen, b. July 15, 1857.

[71½] **V. Margery**[129] Morton (B.), daughter of Ebenezer and Betsey (Boodey) Morton, of Limington, Me., born April 28, 1802; married, Dec. 6, 1827, Michael Sawyer, of Limington, born June 7, 1795, and died Oct. 28, 1876. Children: —

[507] ABBIE A. SAWYER, b. Feb. 12, 1828.

[508] ELIZA J. SAWYER, b. Jan. 10, 1831; m. Feb. 1, 1852.

[509] MARGERY A. SAWYER, b. Sept. 4, 1832; m. Nov. 1853.

[510] SALOME M. SAWYER, b. Dec. 20, 1834; m. Nov. 25, 1857.

[511] HARRIET A. SAWYER, b. Dec. 27, 1836; m. Dec. 1861.

[512] ELLEN M. SAWYER, b. March 15, 1840; m. May 2, 1865.

[513] MERRILL H. SAWYER, b. April 24, 1843.

[514] MARTHA F. SAWYER, b. Aug. 14, 1846; m. Dec. 11, 1868.

[172] **V. Jacob P.**[87] Boodey, son of Rev. Joseph, 2d, and Mercy (Pike) Boodey, born in New Durham, N. H., Sept. 15, 1810; remained at home up to his 18th year;

clerk in a store in Middleton, 1828; clerk in store in Portsmouth, 1829; was clerk in the law-office of James Bartlett, Esq., Dover, N. H., 1830 and 1831; was clerk in the
registry of deeds, Bangor, Me., 1833, '34, '35, and '36;
married Louise M. Dane, of Bangor, Me., Sept. 6, 1836;
was clerk in registry of deeds, Dover, N. H., 1840, '41;
was financial clerk in the Dover Gazette office from
1845 to 1851; moved to Alton, N. H., 1851, and went
into store with John W. French; was postmaster at
Alton, N. H., under President Pierce, 1853, '54, and '55;
was elected a road commissioner for the county of Belknap, 1855; was elected county commissioner for said
county, 1856, holding the office three years; in 1859 was
elected register of deeds for Belknap County, N. H.,
which office he continued to hold through twenty-one
re-elections to the date of his death. His late residence
was at Laconia. Mr. Boodey died on the 28th day of
February, 1880. Mrs. Boodey, born Feb. 8, 1819, survives him. Previously (Dec. 25, 1879), his neighbors,
having noticed his declining health, numerously gathering together, made him a kindly call, each bearing to
him, whose life-long generosity they desired to recipro-
cate, some substantial token of their love and esteem, to
which, on the next day, in a public print of the place, he
thus replied : —

" CARD.

" To my warm-hearted, generous friends,— the business men of
this vicinity, — I desire to express my keen appreciation of the
kindly sentiments which prompted their magnificent New Year's
gift to me. It is, indeed, a 'Happy New Year,' not alone for
the substantial tokens it brings, but for the expressions of
neighborly good-will and kindness from those whose respect is
more to me than gold. I thank you with the tongue, with the
pen, and with the heart.   JACOB P. BOODEY."

At the March session of the court for the county of
Belknap, according to a notice previously ordered, of
which ex-Sheriff Everett and E. P. Jewell, Esq., served
as a committee of arrangements, a memorial service was
held at the Unitarian church. The court for that day
was accordingly adjourned, and the congregation, made up
of the honorable court, members of the Belknap bar, the
county officials, the jurors and citizens at large from
many parts of the county, moved in procession to the
place of appointment. Flowers were in abundance.
The Rev. Enoch Powell opened the service by appropriate readings and prayer; sacred song by Messrs.
Stone and Baker, Mrs. Muncy, Mrs. Gould, Mrs. Young,
excellent vocalists, with the skilful Miss Clara Davis at
the solemn organ, followed. The generous speakers
bringing grateful garlands in tribute to the memory
of their deceased officer and friend, were Judge Hib-
bard, Col. M. A. Haynes, Hon. Daniel Barnard, Col.
Thomas Cogswell, J. H. Currier, Esq., and Mr. Everett.
The last-named orator read appropriate letters from
John II. Pearson, Esq., of Concord, N. H., and from
Robert B. Caverly, Esq., of Lowell, Mass. Mr. Barnard
read a beautiful poem from the skilful pen of Mary
Helen, only daughter of the deceased, written long
ago, — sweetly sentimental; appropriate to the occasion;
moving the heart. At length came the closing song; a
benediction; and then that day's numerous assembly
silently, sadly turned away, moved by the continued
entrancing trills of the solemn organ, — all, as we trust,
made wiser and better for having known and cherished
the many dutiful deeds and precepts which they long

25

and constantly had seen and found in the noble, generous life of Jacob P. Boodey. He had but one child : —

515 MARY HELEN.

This young lady, known to the literary world as the sweet singer of Laconia, was born at Dover, N. H., Dec. 11, 1847; was his only daughter, the pride of his heart, and the darling child of the amiable mother. For these, the mother bereaved, and the daughter being upon her dying bed, the kind father had much solicitude at his departure. He had nothing to leave to them but a long, last farewell, his own good name and fame, and a train of generous, God-serving neighbors.

Below we give place to two of the songs of this poetess, clipped from a public journal, — the one a lyric addressed to the memory of her affianced lover, deceased; and the other a reply to S. F., a young lady friend, who had reproved Mary for her apparent sadness.

LINES TO THE MEMORY OF MR. CHARLES FRANCIS HOLDEN, OF BOSTON, MASS.

(Author of " Holden's Book on Birds," who died Nov. 4, 1875.)

"The noblest work below the sun
Is such a one as he."

We love the sunshine, and when storm-clouds come
   To veil the sky in darkness, earth grows sad,
And moaning winds from out their cavern home
   Wail through the bowers that once were bright and glad.
So do we mourn for thee, thou noble one!
   Thy presence was like sunshine to our hearts,
And now, alas! thy earthly life is done,
   And hope, that came with thee, with thee departs.—
O Death! couldst thou not spare a heart so kind?
Couldst not some less endeared, less cherished victim find?

Thou wert like sunshine, and didst live to bless
   Where'er the influence of thy life was felt;
Not thine the heart to turn from all distress,
   For kindly pity in thy bosom dwelt.
Thy hand was ever swift to help the poor,
   Thine ear unto their sorrows would attend;
And when deserving merit sought thy door,
   It found in thee a kind and generous friend.
Gloom fled from sorrowing hearts at thy advance,
And flowers of grateful joy sprang up beneath thy glance.

Thou wert like sunshine; few are like to thee;
   Mind, manners, person, all combined to form
A being such as Heaven delights to see, —
   A rainbow on the darkness of life's storm.
The light of an undaunted spirit shone
   From the clear depths of thine unsullied eyes,
Where one might gaze, nor fear to look upon
   Some hidden treachery or low disguise;
Strength joined to kindness, kindness joined to mirth,
Stainless integrity, there beamed and blessed the earth.

There shall be many praises said of thee,
   And many hearts be saddened at thy loss,
And words more worthy than mine own can be
   May do thee justice; but the heavy cross
Of this bereavement will not pass away
   Until 'tis lifted by the Father's hand,
Until the golden morning of that day
   Which waits the spirit in the Better Land
Shall shine upon the soul, excelling far
The light of all our dreams of what its glories are.

Often we prayed, with lips that longed to bless,
   That God would guard thee, keep thee from all harm;
But ah, how little did our full hearts guess
   How He would bless thee, *how* all troubles calm!
The prayer is answered; thou, indeed, art blest;
   No earthly ills can now thy spirit fret;

God loved thee, and He gave His peace and rest;
  Nor will He, in His mercy, us forget.
O heavenly sunshine! from thy heavenly home
Wilt thou not to our sad and shadowed spirits come?

God's compensations are on every hand;
  He hath a healing balm for every wound;
By His kind providence the earth is spanned,
  In Him all light and wisdom may be found.
He gives His strength in dark affliction's night,
  His own eternal sunshine never fails;
His gifts are ours; but sometimes from our sight
  He for a season their effulgence veils:
But what He gives He ne'er will take away,
The deathless soul can claim all but the senseless clay.

Thou wert like sunshine—thou wilt ever be!
  The brightness of thy nature is not lost;
It lives, and beams above life's stormy sea,
  Whereon our feeble barks must still be tossed.
The star of memory shines upon our way,
  Its light is sweet as we recall the past,
Whose golden glory was too bright to stay
  And gild a life by sorrow's shades o'ercast.
In Heaven's congenial light thy soul exists,
And some day we shall see beyond these earthly mists.

LACONIA, N. H.   MARY HELEN BOODEY.

To this manifestation of sadness Miss S. F., as appears,
interposes reproof, to which Mary advances as follows:—

THE ANSWER.

You do not chide the blasted, prostrate tree,
  Shivered to fragments by the bolt of heaven,
Because it rises not in verdancy,
  Fair as before the fatal stroke was given;
But look with mournful sympathy to see
The once proud monarch's fallen majesty.

You do not murmur at the blighted flower
　That greets your saddened gaze, whose withered form
Tells with a wordless eloquence, of power
　More fatal than the summer's fiercest storm ;
But sorrow as you see the blossom lie
Prone to the earth, robbed of its beauteous dye.

And you reproach not the sweet bird of song,
　When, mourning for her mate, she will not sing,
And droops her pretty head amidst the throng
　Of feathered songsters, — folds to rest her wing,
Resolved to unconsoled, unmated die,
The sweetest model of true constancy.

Then wilt thou chide me, if I give not forth
　The gladsome strains that speak of naught but mirth,
And deem my song has lost its all of worth,
　Because it quivers with the wrongs of earth?
My harp hath lain in shades of grief so long,
It often blends in wailings with my song.

I have my sorrow; though the thoughtless world
　May look upon my life and deem it glad,
And say affliction's bolt was never hurled
　Across the sky so free from every shade,
Lit by the glowing radiance of love,
No clouds to dim the smiling heaven above.

Thank God! I *do* have love, — a priceless gift, —
　And sympathy so sweet it seems like heaven.
These have more power the clouds of grief to lift
　Than aught to take their place that could be given,
These are the precious blessings that I hold
More value than earth's store of shining gold.

Yet still there breathes a sadness in my song,
　My harp must yield a plaintive, sad refrain,
For ever I am conscious of the wrong
　And cruel hardships in the world ; in vain
Are all my efforts to forget the grief
Of myriad ones who toil without relief.

Let those who will, turn from the sorrowing ones,
　Earth's martyrs, — though consumed not in the flames,
A mournful prelude o'er my harp-strings runs,
　As I recall their oft-neglected claims,
And how their pleading prayers to God ascend,
Turning from countless foes to one great Friend.

I would not change the fate my God has given,
　But rather thank him for his tender care;
I know that sorrow brings us nearer Heaven,
　And crowns us with immortal glory there.
This life to some would be a weary way,
Caught they not glimpses of eternal day.

Long as the foaming billows hover near,
　And loud the murmuring breezes sweeping by,
I'll face the troubled storms without a fear,
　With this sweet thought, "I know that He is nigh."
My heart is but a wild, impatient thing,
But *He* hath patience with my wandering.

LACONIA, N. H.　　　　　　　　　　　　　　　　　M. H. B.

DEATH OF MARY HELEN.

The father, as we have seen, died on the 28th of
February, 1880; and now, on the 29th of April, a
startling telegram announces to us the decease of the
daughter poetess.　Her funeral brought to her many a
"lily sweet, the rose in beauty full in bloom."

From among the many letters of condolence received
by the widowed mother of the late Mary Helen Boodey,
we make a few brief extracts.

Messrs. Thomes & Talbot, of Ballou's Magazine,
write: "With profound regret we received the intel-
ligence of the death of Miss Boodey, although the
announcement was not quite unexpected.　We have
many pleasant remembrances of the lady while she was

associated with us, and our friendship for her was not broken when her ill health had compelled her to relinquish the labors which she loved so well."

Robert B. Caverly, the poet, writes: "I have known Miss Boodey by reputation and by her literary accomplishments during the most part of her short but brilliant life. Proudly do I cherish her memory, regarding her as having been one of the best poetical and prose writers of her time. Among many others, her pathetic poem on life and death, entitled 'The Two Angels,' was, to my mind, a production of which even a Bryant or a Milton might well be proud."

Mrs. Henrietta E. Page, the authoress, writes: "Mary Helen Boodey was one of the sweetest women it has ever been my lot to know."

The Manchester Union pays a warm tribute to the memory and literary ability of the late Mary Helen Boodey, and makes the following suggestion, which will be heartily endorsed by her friends in this vicinity: "It is sincerely to be hoped that some friendly hand will gather the stray flowers of poesy which she scattered along the way of life, and bind them in one fair garland. Many of her verses are touchingly tender and sympathetic, while holy trust and spiritual aspiration are manifested in almost every line. No richer contribution can be made to the permanent literature of New Hampshire, than a volume embracing the poems of Mary Helen Boodey." [From the Laconia Democrat, of April, 1880.]

To this we add a quotation from the poetic pen of
Mary's friend, Henrietta C. Page, of South Boston.

In Memoriam.

A bird let loose from prison bonds
    Flies singing upward high for heaven,
As though in having freedom gained,
    Its beauteous breast with joy is riven.

So, from the prison of thy form,
    Thy soul flies singing to its God,
Thrilling with joy in love released,
    From weary pathways lately trod.

With softly folded waxen hands,
    Peaceful, at rest, thy form now lies;
Dumb are thy ever-loving lips,
    Closed are thy gentle, dove-like eyes.

No whiter spirit God had given
    To mortal, than on thee bestowed;
No sweeter songs were ever sung,
    Than those which from thy pen have flowed.

Thy fragile form enshrined a soul,
    Sparkling and bright as rarest gem;
Pure as the sweet arbutus buds
    Nestling upon the parent stem.

.   .   .   .   .

Farewell, sweet friend, a little while,
    A span, and we shall meet again;
Meet where the weary are at rest,
    Where there no parting is, nor pain.

                                        II. C. P.

173 **V. Zechariah[88]** Boodey, Col., son of Rev.
Joseph, 3d, and Mercy (Pike) Boodey, born in New
Durham, N. H., June 20, 1813; married, Feb. 19, 1837,
Joan O. Runnals, of Portland, Me. An independent

husbandman, he resided for some years in New Durham,
and from thence they settled on a farm in Watertown,
where he still lives in sweet content, after the manners
and customs of the healthy, economical, prosperous
fashion of the olden time. Mr. Boodey in early life
was honored in the military of New Hampshire with
various offices, among which was that of colonel of its
33d regiment. Of late he has greatly favored his
kindred race in his contributions to the publication of
these annals. May the venerable, ancient name which
he still lives to honor, be cherished in the far-off future
as in the past. Children : —

520 CHARLES H., b. Dec. 27, 1838; now a physician
and surgeon, at Cochituate.   181
521 DANIEL EDWIN, b. Aug. 23, 1840; d. Nov. 27,
1840.
522 ELLEN AMILLA, b. Jan. 3, 1847; m. F. W. Colbath.   182

89 **V. Socrates Harrison**[174] Boodey, son of
Rev. Joseph, 3d, and Marcy (Pike) Boodey, born Nov. 2,
1816; married, Aug. 16, 1840, Tamson L. Ham, born
Jan. 3, 1821, and resides in New Durham, N. H. Children : —

523 LEZETTE E. A., b. Sept. 12, 1841.
524 HORACE P., b. April 14, 1844.   183
525 ORISA, b. Sept. 25, 1846; m. Albert Labounty.
526 MARIETTA, b. Nov. 1, 1848; m. Henry Hurd.
527 BELLE, b. Jan. 19, 1856.
528 NAT H., b. Oct. 25, 1860.

89½ **V. Joseph M. and Betsey P.** Boodey, son
and daughter of Rev. Joseph, 3d, and Marcy (Pike)
26

Boodey, the one born Sept. 10, 1821, and the other, Jan.
9, 1819; still reside on the old homestead of their father
and of their grandfather, Zechariah the 2d, and in the
same old mansion of more than one hundred years'
standing (see pages 130–180 of this book). On the twen-
ty-ninth day of July, 1880, a delegation of a thousand
Free Baptist clergymen, among them some from England, visited Randall's grave in New Durham, N. H.
(see page 153), where the covenants of their first church
had been drawn by the Boodeys, and where its first
church organization was formed on June 30, 1780, in
reference to which meeting the Boston Journal of July
30, 1880, has an account as follows:—

"THE BOODEY HOUSE.

"A short distance from the village centre, on the road
to Barnstead, is the celebrated Boodey House, in which
was formed one hundred years ago the first Freewill Baptist Church. It is an ancient, weather-beaten structure,
which was built by Zechariah Boodey in 1777. One son,
Rev. Joseph Boodey, was a Freewill Baptist minister,
and the house is now owned by a granddaughter, Mrs.
Betsey Boodey, and a brother. The room in which the
few brave pioneers of the denomination assembled a
century ago remains substantially in the same condition
as then. As many as possible gathered into this apart-
ment; after which those in the house as well as those in
the yard outside joined in singing the Doxology. Prayer
was then made by Rev. Professor Dunn, D. D., of Hills-
dale College."

    90 V. Xra[184] Boodey, son of John, 2d, and Susanna
(Hayes) Boodey, born April 26, 1801; married, Nov. 11,

1824. Joanna Sewards; resides in Strafford, N. II., an industrious man, a kind neighbor, and a faithful friend. Children : —

529   JOHN, b. May 13, 1825; d. March 29, 1826.
530   ARIANNA, b. Aug. 21, 1828; m. Joseph
      O. Foss.   } Twins.   184
531   SARAH A., b. Aug. 21, 1828; m.   }   185
532   MARY S., b. June 22, 1831; m. Joseph Hill.   186
533   MARTHA, b. Sept. 16, 1834; m. Geo. A. Caverly.   186½
534   GEORGE S., b. Jan. 23, 1839; m. April 1, 1859,
      Eliza J. Carter, born April 4, 1842.

91   V.   Zechariah[185] Boodey, 4th, son of John, 2d, and Susanna (Hayes) Boodey, born Sept. 4, 1802; married, Sept. 28, 1823, Abigail Watson, of Strafford, N. II., born March 28, 1801. He, an industrious farmer, died Feb. 5, 1869. His widow died Jan. 8, 1874. Children : —

X 535 MARTHA A., b. May 30, 1824; m.   187
536   CHARLES H., b. Dec. 16, 1826; d. Sept. 25, 1829.
537   ALONZO H., b. March 28, 1829; m. Nov. 11, 1856. 188
538   ELIZABETH S., b. Dec. 16, 1831; m. Aug. 10, 1847. 189
539   GEORGE W., b. Nov. 22, 1834; m. Feb. 16, 1856.   190
540   ASENATH A., b. Feb. 17, 1838; m. July 3, 1855.   191
541   JOHN O., b. Nov. 27, 1842; m. Nov. 27, 1863.   192

92   V.   Lucinda[186] Boodey, daughter of John, 2d, and Susanna (Hayes) Boodey, born March 26, 1804; married Oliver Leathers, born Oct. 12, 1796. They settled in Palmyra, Me. She died Sept. 22, 1873. Children : —

542   ABBIE LEATHERS, b. Feb. 6, 1822; m. James
      Greenacre, b. May 17, 1820. One son, James
      A., b. Aug. 15, 1843.

543   JOHN B. LEATHERS, b. April 26, 1823; d. March
18, 1864.

544   GILBERT H. LEATHERS, b. Dec. 12, 1824; was a
Union soldier in rebel prison.

545   LOUISA M. LEATHERS, b. Feb. 17, 1827; d. Jan.
10, 1868.

546   SARAH J. LEATHERS, b. Jan. 9, 1830; d. July 27,
1870.

547   OLIVER W. LEATHERS, b. Jan. 9, 1832.

548   JOSEPH B. LEATHERS, b. April 17, 1834.

549   CHARLES H. LEATHERS, b. July 9, 1836.

550   FREDERICK A. LEATHERS, b. March 20, 1839.

551   ALPHONSO D. LEATHERS, b. April 17, 1842.

552   LUCINDA H. LEATHERS, b. Sept. 24, 1843.

93   **V. Aaron**[187] Boodey, son of John, 2d, and
Susanna (Hayes) Boodey, born Sept. 28, 1805; married,
April 12, 1827, Charlotte Hill, born March 24, 1803.
They resided in Northwood, N. H., and lived faithful,
exemplary lives.   Children: —

553   ELBRIDGE G., b. Sept. 14, 1827; m.   193

554   CHARLES H., b. Sept. 21, 1829.   194

555   SAMUEL H., b. Aug. 13, 1831; m. Lucinda M.
Patch.   195

556   AUGUSTA, b. Sept. 28, 1833; d. September, 1876.

557   JOHN W., b. Dec. 16, 1835; d. June 16, 1864.   196

558   JUDITH C., b. Aug. 8, 1839; m. Dudley Ladd, of
Vermont.

559   MARTHA M., b. May 14, 1842, ⎫
560   MARY E., b. May 14, 1842,   ⎬ Twins.
                                   ⎭

661   EDSON H., b. March 28, 1845; m. Abbie Savage,
of New Market, now of South Berwick.

⁹⁴ **V. Joan**[188] Boodey, daughter of John, 2d, and
Susanna (Hayes) Boodey, born Nov. 29, 1807 ; married,
May 27, 1827, Enoch B. Caswell, of Strafford, and then
of Manchester, N. II., born Dec. 19, 1799. He died
April 4, 1864. She then, surviving, died Dec. 19, 1865.
Children : —

562   JOHN M. CASWELL, b. Oct. 27, 1827; m.; d. Oct.
      1, 1864.   197

563   ELIZABETH J. CASWELL, b. June 6, 1829.   198

564   ALONZO M. CASWELL, b. April 26, 1832; m.   198½

565   MELISSA A. CASWELL, b. Nov. 24, 1833; died
      March 3, 1835.

566   MELISSA A. CASWELL, b. Jan. 28, 1835.

567   MARY S. CASWELL, b. Sept. 27, 1841.   199

568   ENOCH I. CASWELL, b. July 6, 1844; d. Jan. 5, 1845.

569   HENRY I. CASWELL, b. Nov. 5, 1847.   200

⁹⁵ **V. Daniel**[189] Boodey, son of John, 2d, and
Susanna (Hayes) Boodey, born April 14, 1809; married
Sarah Wiggin, born May 25, 1812. He is settled, an
industrious, thrifty husbandman, upon the old homestead
of his father and grandfather, the John Boodeys of
Canaan, in Barrington, N. H. Daniel holds the confidence of his fellow-townsmen, and has been honored as
their representative in the State legislature, and in other
places of trust. His amiable lady has much favored us in
obtaining materials for these annals. This husbandman
has the possession and care of the graves of many of our
first kindred, who died at Canaan, and whose ashes peacefully rest there on a pleasant hill-side sacredly enclosed.
Let the glorious sun light it up at morn ! At its going
down, let it linger there ! And let the moonbeams of

night cast down her honors there as the eternal years rolling onward shall come and go ! Children: —

570   JOHN G., b. Feb. 13, 1834; d. Aug. 13, 1836.
571   SUSAN H., b. Aug. 19, 1835 ; m. John W. Gear, July 12, 1853, b. June 6, 1840 ; d. Aug. 7, 1874.
572   D. WEBSTER, b. July 9, 1842; m.   201
573   WILLIAM, b. July 10, 1853 ; m. Mary Caswell.

96   **V. Susanna**¹⁹⁰ Boodey, daughter of John, 2d, and Susanna (Hayes) Boodey, born Jan. 31, 1811; married, January, 1827, Israel Huckins, born April 29, 1791; d. March 11, 1855. Children: —

574   HANNAH B. HUCKINS, b. July 18, 1828; m. Frank Knowlton.   202
575   AZARIAH W. HUCKINS, b. Oct. 3, 1831; ⎫
        m. Betsey Paige, Nov. 30, 1854; d.   ⎪   203
        Aug. 20, 1862.   ⎬ Twins.
576   ZECHARIAH B. HUCKINS, b. Oct. 3, 1831; ⎪
        m. Caroline Gear.   ⎭   204
577   RUHANNA HUCKINS, b. Sept. 18, 1835.   205
578   WARREN HUCKINS, b. May 10, 1838; capt. in war.   206
579   MINOT HUCKINS, b. Dec. 29, 1842; d. June, 1861.

97   **V. John B.**¹⁹¹ Boodey, son of John, 2d, and Susanna (Hayes) Boodey, born Nov. 28, 1812; married, March 5, 1837, Abigail R. Smith, of Exeter, N. H. He settled, and now resides, a farmer, in Epping, N. H. In youth John was a good scholar, and in advanced years is a good citizen. Children: —

580   ABIGAIL S., b. March 7, 1838; d. Jan. 7, 1847.
581   JOHN S., b. Sept. 2, 1845.   207
582   ALFARATA A., b. Aug. 21, 1849.   208

⁹⁸ **V. Robert W.**[192] Boodey, son of John, 2d, and Susanna (Hayes) Boodey, born March 7, 1815; married, Feb. 18, 1847, Martha A. Proctor, born Aug. 2, 1822. He resides in Northwood, N. H., an honest farmer. Children:—

⁵⁸³ CHARLES P., b. April 25, 1848; m. Marilla Hoyt.
⁵⁸⁴ JENNIE M., b. July 8, 1851; m. Jeremiah French, of Farmington.

⁹⁸½ **V. Mahala**[217] Howe, daughter of James and Molly (Boodey) Howe, born Dec. 27, 1812; married, May 29, 1842, Samuel Laking, born Oct. 28, 1813. They resided in the city of Lowell, Mass., and by diligence in duty and frugal industry, made the most of life. He died July 19, 1880. Children:—

⁵⁸⁵ MARY A. LAKING, b. Aug. 3, 1849.
⁵⁸⁶ LORA ANN LAKING, b. Dec. 24, 1852.

⁹⁹ **V. Cyrene**[218] Howe, daughter of James and Molly (Boodey) Howe, born Nov. 15, 1815; married Stephen Bartlett, born Jan. 11, 1819, an intelligent, enterprising citizen of Massachusetts. They reside in the city of Lowell, and have children:—

⁵⁸⁷ MELISSA I. BARTLETT, b. Sept. 18, 1842; m.
⁵⁸⁸ SAMUEL B. H. BARTLETT, b. Oct. 31, 1843; m. **209**
⁵⁸⁹ EDWIN W. BARTLETT, b. April 10, 1845; m. **210**
⁵⁹⁰ STEPHEN E. BARTLETT, b. Sept. 23, 1847; m. **211**

¹⁰⁰ **V. Lot**[219] Boodey, son of Jonathan and Nancy (Evans) Boodey, born in 1799, in Stanstead, Lower Canada; married Rebecca Durham Eastman, and being a husbandman, settled in that occupation, first in Illinois

and afterwards in Iowa, where he lived prudently and prosperously to the date of his death by cholera morbus, July 8, 1854. He had seen much of the world and many of its hardships, among which it happened, when in the winter of ——, he, with a brother, had embarked in a boat upon the St. Lawrence, in the midst of a cold wave they became frozen into the ice, and were obliged to remain there until the adjoining ice became strong enough to sustain them on foot from the boat to the shore. Arriving there, his feet proved badly frozen, and both had to be amputated at the ankle. Afterwards, about the year ——, while superintending the building of a bridge, an embankment gave way, and falling upon him, broke both legs. They were amputated, which he valiantly endured without breathing a groan or a sigh. He, as seems, was a man having great force of character. Children : —

[591] BENJAMIN FRANKLIN, b. Dec. 14, 1848; m.   [212]

[592] GEORGE WASHINGTON, b. May 17, 1852.

[593] ELIZA EMERINE, b. Oct. 25, 1853; d. Sept. 11, 1854.

[101] **V. Joseph Warren**[220] Boodey, M. D., son of Jonathan and Nancy (Evans) Boodey, born in 1800, in Burlington, Vt.; graduated at the college at Burlington, and subsequently at Smith's Medical College at Montreal, and there received his diploma of M. D. Sometime after this he left the medical profession and gave his attention more generally to scientific matters, and did much towards the development of mineral wealth, which theretofore seemed to lie hidden in the mountains which skirt the Juniata valley. In this he was abundantly successful. Mainly by his own genius

and enterprise, the iron and coal mines and furnaces at
Bennington, and the ocre mines and paint mills at Newton Hamilton, Pa., were developed, became famous, and
were made progressively useful. At his death a public
obituary declared him to have been "a man of pure
character, honest purpose, and of uprightness in all his
transactions." He died at his residence at Newton
Hamilton, Pa., June 4, 1867, in the 64th year of his age.
"In his death the poor have lost an almoner, the public
a benefactor, and the community an honest, upright, and
generous citizen."

[102] **V. Mary**[221] Boodey, daughter of Jonathan
and Nancy (Evans) Boodey, born Dec. 14, 1804; married
Jeremiah K. Sias, May 4, 1828, at Derby, Vt., and settled
in the farming business at Spencerport, N. Y. She lived
and died a Christian. Her last hours were at the
residence of her sister, Mrs. Jona. Nelson, in Brighton,
N. Y., May 19, 1879. Her husband had died at Rochester, Minn., May 1, 1879, at the advanced age of 75 years.
Children: —

[594] CHARLOTTE SIAS, b. Jan. 26, 1830; m. March 4,
1850. [213]
[595] MARY M. SIAS, b. May 24, 1831; m. Dec. 7, 1853. [214]
[596] ALONZO W. SIAS, b. May 30, 1832; m. May 30,
1863. [215]
[597] DANIEL B. SIAS, b. May 21, 1834. [216]
[598] IRA E. SIAS, b. July 31, 1836; d. Dec. 31, 1878. [217]
[599] NANCY E. SIAS, b. April 26, 1838. [218]
[600] ANNA SIAS, b. Jan. 26, 1841; d. March 3, 1842.
[601] ROXANNA M. SIAS, b. Sept. 22, 1842; m. John D.
Ostrom, Esq. [219]

27

103   V. 𝕿𝖍𝖔𝖒𝖆𝖘 𝕵.[223] Boodey, son of Jonathan
and Nancy (Evans) Boodey, born in 1809; obtained a
liberal education, and through talent, industry, and good
faith, made himself a lawyer. But the service and usefulness of his years were made short. He died in August,
1832, at the early age of 23 years, beloved.

104   V. 𝕹𝖆𝖓𝖈𝖞[224] Boodey, daughter of Jonathan
and Nancy (Evans) Boodey, born April 11, 1812; married, Nov. 27, 1839, Carley Gerald, born June 15, 1805.
Children : —

602   ELIZA A. GERALD, b. Oct. 4, 1840; d. Oct. 15, 1841.
603   CARLOS GERALD, b. May 22, 1843; d. Oct. 23,
         1862, in the service of the U. S. A.; a soldier
         in the 140th Regt. N. Y. Volunteers; and
         rests at the homestead, Brighton, N. Y. He
         lives long who dies for his country.
604   MARSHAL N. GERALD, b. May 27, 1847.
605   AMBIA A. GERALD, b. April 2, 1849; m. Oct. 23,
         1873, Clayton J. Benjamin.   220

104½   V. 𝕬𝖟𝖆𝖗𝖎𝖆𝖍[225] Boodey, son of Jonathan and
Nancy (Evans) Boodey, born in 1815, at Stanstead,
Canada East; after obtaining an education, settled in
New York City, where he still lives. He is an active,
sagacious business man. Many years ago he, under contract, superintended the building of a bridge across the
Merrimack, in the city of Lowell, Mass., and long afterwards, in the same city, under a contract, he constructed
the great Pawtucket canal, which feeds many of the man-
ufactories of that thriving city. We have not learned
anything of his family.

[105] **V. Eliza A.**[226] Boodey, daughter of Jonathan and Nancy (Evans) Boodey, born Nov. 25, 1822; married, March 17, 1842, Jonathan Nelson, born Dec. 25, 1812. They settled in Brighton, N. Y., about the year 1853. He employed himself in the nursery and in the farming business. They have done much for charitable institutions; have always been friends to the poor, as found and acknowledged in the city of Rochester and elsewhere. Losing their only child, they generously adopted and educated six of their nephews and nieces. Their faith is Presbyterian. Child: —

[606] GEORGE C. B. NELSON, b. July 8, 1857; d. May 28, 1858.

[106] **V. Clarissa A.**[233] Foss, daughter of George and Olive (Boodey) Foss, born Nov. 26, 1823; married Nathaniel E. Hanson, of Strafford, N. H. Children: —

[607] GEORGE E. HANSON, b. Jan. 21, 1843.
[608] MARY A. HANSON, b. Jan. 31, 1844.

[107] **V. Joseph B.**[236] Caverly, son of Charles and Comfort (Boodey) Caverly, born April 21, 1814, at Strafford, N. H.; died Sept. 14, 1843, in New Orleans, of yellow fever.

[108] **V. Leonard W.**[238] Caverly, son of Charles and Comfort (Boodey) Caverly, of Strafford, N. H., born Nov. 17, 1818; married Esther L. Hammon, Dec. 1, 1844. She died April 16, 1846. Second marriage, with Martha T. Washton, of Charlestown, Mass., March 28, 1853; died Nov. 25, 1870. Children: —

[610] FLORENCE E. CAVERLY, b. Sept. 7, 1845; m. E. C. Benson.

[611] CHARLES F. CAVERLY, b. May 20, 1855; m.
Emma E. Davis.
[612] EDWIN A. CAVERLY, b. Aug. 16, 1858.
[613] HERVILL V. CAVERLY, b. April 1, 1860.
[614] NETTIE E. CAVERLY, b. Sept. 16, 1862.
[615] MARY L. CAVERLY, b. Jan. 2, 1867.

[109] **V. Charles B.**[239] Caverly, son of Charles
and Comfort (Boodey) Caverly, born May 26, 1823.
Second marriage, with Lovina D. (Caverly) Rowe, widow
of John W. Rowe. He died in 1865, leaving one daughter by this marriage, and by the first wife a son and
daughter. Children: —

[616] ALONZO.   [617] EMMA.   [618] ELSIE ETTA.

[110] **V. Cyrus G.**[240] Caverly, son of Charles and
Comfort (Boodey) Caverly; married, May 5, 1851, Sarah
A. Twombley, born July 16, 1832; was a soldier for the
Union three years; was taken prisoner by the rebels, and
lost his life at Andersonville, Nov. 25, 1864. Children: —

[619] MARTHA J. CAVERLY, b. Dec. 30, 1852; m.   [222]
[620] NELLIE M. CAVERLY, b. June 4, 1854; m.
[621] JOSEPH H. CAVERLY, b. Aug. 22, 1855; m.
[622] LEWIS P. CAVERLY, b. April 26, 1857.
[623] HORACE IRVIN CAVERLY, b. Nov. 3, 1859.
[624] LAURA EVA CAVERLY, b. June 3, 1860; m.
[625] SARAH SUSAN CAVERLY, b. Dec. 1, 1861.

[110½] **V. Joseph B.**[242] Boodey, son of John and
Sally (Hall) Boodey, and grandson of the Rev. Joseph
Boodey, late of Barrington, N. H., born June, 1821;
married, at Stockton, Cal., Dec. 30, 1857, Lizzie (M.)
Boodey, and near that place he established his residence.

His landscape is beautiful, and his wealth in flocks and herds appears to abound. Long may he live.

110¾ V. John W.[244] Boodey, son of John, late of Lowell, and Sally (Hall) Boodey, born July 20, 1828; married, in 1849, Harriet Cheney, and lives in Nottingham, N. H. Children:—

[626] LEON, b. in 1850; d. in May, 1853.

[627] EMMA, b. September, 1853; d. Dec. 15, 1874.

[628] FEN.

[629] GRACE.

111 V. Emily S.[245] Boodey, daughter of John and Sally (Hall) Boodey, born May 14, 1831; married, April 30, 1849, George W. Foss, machinist, residing in Dover, N. H. Children:—

[630] FRANK P. Foss, b. April 29, 1855; m. Oct. 25, 1875. **222½**

[631] EMMA J. Foss, b. May 20, 1857.

112 V. John C.[263] Waldron, son of Daniel (B.) and Louis (Glass) Waldron, born Feb. 13, 1823; married, Jan. 14, 1849, Hannah H. Lang, born Sept. 10, 1821; she died May 1, 1854. Second marriage, Oct. 1, 1854, Lydia A. Seward, of Wakefield, N. H., born Dec. 18, 1825. Children:—

[632] LUCY A. WALDRON, b. Aug. 13, 1850.

[633] LLEWELLA G. WALDRON, b. Dec. 12, 1862.

113 V. William W.[278] Waldron, son of Isaac (B.) and Hannah (Whitcher) Waldron, born March 10, 1822; married Mary E. Peavey (daughter of John, Esq., and Mary (B.) Caverly Peavey), born May 5, 1828.

This intermarriage was the union of prior distant kindred ties, and yet it has proved pleasant, prosperous, and successful.   Children: —

634   JOHN P. WALDRON, b. Aug. 3, 1852.
635   GEORGE W. WALDRON, b. May 15, 1859; d. Oct. 19, 1859.
636   ELLA M. WALDRON, b. Oct. 2, 1860.

113½   **V. John** Huckins, son of Joseph and Hannah (Waldron) Huckins, born in Strafford, March 16, 1815; married Hannah Abbie Hill, daughter of Neal Hill, Esq. Theirs is a successful life; plenteousness abounds within their walls.

113¾   **V. Hannah** Huckins, daughter of Joseph and Hannah (Waldron) Huckins (B.); married, in 1833, Joshua Woodman, Esq., of Strafford.   Children: —

637   JOHN WOODMAN, b. July 10, 1835; d. July 30, 1835.
638   MIRA A. WOODMAN, b. July 28, 1836; m. Judge B. W. Jenness, late deceased.
639   HANNAH M. WOODMAN, b. Feb. 26, 1839; d. April 26, 1844.
640   CHARLES A. WOODMAN, b. May 1, 1841.
641   AARON H. WOODMAN, b. Aug. 5, 1843; d. Jan. 20, 1853.
642   DANIEL S. WOODMAN, b. Dec. 11, 1845.
643   ABBY C. WOODMAN, b. April 7, 1848; d. Oct. 16, 1854.
644   DANA J. WOODMAN, b. May 18, 1851.

114   **V. Zechariah**[296] Leighton, son of Richard and Lovey Waldron (B.) Leighton, born March 9, 1818;

married, in August, 1841, Mishel Bartlett, born April 18, 1812. Children: —

⁶⁴⁵ JAMES W. LEIGHTON, b. March 31, 1842; d. Nov. 13, 1864.

⁶⁴⁶ PHENA L. LEIGHTON, b. Sept. 2, 1846; m. Dec. 31, 1873, Charles Marden. He died May 31, 1874. **223**

⁶⁴⁷ ALBERT R. LEIGHTON, b. Dec. 8, 1849; m. Jennie E. Martin; has one son, Forest A. Leighton, Haverhill, Mass. **224**

⁶⁴⁸ JOHN F. LEIGHTON, b. May 6, 1853; married Katie H. Bean, May 19, 1878; one son, Arthur J. Leighton. **225**

⁶⁴⁹ HORACE G. LEIGHTON, b. April 23, 1857.

114½ V. 𝕳𝖆𝖓𝖓𝖆𝖍 𝕰.²⁹⁷ Leighton, daughter of Lovey Waldron (B.) Leighton and Richard, born July 14, 1822; married, in 1842, William Meader. Child: —

⁶⁵⁰ LIZZIE A. MEADER, m. Hiram Moores, of New Market, N. H. **226**

115 V. 𝕬𝖑𝖒𝖎𝖗𝖆³⁰⁰ Leighton, daughter of Richard and Lovey Waldron Leighton, born May 8, 1833; married, in 1856, Oliver J. Gray, of Northwood (Narrows), born Feb. 26, 1832. Children: —

⁶⁵¹ ANNA L. GRAY, b. at Northwood, April 12, 1862.
⁶⁵² LIZZIE E. GRAY, b. at Northwood, Dec. 25, 1864.

116 V. 𝕬𝖆𝖗𝖔𝖓 𝖂.³⁰³ Foss, Esq., son of James B. and Sarah Waldron (B.) Foss, born July 20, 1824; married, in 1849, Elizabeth O. Caverly, only daughter of the late Rev. John Caverly, of Strafford, N. H. He is thus far a prosperous, industrious husbandman, and his household

is active, enterprising, upward and onward. Mr. Foss
has been called to many responsible places of trust.
Among other offices, he has held the place of representative in the New Hampshire halls of legislation, and in its
constitutional convention.   Children: —

653   CLARA C. Foss, b. Jan. 18, 1850; m. Calvin Rea,
      of Andover, Mass.   She died at her father's
      residence in Strafford, N. H., Oct. 10, 1877,
      aged 27 yrs. 9 months; and there on the
      homestead of her father she rests, —
            "Upon the beautiful hill-side slope,
            Where the sunbeams love to linger."*
      Children: —

654   ALBERT C. Foss, b. Oct. 21, 1851; m. L. E. Tasker.
655   SARAH A. Foss, b. Aug. 28, 1853; m. G. W. Brock.
656   JOHN JAMES Foss, b. Nov. 12, 1855; of Straf-
      ford, N. H.
657   AARON H. Foss, b. Oct. 31, 1857; also of Strafford.

132   **V. John Boodey**[333] Caverly, son of Rev.
John and Nancy (French) Caverly, born Jan. 15, 1836;
married, May 26, 1861, Abby M. Swaine, of Atkinson,
Me., born June 20, 1837.   They reside in Ipswich, Mass.
Fanned by the invigorating breezes of old ocean, they
are inspired by the enduring realities of vigorous health,
which is usually possessed through an enterprising industry.   Children: —

658   IRVIN W. CAVERLY, b. at Strafford, N. H., Jan.
      29, 1864.
659   ROSCOE CAVERLY, b. at Strafford, May 2, 1866.
660   CARL A. CAVERLY, b. at Strafford, March 16, 1868.
661   CHESTER B. CAVERLY, b. at Ipswich, Mass., March
      18, 1874.

---

* For her obituary, see Annals of Caverly Family, p. 156.

[117] **V. Asa**[310] Huckins, son of Robert and Hannah (B.) Caverly Huckins, of Madbury, born in Strafford, N. H., Dec. 21, 1807; married, Feb. 14, 1835, Eliza Seaver, of Chichester, N. H., born Dec. 27, 1807. He died Sept. 29, 1878, much respected. Children: —

[662] GEORGE W. HUCKINS, b. Nov. 12, 1836.

[663] CHARLES A. HUCKINS, b. July 19, 1845.

[118] **V. Robert**[312] Huckins, son of Robert and Hannah (B.) Caverly Huckins, born July 8, 1821; married, July 3, 1852, Mary A. Paul, of Rollingsford, N. H., born March 3, 1828. They are frugal and industrious in the farming interest. Children : —

[664] LYDIA E. HUCKINS, b. Feb. 15, 1856.

[665] FRANK W. HUCKINS, b. Sept. 9, 1860.

[666] EDGAR I. HUCKINS, b. Sept. 19, 1862.

[119] **V. Elizabeth Lydia**[313] Huckins, only daughter of Robert and Hannah (B.) Caverly Huckins, of Madbury, N. H., born May 20, 1829; married Samuel N. Towle, Esq., Oct. 1, 1855, then of Barnstead, now of Northwood, N. H. Encouraged by an intelligent, active household, Mr. Towle has become a thrifty farmer as well as a skilful mechanic, and has sometimes represented his enterprising town in the New Hampshire halls of legislation. Mrs. Towle is an exemplary, progressive inmate of the mansion. "He strengtheneth her arms; her candle goeth not out at night." Children : —

[667] ALBERT W. TOWLE, b. Nov. 15, 1856; d. Feb. 24, 1857.

[668] MARTHA ELLEN TOWLE, b. July 31, 1858; d. Feb. 24, 1869.

[669] JOHN G. TOWLE, b. Jan. 17, 1860.

[670] ALICE L. TOWLE, b. June 10, 1871.

28

[120] **V. Louisa**[314] Foss, daughter of George and Betsey (B.) Caverly Foss, born Nov. 17, 1815; married James F. Berry, of Strafford, N. H., July 4, 1841. He is an industrious farmer, and she faithful to the interests of the husband, and the household accomplishes much by their own enterprises. Children : —

[671] GEORGE A. BERRY, b. Jan. 28, 1842.

[672] VEANNA S. BERRY, b. Feb. 4, 1846; m. Jan. 12, 1867.

[673] FIDELIA A. BERRY, b. Dec. 27, 1847.

[674] ALMIRA BERRY, b. July 30, 1863.

[121] **V. John C.**[315] Foss, Capt., son of George and Betsey (Caverly) Foss (B.), born Jan. 12, 1819; married Mary E. Foss, born Nov. 19, 1818, who died April 13, 1862. He was a commander of a militia company, and lived in Strafford; farmer. Children : —

[675] ALBERT M. FOSS, b. September, 1853.

[676] EDWIN P. FOSS, b. Jan. 20, 1855.

[122] **V. Azariah**[316] Foss, son of George and Betsey (Caverly) Foss (B.), born Jan. 24, 1821; married, June 18, 1848; lives in Strafford, N. H.; a farmer; industrious and successful. He has been honored by his townsmen with a seat in their State legislature, and has been favored with an exemplary and frugal household. Children : —

[677] EDRICK I. FOSS, b. March 25, 1852.

[678] LAURA J. FOSS, b. June 9, 1855.

[122½] **V. Betsey C.**[318] Foss, daughter of George and Betsey (Caverly) Foss (B.), born March 2, 1825; married, in 1846, Charles T. Hayes, born in 1822. He was a farmer, and died Jan. 31, 1861.

¹²³ V. 𝕰𝕷𝕴𝖟𝕒³²⁰ Hill, daughter of Joseph and Sarah (Caverly) Hill (B.), born Dec. 11, 1809; married Ira Clark, formerly of Strafford, now of Sheffield, Vt. She died March 5, 1867. Children:—

⁶⁷⁹ AMANDA E. CLARK, b. in Dover, N. H., in 1837.
⁶⁸⁰ JOSEPH H. CLARK, b. in Strafford, July 30, 1840.

¹²⁴ V. 𝕾𝖚𝖘𝖆𝖓³²¹ Hill, daughter of Joseph and Sarah (Caverly) Hill (B.), born Feb. 12, 1811; married Hiram Ham, then of Strafford, a carpenter, born Feb. 26, 1810. Susan died April 14, 1861. Mr. Ham resides in Ossipee, N. H., in peace and prosperity. Children:—

⁶⁸¹ DARIUS W. HAM, b. July 21, 1833; m. Susan A. Chamberlin.
⁶⁸² CHARLES E. HAM, b. July 24, 1835; m. Nellie Chase.
⁶⁸³ ELIZABETH E. HAM, b. Sept. 27, 1837; m. Augustus Horne.
⁶⁸⁴ HANNAH S. HAM, b. Aug. 27, 1840; m. John Libby.
⁶⁸⁵ CLARA A. HAM, b. Nov. 13, 1842; m. Frank Vanfleet.
⁶⁸⁶ MARY A. HAM, b. Jan. 1, 1846; m. Allen Howard.
⁶⁸⁷ EMMA F. HAM, b. May 20, 1849.
⁶⁸⁸ HIRAM B. HAM, b. May 2, 1852; m. Elizabeth Hasty.
⁶⁸⁹ LUCERN R. HAM, b. Jan. 24, 1855.

¹²⁵ V. 𝕸𝖊𝖍𝖆𝖑𝖆³²² Hill, daughter of Joseph and Sarah (Caverly) Hill (B.), born March 20, 1814; married, June 26, 1839, Abram Smith, b. Dec. 8, 1817. They reside at Manchester, N. H.   Mr. Smith is an industrious mechanic.   Children: —

690   GEORGE E. SMITH, b. March 9, 1840; was a
Union soldier, and died at Beaufort, S. C.,
Oct. 9, 1863, while in the line of duty, in the
service of his country.   Sweet peace to the
soldier!

691   SARAH A. SMITH, b. July 6, 1843.

692   CHARLES A. SMITH, b. Nov. 26, 1847.

693   ´ EMMA M. SMITH, b. June 13, 1853.

126   V. Azariah Boodey[323] Hill, son of Joseph
and Sarah (Caverly) Hill, born Dec. 26, 1817; married,
in 1839, Hannah Hall, born in 1821.   They reside at
Strafford Centre.   He by trade is a carpenter, and his
family are energetic and enterprising.   Children: —

699   SAMUEL H. HILL, b. in 1839.   227

700   CHARLES M. HILL, b. in 1842.   228

701   HIRAM S. HILL, b. in 1846.   229

702   LAURA J. HILL, b. in 1851.

703   IDA F. HILL, b. in 1854.

127   V. Sarah[324] Hill, daughter of Joseph and
Sarah (Caverly) Hill (B.), born April 20, 1819; married
Albert B. Chamberlin, Esq., May 3, 1836, born Aug. 3,
1812; resided formerly in Brookfield, N. H., now at
Waverly, Mass.   They are faithful, active, and enterprising.   Children: —

704   ELLEN A. CHAMBERLIN, b. March 29, 1848, in
Waverly.

705   JAMES A. CHAMBERLIN, b. Sept. 29, 1850.

706   EVA M. CHAMBERLIN, b. Sept. 27, 1854; m.
Herbert H. Russell, March 6, 1875.   230

[128] **V.** **Nancy**[325] Hill, daughter of Joseph and Sarah (Caverly) Hill (B.), born May 22, 1821; married, Sept. 28, 1848, Thomas H. Benton, born Feb. 12, 1824. He died Sept. 5, 1867. Children:—

[707] GEORGE H. BENTON, b. Aug. 16, 1849; m. Mary
T. Lathrop. 231

[708] EUGENE A. BENTON, b. Oct. 26, 1851; m. Ada
Van Norman.

[709] IDA A. BENTON, b. June 29, 1854; d. Nov. 8, 1867.

[710] ALBERT C. BENTON, b. May 4, 1857; now of
Manchester, N. H.

[711] THERESO BENTON, b. Feb. 22, 1859.

[712] LEVI S. BENTON, b. Aug. 2, 1864; d. March 5, 1867.

[129] **V.** **Almira W.**[326] Hill, daughter of Joseph and Sarah (Caverly) Hill (B.), born April 12, 1830; intermarried with Seth T. Hill, Esq.,* of Manchester, N. H., Nov. 27, 1851, where they still reside. Child:—

[713] A daughter.

[130] **V.** **Lovina**[327] Hill, daughter of Joseph and Sarah (Caverly) Hill (B.), born Sept. 12, 1832; married, in October, 1852, Josiah Hills. They now reside in Illinois. Children:—

[714] FRANK HILLS, b. Nov. 1854; d. June 6, 1862.

[715] ELLA F. HILLS, b. June 26, 1859.

[716] CORA M. HILLS, b. Jan. 8, 1862.

[717] EDDIE HILLS; now in Illinois.

[718] FRED A. HILLS; now in Illinois.

[131] **V.** **Zechariah Boodey**[328½] Caverly, son of Rev. John and Nancy (French) Caverly, born in Straf-

---

* See further as to Mr. Hill in the Annals of the Caverly Family, pp. 120, 121.

ford, N. H., March 20, 1822; married Rebecca M. Crosby, of Lowell, Mass., born Nov. 13, 1836; was a lawyer; died May 24, 1862, while in office as secretary of legation to Peru. Mrs. Caverly and daughter were lost at sea, May 7, 1875.* Children: —

719   AMY CAVERLY, b. at Lima, Peru, June 28, 1858; d. May 7, 1875. Lost at sea.

720   CECIL M. CAVERLY, b. at Lowell, Mass., Sept. 19, 1859.

132   **V. John Boodey**[333] Caverly, son of Rev. John (B.) and Nancy (French) Caverly, born June 16, 1836; married, May 26, 1861, Abbie M. Swaine, of Atkinson, Me., born June 20, 1837. They reside in Ipswich, Mass., where the wild old ocean brings healthful, pleasant breezes.* Children: —

721   IRVIN W. CAVERLY, b. at Strafford, N. H., Jan. 29, 1864.

722   ROSCOE CAVERLY, b. at Strafford, May 2, 1866.

723   CARL A. CAVERLY, b. at Strafford, March 16, 1868.

724   CHESTER B. CAVERLY, b. at Strafford, March 18, 1874.

132½   **V. Luther M.**[334] Caverly, son of Rev. John and Nancy (French) Caverly, born Dec. 15, 1838; married, April 11, 1877. He is at Dover, N. H. Mrs. Caverly died Oct. 3, 1878. Child: —

725   VICTOR L. CAVERLY, b. July 2, 1878.

133   **V. Betsey**[335] Caverly, daughter of Capt. Azariah and Sarah (Adams) Caverly; married Joseph

---

* For biographical sketch, see Annals of Caverly Family, pp. 121, 122.

T. Clark, born Aug. 22, 1820, and who died in 1851.
Children: —

726   SUSAN E. CLARK, b. Sept. 29, 1839; m. June 15,
       1855.   232
727   JOSEPHINE CLARK, b. Feb. 9, 1841; m. June,
       1858.

134   V.   John H.[339] Caverly, son of Capt. Azariah
and Sarah (Adams) Caverly, born at Strafford, N. H.,
Oct. 17, 1828; now at Maiden Rock, Wis.; was an
editor; is now a husbandman; married, Dec. 24, 1864,
Melvina E. Butcher, of Iowa, born Aug. 22, 1846.*
Children: —

723   CORA CAVERLY, b. at Osceola, Ia., Oct. 17, 1865.
729   DELLA CAVERLY, born at Maiden Rock, Wis.,
       Feb. 15, 1867.

135   V.   George A.[340] Caverly, son of Capt. Azariah
and Eliza (Tasker) Caverly, born Jan. 28, 1833, as more
fully mentioned in No. 286½; resides in Strafford, N. H.;
is a farmer, and near by him resides his friend Huckins.
During a bright spring morning, on a visit to his neighbor's plantation, being poetically inclined, he sang as
follows: —

HUSBANDRY.

Farmer Huckins stood in his open door,
  Looked north and southward, east and west;
Then turning, said: "I'll ne'er be poor,
  Abbie, good wife, why should we rest?
The day hath dawned, is beaming now,
  And the swallow is back to his native nest.

---

* For biographical sketch, see Annals of Caverly Family, pp. 121, 122.

Call all the boys, I'll speed the plow,
The bird is busy on the bough,
   The skies are seeking their summer blue,
   The trees are feeding their lovely leaves,
And I have a dream (God make it true)
Of full-grown harvests, heavy sheaves,
Where the meadow is sweet with new-made hay,
And the reapers rejoice at the dawn of day."

Our farmer, frugal, onward went;
   He plowed and sowed at early morn,
God gave him health, strength, sweet content,
   And crowned his crib with golden corn.

G. A. C.

ADVICE.

Take courage, then, my farmer boy,
   And plow and sow 'neath morning skies!
Life's duteous labor full of joy,
   Shall make thee valiant, strong, and wise.

R. B. C.

136 V. Hiram P.[342] Caverly, son of Capt.
Azariah and Eliza (Tasker) Caverly, born May 10, 1839;
resides at Dubuque, Iowa. He has long been a teacher of
youth. Of late changing occupation, is at present city
clerk of Dubuque. Married, Nov. 21, 1861, Lizzie M.
Anderson, born Feb. 17, 1843. Children:—

730   MARY L. CAVERLY, b. in Washington, May 27,
         1863.

731   BERTHA CAVERLY, b. in Galena, Ill., Oct. 19, 1864.

732   CORA CAVERLY, b. in Galena, April 6, 1867.

733   CLARENCE CAVERLY, b. in Hanover, Ill., May 7,
         1869.

137 V. Elizabeth A.[343] Caverly, daughter of
Capt. Azariah and Eliza (Tasker) Caverly, born April

29, 1843; married, Oct. 1, 1868, Stephen W. Hanson, of Barrington, born May 12, 1836.* Child: —

734 MAMIE E. HANSON, b. April 15, 1870.

189 **V. John B.**³⁴⁹ Caverly, Esq., son of Daniel and Nancy (Hill) Caverly, born June 2, 1826; married Miss Susan A. Quimby, Aug. 4, 1859; owns and resides upon a very extensive, pleasant, and productive farm in the northeast part of Dover, N. H.†

140 **V. Darius E.**³⁵⁰ Caverly, son of Daniel and Nancy (Hill) Caverly, born May 21, 1828; married, July 22, 1856, Abbie A. Caverly. He fell in the contest at S. C., July 19, 1863. Children: —

736 ANNIE B. CAVERLY, b. in Strafford, N. H., June 20, 1858.

737 HERBERT D. CAVERLY, b. in Barrington, Nov. 21, 1859.

Darius was a Union soldier in the rebellion, valiant for the fight. He fell in the battle-storm of Fort Wagner. Oh, how noble such a heart and such a death! Of the heroic soldier the immortal Homer poetizes thus: —

> "The gallant man, though slain in fight he be,
> Yet leaves his country safe, his nation free,
> Entails a debt on all the grateful state;
> His own brave friends shall glory in his fate;
> His wife live honored, and his race succeed,
> And late posterity enjoy the deed." ‡

---

* See also Annals of the Caverly Family, p. 126.

† See further sketch in Annals of the Caverly Family, p. 127.

‡ A new National Cemetery of late having been consecrated at Beaufort, S. C., Darius, removed from the battle-ground, now rests there, at Section 18, in grave numbered 74.

[141] **V. Nancy I.**[351] Caverly, daughter of Daniel and Isabel (Morrison) Caverly, born Aug. 25, 1831; married Charles A. Waterhouse, Esq., of Barrington, N. H., born Sept. 17, 1835. His active family have aided us much in the collecting of materials for these annals.* Children: —

[738] C. FRANK WATERHOUSE, b. July 8, 1859.   234
[739] DANIEL C. WATERHOUSE, b. May 14, 1864.
[740] M. ISABEL WATERHOUSE, b. Feb. 20, 1870.

[142] **V. Jane E.**[352] Caverly, daughter of Daniel and Isabel (Morrison) Caverly, born April 17, 1833; married, March 20, 1854, Matthew Hale, Esq., born Nov. 26, 1829. They reside at Conway, N. H. He is a thrifty farmer.† Children: —

[741] FRANK M. HALE, b. at Conway, July 18, 1860.
[742] ISABEL HALE, b. at Conway, Feb. 15, 1862.
[743] ELIZA A. HALE, b. at Conway, April 17, 1866.
[744] MARTHA S. HALE, b. at Conway, Jan. 2, 1871.
[745] JENNIE C. HALE, b. at Conway, Feb. 19, 1873.

[144] **V. Robert Boodey**[354] Peavey, Esq., son of Capt. John and Mary Caverly (B.) Peavey, born Jan. 17, 1824; married, in 1848, Emily P. Montgomery. Emily died May 6, 1876, and rests at the old homestead inherited by Robert from his father.†

[146] **V. Daniel D.**[356] Caverly, son of Dea. Ira (B.) and Lydia (Libbey) Caverly, born Jan. 29, 1825; married, June 2, 1845, Abbie E. Hutchins, born March 15, 1827; a farmer and clerk, residing in Lowell, Mass. He

---

* See further sketch, Annals of Caverly Family, p. 128.
† For further sketch, see Annals of Caverly Family, pp. 129, 130.

served in the Union army to the end of the war, and up
to the falling off of fetters from the black man. Child:—

⁷⁴⁶ ANNIE B. CAVERLY, b. Jan. 12, 1863.

¹⁴⁷ V. Susie E.³⁵⁷ Caverly, daughter of Dea. Ira
(B.) and Lydia (Libbey) Caverly, born Dec. 4, 1828;
married, Oct. 15, 1857, Hon. Wm. R. Frye, born in May,
1808. He was a Maine senator, and for a long time postmaster of Lewiston. Mrs. Frye resides in the city of
Lowell. Children:—

⁷⁴⁷ MILLIE FRYE, b. in Lewiston, Me., Feb. 24, 1859.
⁷⁴⁸ FRED M. FRYE, b. in Lewiston, April 2, 1861.

¹⁴⁸ V. J. Henry³⁵⁹ Caverly, son of Dea. Ira (B.)
and Sarah (Colcard) Caverly; married, Aug. 2, 1865, Miss
Mary S. Severance, born at Uxbridge, Mass., July 17,
1844; was a Union soldier to the end of the conflict.
In faith, skill, and care, being worthy of confidence, he
has long held the office of paymaster on the Merrimack
Corporation in the city of Lowell. Children:—

⁷⁴⁹ SUSIE A. CAVERLY, b. in Lowell, Feb. 15, 1866;
d. Dec. 10, 1876.
⁷⁵⁰ SARAH L. CAVERLY, b. in Lowell, June 9, 1868.
⁷⁵¹ ORRIN GUY CAVERLY, b. in Lowell, Oct. 10, 1871.
⁷⁵² ALICE MAY CAVERLY, b. in Lowell, Oct. 5, 1874;
d. Dec. 10, 1876.
⁷⁵⁸ ROY HENRY CAVERLY, b. in Lowell, June 28,
1878.

¹⁴⁹ V. Edward³⁶² Caverly, son of Robert B.,
born Oct. 4, 1844; married Julia Irving Holloway; was
a musician in the Union army, also a soldier in Sheridan's

cavalry and in his raids; now a merchant in the city of Washington, D. C.*   Children : —

754   ROBERT BRIARD CAVERLY.
755   GRACE MIDDLETON CAVERLY, d. July 2, 1877,
    aged 7 years.
756   CHARLOTTE LOUISE CAVERLY.
757   EDWARD FOYE CAVERLY.

150   V. Mary[365] Caverly, daughter of Robert Boodey and Emily (Parker) Caverly, born Sept. 4, 1857; married, Sept. 23, 1879, Isaac S. Daly, Esq., an attorney and counsellor at law, Lowell, Mass.   Child : —
758   HAROLD CAVERLY DALY, b. June 13, 1880.

Sixth Generation.

153   VI. Simeon S.[385] Hasty, son of William and Polly (Strout) Hasty, born July 23, 1812; married Sarah Watson; resided in Limerick, Me.   Children : —

758½ EMMA E. HASTY.	762 FRANCIS A. HASTY.
759 SARAH A. HASTY.	763 HANNAH A. HASTY.
760 MARY C. HASTY.	764 SIMEON M. HASTY.
761 ABILDA HASTY.	765 CHARLES B. HASTY.

154   VI. Mary Ann[386] Hasty (B.), daughter of William and Polly Hasty, born Sept. 13, 1814; married Thurston McKusick, of Cornish, Me.   Children : —
766   MARY McKUSICK, m. —— Trafton.
767   FANNY McKUSICK, m. —— Libbey.
768   NANCY McKUSICK, m. —— Favor.
769   JENNIE McKUSICK, m. —— Smith.
770   CHARLEY McKUSICK.

---

* See further in Annals of Caverly Family, pp. 132, 133.

154½ VI. Esther S.[387] Hasty, daughter of William and Polly (Strout) Hasty, born Aug. 29, 1818; married Eliab Day, of Cornish, Me. Children : —

[771] ELLEN MARIAH DAY, m. —— Strout.
[772] ELIZABETH DAY, m. —— Dearborn.
[773] THURSTON DAY, m. —— Bean.
[774] LYDIA DAY, m. —— Garland.
[775] MARY ANN DAY.
[776] WILLIE DAY.
[777] EMMA DAY.
[778] JOHN DAY.
[779] ROBERT DAY.
[780] HENRY DAY.

156 VI. William G.[391] Hasty, son of William and Polly (Strout) Hasty, born June 26, 1832; married, Feb. 7, 1856, Lydia G. Stover, of Limerick, Me., born Aug. 5, 1830. He died Sept. 4, 1879. Children: —

[781] JOHN WILLIS HASTY, b. Dec. 14, 1856.
[782] SIMEON OSCAR HASTY, b. March 20, 1859.
[783] EVA OSTELLA HASTY.
[784] EDWIN ELLSWORTH HASTY, b. Jan. 2, 1862.
[785] LYDIA HASTY, b. Jan. 2, 1872.

157 VI. Sylvester G.[409] Boodey, son of Joseph B. and Abigail (Nason) Boodey; married Ruth Bean, who was born in a log cabin in the east of Maine, and was cradled in a box of birch bark. Children : —

[786] MARY A., b. in 1854. [788] MILTON, b. in 1858.
[787] FRANK E., b. in 1856. [789] CORA, b. in 1860.
[790] ELARETTA, b. in 1868.

158 VI. Robert Milton[411] Boodey, son of Joseph B. and Abigail (Nason) Boodey, born March 6, 1838;

married, Nov. 22, 1865, Mary Winkley Osgood. He left
home at the age of seventeen, and at first obtained the
useful trade of a hatter. He is now, as we are informed,
an owner and agent in a large and thriving manufacturing company, in the county of Essex, in the State of
Massachusetts, at an opulent thriving income. Children: —

791   LOUIS MILTON, b. Sept. 6, 1866.
792   FREDERICK WILLIS, b. Nov. 27, 1869.
793   MAMIE LOUISE, b. Aug. 23, 1872.

In the late rebellion this captain served his country as
a Union soldier, lieutenant, and for a long time was the
commander of Company B, 40th Regiment New York
Volunteers. He most valiantly braved the fire and flame
of nineteen battles. His was the famous Mozart Regiment, and it is said "a better one was never enlisted."
The following are some of the conflicts in which he par-
ticipated: in the fight at Yorktown, Va., and in the battle of Williamsburg, at Fair Oaks, wounded; at Malvern
Hill, at the Second Bull Run, at Chantilly, at Freder-
icksburg, and at Chancellorsville, full of fight. Ah! we
well remember when the news of this great battle at
night reached Washington city, how we were moved,
and among other things, how, in a brief letter, we wrote
of it as follows: —

AGAIN 'TIS NIGHT.

D. C., MAY 4, 1863.

Again 'tis night; — yet the moon afar
Brings radiant light to the tents of war,
While the tramp of steed and the tap of drum
Have waned away at Washington.

Yet many a soldier, brave and bright,
Are sad within their tents to-night,
For the battle hath raged, and comrades true
Are pale beneath yon hills of blue.

Wild now in dreams the country maid
Awakes to memories of her dead;
And hearts afar in grief must yield
To the cry of a crimson battle-field.*

Our brave captain was also in the battle of Gettysburg, and there he received a severe wound; also in the fight at Mine Run, and at Locust Grove he was again wounded. He was also at the fight on the Po, in the Wilderness, near where the noble Sedgwick fell at the cowardly aim of a sharpshooter, of which we then sadly sang, and now give place to the song: —

On Dixie's Woodland.

On Dixie's woodland hill and plain,
    Where treason stalks in ghost-like form,
The deadly mortars belch again;
    Earth, troubled, quakes beneath the storm.

Down on the foe to battle led,
    Brave gallant legions, fired of hope,
Out through the heaps of mangled dead,
    They bear a nation's banner up.

Firm yet again, though comrades fall,
    And undismayed at Fate's decree,
Onward they heed their country's call,
    Their noble hearts shall make her free.

Lo! there, amidst the valiant slain,
    Is he who bore that banner high
O'er many a gory battle plain,
    Where "Greek met Greek" — met there to die.

---

* From Epics, Lyrics, and Ballads, pp. 215, 216.

Clouds clad in crimson intervene,
  Our dear old flag is bending low
Where Sedgwick fell, — the willow green
  Trails, weeping o'er him on the Po.

Ah! 'tis of earth, man can but know
  How truth eternal, right divine,
Must from the blood of martyrs flow,
  'Tis wondrous wisdom's vast design!

Yet far from fields of valor blest,
  Though Freedom's flag may rend in twain,
Though race and nation be oppressed,
  Shall not the hero live again!

Brave, noble spirit! — higher hence,
  A leader in that land of light;
What though no traveller comes from thence,
  We'll hail thee there in armor bright.

Go, ye that linger where he fell,
  With guards of honor, bear him thence,
Yet pageant praise shall fail to tell
  The general care, the gloom intense.

In vain the solemn organ trills,
  While true to trust ye homeward come;
In vain the echo from the hills
  Of plaintive airs and muffled drum.

And vain, indeed, the soldier's shot,
  Or thunders breaking o'er the tomb;
A nation weeping heeds it not,
  She hath an impulse of her own.

Rest! let him rest in the high land fair,
  Where golden sunsets glow and gleam,
Where wild birds warbling fill the air,
  And the pine-tree sings its love serene.

Oft here the patriot's heart shall burn
In mournful lays, in generous tears,
And pilgrim feet shall hither turn,
As come and go the rolling years.

Bring lilies sweet, in hands-full bring
The rose in beauty, full in bloom;
Bring garland flowers of grateful spring,
And crown for aye the hero's tomb.*

Our gallant Robert M. was also in the battle at
Spottsylvania, May 12, 1864, and there he was slightly
wounded. He was at the fight at Seven Pines, and was
in the seven-days' conflict before Richmond. On that
terrible retreat, the soldier of that (last) day witnessed
the following incident: —

It happened our troops, while on that dread retreat,
were hailed by a wounded rebel soldier, who rising up from
beneath a tree as they passed, swinging his hand, saluted
them thus: "Hurrah for that old flag yet." We described
this incident at the time, and here give place to it.

"That Old Flag Yet."

It floated long — the foe defied, —
Proud o'er our brave ones when they died,
    Its destiny completing;
On wide old Ocean's dread domain,
Or down on Richmond's bloody plain,
    In victory or retreating.

On that sad field, beneath a tree
A soldier falls; — fighting for Lee,
    A shaft his heart had met;
Yet while our troops retreating flee,
He hails them — shouting (faintly free),
    "Hurrah! — for that old flag yet!"

---

* From my Epics, Lyrics, and Ballads, p. 177.

30

He'd lived beneath a southern sun,
Had been conscribed when the war begun,
　　But against the wrong had set;
Still leaning on a rebel gun,
High now that dying voice, it run,
　　"Hurrah!—for that old flag yet!"

All day, all night, our cohorts fly,
While oft they turn a tearful eye,
　　Back where that soldier sat;
Although they'd known him there to die,
At every step they heard the cry,
　　"Hurrah!— for that old flag yet!"

The din of danger far and nigh,
A sultry sun;— that crimson sky
　　At night, they heeded not;
Above that clamorous battle-cry,
They knew that voice ('t was from on high);
　　They waved— "that old flag yet!"

And when next day at dawn of light,
Our squadrons wheeling, left and right,
　　The foe aback beset;
They rallied nobly, full of fight,
And headlong drove him out of sight;
　　Hurrah!— 't was "that old flag yet!"

That voice will never wane away,
'T is in the air, the cloud, the clay,
　　Deep in the soul 't is set;
In every form, in every way,
They'll hear it till their dying day,
　　"Hurrah!—for that old flag yet!"

Yes!—let it wave on every hill;
In every land, triumphant still,
　　In freedom fair as ever;
High o'er the deeds the brave have done,
A Nation's glory they have won,
　　Yes, let it float forever!*

* From my Epics, Lyrics, and Ballads, p. 211.

Our captain, Robert M., was also in the battle at the
North Anna River, at Cold Harbor, and at Petersburg,
as well as in several other severe conflicts not already
named, as against the

REBELLION.

True, true it is, yet dread in deep disgrace,
An oligarchy of a southern race,
Born there of hell, and bred in slavery's school,
"Let loose their dogs of war," and sought to rule,
And Sumter falls. "To arms!" the patriot cries;
To arms provoked, the northen legions rise;
Nor age, nor caste, nor different race, decline;
Alike in zeal, alike in faith combine
In manly strength. From all the vales and hills,
Out from mechanic shops, from noisy mills;
Physicians even, divines, and legal bar
Turn heroes brave and rally for the war.

As when a bull disturbs a native hive,
The bees ten thousand buzz and outward drive,
Black in the air the vast battalions bring
Their horrid weapons down, fierce on the wing,
Upon the herd. So bent on war, alive
Legions of Yankees from the northern hive
Leap forth aflame, in native strength and power,
Wielding dread engines yet unknown to war;
Countless in cost, the preparation grand,
For deadly conflicts on the sea or land;
The monitor, in iron mail afloat;
The monstrous mortar with a yawning throat,
Vast shells and shot within, of strange invention;
Six-hundred-pounders, slugs of huge dimension,
The new-capped rifle keen, the seven-shooter,
Ten thousand tons of iron, lead, or pewter.

Armed thus the cohorts tramp the trembling plain,
And crowd the mighty ships that plow the main;
The conscious thunders, muttering from afar,

Bemoan the horrors of impending war.
Not less the bolt, oft breaking from the sky, ·
Bespeaks dread vengeance, threatened from on high;
Four years of darkness curtains all the plain,
Four years of conflict on the land and main,
Earth deep in sorrow for the thousands slain,
Prove but the fruit, the penalty, and pain
Of sin. Yet high o'er all that earth betides,
Th' eternal Jove in majesty presides;
And in His mercy, sovereign will, and power,
Forgives the crime and turns the tide of war.
Now tumbling from her bulwarks, treason falls;
Loud ring the batteries, crashing in her walls,
The sweeping navies press the rebel shore,
From field to field the belching mortars roar.
Yet doth dread carnage cease at Heaven's will;
The curse is but removed, and all is still.
Great God of armies, we adore thy name
For thy forgiveness of a nation's shame!
Who, through the sea "led Israel like a flock,"
Hath led this modern Israel to "the rock
Beyond the flood." Oh, let us learn thee still;
Who bears thy image, must obey thy will!
To whom but man should noble deeds belong,
To learn the right divine, to spurn the wrong?
What we would have of others, do to them,
Alike the work of nations as of men.*

TRUE VALOR.

This is a leading characteristic in the gallant soldier
(R. M. B.), whose record in brief we have given above,
and which, to a praiseworthy extent, is quite common to
our race; we hope and trust it will ever prove to be
hereditary. In tracing out the peculiar traits of the
Boodeys, none appear more prominent than their faithfulness to their God, their kindred, and to their fellow-

---

* From my Epics, Lyrics, and Ballads, p. 384.

man. Strange to say, this benign virtue is nowhere more strikingly affixed, than in the hearts of the canine race. For illustration: in our great battle of Shiloh, Aug. 10, 1861, the noble mastiff of Lieutenant Phelps, of Chicago, closely following him from the beginning of the war, still stood by him in this battle, and when he fell, he lay down by him, and the officer being buried there, Tray still adhered to the grave, until the arrival, twelve days afterwards, of Mrs. Phelps from afar, when old Tray, being found, proved her only pilot to the body of her dear dead husband.

On March 4, 1869, the rebellion being at an end, and the great American general having this day been inaugurated (in the presence of a hundred thousand people) to the presidency, we, in the evening, wandered away, taking a stroll through the shades in and over Arlington Heights, where repose many thousands of the braves who fell in the various battles of that war. On this evening walk, among the many other incidents which appeared to awaken our imagination, was the sight of a stranger in black, a lady with her dog then and there in search sacredly among the graves. As it reminded us of the same old Tray, we then sang this story among other incidents of that night, and here for the interest of the generations, we repeat in verse this manifestation of true

FAITHFULNESS.

'Tis late! The groups have left the ground,
As they were wont at daylight down,
   Who'd firmer steps, yet faster;
Still lingering long, inclined to abide,
A lady and her dog beside,
   The widow of his master.

And now I turn to look at Tray,
A tale we'd heard of him one day,—
　　('T was no unfounded tattle;)
How firm he'd followed, prompt and warm,
Close to his master, 'mid the storm
　　That shook the field of battle; —

How the master fell at one of the rounds, —
Then how he licked his dying wounds,
　　And then lay down beside him;
And when, next day, they buried him low,
Old Tray refused away to go;
　　In truthful trust abiding.

'T was long — 't was many a trial day,
Ere the lone widow found her way
　　To the field of dread disaster;
Dark, humid nights of storm and hail
Had intervened.　And she grew pale,
　　Yet came to find the master.

Long, long she wandered, none could tell
Where the hero lay, nor where he fell,
　　And daylight was departing;
While tearful, thence to turn away,
She heard a voice, — 't was the same old Tray, —
　　He hailed her howling, barking:

The instinct of his nature rare,
His head was high to the tainted air,
　　As if in expectation;
His eye, his ear, his faith expressed,
He ran, he flew to greet the guest,
　　To hail her visitation.

Three times he crouched upon the ground,
And three times more he made a bound,
　　Then whining, told the story;
And then he turned, and led the way,
Where did her hidden treasures lay, —
　　The end of earthly glory.

Cold were the curtains overhead,
And cold the clods that bent his bed,
Above the master's ashes;
Yet there, when Tray lay down again,
A ray of hope, from the heavens it came,
Beneath a cloud it flashes!

Great God of grace, of love profound,
Could we to Thee as true be found?
Thy frown, we'd never fear it;
Dread war hath waned, the years go by,
That treasure still is hidden nigh,
And the widow's dog stands near it.*

[159] **VI. Alvin B.**[419] Emery, son of John and Sally (Boodey) Emery, born July 8, 1845; married, Feb. 26, 1870, Alberta Mills, of Corinna. They, with the mother and Carrie, reside there on the old homestead. Children: —

[793] WALTER L. EMERY, b. Dec. 14, 1870.
[794] EDNA ADEL EMERY, b. July 27, 1879.

[160] **VI. Prucia X.**[420] Emery, daughter of John and Sally (Boodey) Emery, born Dec. 25, 1846; married, May 1, 1866, Charles H. Sprague, of Corinna, Me. They now (1880) reside in the city of Lowell, Mass. Child: —

[795] ELMER E. SPRAGUE, b. April 3, 1867.

[161] **VI. Fitz Henry A.**[422] Boodey, son of David and Lucretia (Mudget) Boodey, born April 27, 1833; married Hannah Jane Ames, of Stockton, Me., born Dec. 5, 1832. Children: —

---

* From my Epics, Lyrics, and Ballads, p. 142.

796 HELEN LUCRETIA, b. June 23, 1850; d. Feb. 22,
1852.
797 WILBERT H., b. April 20, 1860; now a watchman
on the Lowell Corporation, Lowell, Mass.

162 VI. David Augustus[423] Boodey, son of
David and Lucretia (Mudget) Boodey, born Aug. 13,
1837, in the town of Jackson; married, June 1, 1863, to
Miss Abbie H. Treat, of Frankfort, Me.

This gentleman, David Augustus, is now (1880) a
banker in the city of New York, at No. 58 Broadway,
corner Exchange Place. He is an honor to his race, is
independent, and is doing a lucrative business under the
firm-name of Boodey, McLellan & Co. His generosity
has greatly favored us in the publication of these annals.
Children: —

798 HENRY TREAT, b. April 12, 1866.
799 MAUDE LOUISA, b. Sept. 5, 1867.
800 CHARLES AUGUSTUS, b. Aug. 23, 1870.
801 ALVIN, b. Jan. 26, 1873.
802 EDGAR, b. Sept. 19, 1874.

162½ VI. Laura Jane[425] Boodey, daughter of
David and Lucretia (Mudget) Boodey; married Dr.
Samuel Johnson, of Dixmont, Me. Children: —

803 FRED A. JOHNSON, b. Sept. 2, 1875.
804 LULA MAUDE JOHNSON, b. November, 1877.

163 VI. John B.[424] Boodey, son of David and
Lucretia (Mudget) Boodey, born in Scarborough, April
23, 1847; married, in 1874, Nora Pilly, born 1857.
Child: —

805 DAVID BERTRAND, b. Aug. 31, 1877.

163½ **VI. Josephine Z.**[427] Boodey, daughter of David and Lucretia (Mudget) Boodey; married Andrew B. Fogg, of Jackson, Me. Child: —

806¼ LAURA VASHTA FOGG, b. July 11, 1878.

164 **VI. Persis T.**[428] Boodey, daughter of Redman, 2d, and Mary (Twitchell) Boodey, born in 1835; married, in 1856, Coleman Hall. Children: —

807 ETHEL R. HALL, b. March 27, 1859.
807½ ELMER O. HALL, b. 1861.
808 WILMER A. HALL, b. 1862.
808½ MIRA H. HALL, b. 1864; d. 1864.
809 RALPH E. HALL, b. 1866; d. 1867.

165 **VI. Ann Mary**[429] Boodey, daughter of Redman, 2d, and Mary (Twitchell) Boodey, born in 1838; married, Feb. 28, 1858, S. S. Roberts. Children: —

809½ EDITH G. ROBERTS, b. 1859.
810 MAUDE L. ROBERTS, b. Sept. 28, 1869.

166 **VI. Henrietta**[430] Boodey, daughter of Redman, 2d, and Mary (Twitchell) Boodey, born in 1840; married, in 1854, Darius Drake. Children: —

810½ ELLA M. DRAKE, b. in 1858; m. George Hasty.
811 M. ELVER DRAKE, b. in 1859.
812 CHARLES F. DRAKE, b. in 1863.
813 LILLIAN H. DRAKE, b. in 1866.

167 **VI. Clarendon**[431] Boodey, son of Redman, 2d, and Mary (Twitchell) Boodey, born in 1842; married, in 1866, Rose A. Roberts. Child: —

814 LIZZIE A., b. in 1871.

31

[168] **VI. Georgiana M.**[432] Boodey, daughter of Redman, 2d, and Mary (Twitchell) Boodey, born in 1845; married, in 1863, Robert Plummer.   Children: —

[815] BERTRAND L. PLUMMER, b. in 1865.
[816] WILMER L. PLUMMER, b. in 1867.

[169] **VI. Aroline**[433] Boodey, daughter of Redman, 2d, and Mary (Twitchell) Boodey, born 1850; married William T. Putnam.   Children: —

[817] ERNEST R. PUTNAM, b. in 1869.
[818] SAMUEL W. PUTNAM, b. in 1870.

[170] **VI. Edwin C.**[434] Boodey, son of Redman, 2d, and Mary (Twitchell) Boodey, born in 1847; married Dora F. Roberts in 1871.   Children: —

[819] BERTHA V., b. in 1871.
[820] EVERETTE R., born in 1873.

[171] **VI. Wellington R.**[435] Boodey, son of Redman, 2d, and Mary (Twitchell) Boodey, born in 1853; married, in 1877, Cora Jewell.   Children : —

[821] MARY ETTA, b. in 1878.
[822] CARRIE E., b. in 1879.
[823] MYRTIE L., b. in 1880.

[171½] **VI. John Alvin**[436½] Eastman, son of Samuel and Harriet (Boodey) Eastman, born at Bangor, June 6, 1849; married, Nov. 1, 1871, Mary E. Wotton, of Charleston, Me.   Child: —

[824] FRANK EUGENE WOTTON, b. at Bangor, June 14, 1872.

[172] **VI. Lorana**[451] Boodey, daughter of Henry H. and Hannah (Strout) Boodey, of Windham, Me., born Sept. 1, 1847; married, Oct. 14, 1868, Frederick Legrow, born Dec. 2, 1849. Children: —

[825] MAUDE LEGROW, b. May 12, 1869.
[826] CLIFFORD LEGROW, b. Nov. 8, 1875.

[173] **VI. Everett W.**[461] Boodey, son of Edmund T. and Lucinda (Emery) Boodey, of Great Falls, N. H., born April 17, 1848; married, 1871, —— Gilpatrick. Child: —

[827] LORANA, b. October, 1874.

[173½] **VI. Sylvania A.**[462] Boodey, daughter of Edmund T. and Lucinda (Emery) Boodey, born May 17, 1850; married Lillian L. Boynton, in 1871. Children: —

[828] LILLIAN L. BOYNTON, b. February, 1872.
[829] EDMUND T. BOYNTON, b. March, 1877.

[174] **VI. Elizabeth L.**[497] Boodey, daughter of Sewall and Lydia (Jones) Boodey, born Feb. 6, 1833; married, June 5, 1859, Augustus Read, born Aug. 25, 1834, of Windham, Me. Children: —

[830] EDMUND B. READ, b. Sept. 29, 1863.
[831] RUFUS READ, b. September, 1864.

[175] **VI. Francis G.**[498] Boodey, son of Sewall and Lydia (Jones) Boodey, born Aug. 31, 1834; married, May 29, 1856, Irene S. Prime, born Feb. 1834, of Readfield, Me. They reside at Windham. Francis, valiant, served in the Union army. Children: —

[832] CHARLES S., b. Oct. 10, 1857.
[833] NELLIE M., b. Dec. 4, 1868.

176 VI. 𝕰𝖒𝖒𝖆 𝕮.⁴⁹⁹ Boodey, daughter of Sewall and Lydia (Jones) Boodey, born Oct. 18, 1836; married, Dec. 4, 1856, John H. Manchester, born Feb. 19, 1830, of Windham, Me. He died July 7, 1879. Children : —

834 LIZZIE B. MANCHESTER, b. Dec. 24, 1857; d. November, 1859.

835 MARY C. MANCHESTER, b. Sept. 18, 1859.

836 ARTHUR W. MANCHESTER, b. Feb. 12, 1863.

837 BERTHA MANCHESTER, b. June 23, 1874.

177 VI. 𝕷𝖊𝖔𝖓𝖆𝖗𝖉 𝕲𝖗𝖊𝖊𝖓𝖊⁵⁰² Boodey, son of Sewall and Lydia (Jones) Boodey, born Dec. 6, 1843; married, May 3, 1869, Maggie A. Flemming, of N. B. Children : —

838 LILLIAN G., b. June 3, 1871.

839 HERBERT, b. July 15, 1872.

840 GRACE M., b. June 22, 1874.

841 L. PERCIE, b. June 16, 1876.

842 CARRIE L., b. Feb. 4, 1878.

"Leonard G. Boodey gave valiant battle for his country, to the freedom of the slave, and for the over-throw of a southern oligarchy."

178 VI. 𝕮𝖔𝖗𝖓𝖊𝖑𝖎𝖆 𝕬.⁵⁰⁵ Boodey, daughter of Sewall and Lydia (Jones) Boodey, b. July 28, 1852; married, Dec. 21, 1870, Elbridge Lord, born March 4, 1839, of Windham, Me. Children : —

843 WILLARD C. LORD, b. Nov. 28, 1871.

844 RALPH J. LORD, b. July 21, 1873.

845 LENE C. LORD, b. April 30, 1876.

181 VI. 𝕮𝖍𝖆𝖗𝖑𝖊𝖘 𝕭.⁵²⁰ Boodey, son of Zechariah, 3d, and Joan O. (Runnalls) Boodey, born in New Durham,

N. II., Dec. 27, 1838; is a distinguished surgeon and physician in a successful practice at Cochituate, Mass. He, early in life, made himself learned in the law, and then advanced to the science of medicine and surgery, and being endowed with keen perceptive powers, and a sound judgment, together with strong inventive faculties, he obtains confidence, and is fast becoming celebrated. They tell, of a visit to one of his patients, the following story poetically : —

> Mrs. Rogers lay in her bed,
> Bandaged and blistered from foot to head;
> Bandaged and blistered from top to toe,
> Mrs. Rogers was very low.
> Bottle and saucer, spoon and cup,
> On the table stood, to the brim filled up;
> Physic of high and low degree,
> Calomel, catnip, boneset tea;
> Everything anybody could bear,
> Save dearest daylight, water, and air.
>
> Charles opened the blinds, the day was bright,
> And God gave Mrs. Rogers light;
> The window was opened, the day was fair,
> And God gave Mrs. Rogers some air.
> Bottles and blisters, powders and pills,
> Catnip, boneset, sirup, and squills,
> Drugs and medicines, high and low,
> Charles threw them as far as he could, you know.
> "What are you doing?" his patient cried.
> "Frightening Death," he coolly replied.
> "You are crazy," a visitor said,
> And he flung a bottle at her head.
>
> Deacon Rogers, he came to see.
> "Wife is coming round," said he;
> "I really think she will worry through,
> She scolds me just as she used to do."

All the people poohed and slurred,
And the neighbors all have had their word;
'T was better to perish (some of them say)
Than to be cured in such a heedless way.
" Your wife," said Charles, " had God's good care;
His drugs are light, water, and air;
All the doctors, beyond a doubt,
Could n't have cured Mrs. Rogers without.
The deacon smiled and bowed his head,
" Then your bill is nothing," he said;
" God's be the glory, as you say;
God bless you, Doctor; good-day! good-day! "
If called there again, we know full well,
The Doctor will give her cal-o-*mel*.

[182] **VI. Ellen Amelia**[522] Boodey, daughter of
Col. Zechariah, 4th, and Joan O. (Runnalls) Boodey,
born Jan. 3, 1847; married Francis W. Colbath, of
Farmington, N. H., an industrious farmer. Children: —

[846] HERBERT COLBATH, b. May 9, 1869.
[847] ANNIE COLBATH, b. Oct. 11, 1871.
[848] NELLIE COLBATH, b. July 14, 1878.

[185] **VI. Horace P.**[524] Boodey, son of Socrates
Harrison Boodey, of New Durham, and Tamson L.
(Ham) Boodey, born April 14, 1844; married, Feb. 9,
1868, Abbie M. Huckins, of Alton, N. H., born Sept. 9,
1848. Horace, on the 11th of August, 1862, enlisted for
the Union army, and served with Capt. Darius G.
Harriman, Co. I, 10th Regt. N. H. Volunteers, giving
battle for his country in the following engagements: At
Orleans, Va., Nov. 5, 1862; Waterloo, Va., Nov. 10, 1862;
White Sulphur Springs, Va., Nov. 15, 1862; Fredericks-
burg, Va., Dec. 13, 1862; Suffolk, Va., commencing April

10, 1863; Hill's Point, Va., April 19, 1863; Raid up the Peninsula, July 1, 1863; Hanover Court House, July 4 and 5, 1863; Burning bridge on the Pamunky, 1863; Raids in North Carolina in pursuit of guerillas, March, 1864; Clover Hill, Va., May,.1864; Drury's Bluff, Va., May 23 to 26, 1864; Bermuda, Va., May 28, 1864; Cold Harbor, Va., June, 1864. This valiant soldier, on the 3d of June, 1864, was wounded in the foot by the explosion of a shell from the enemy; was carried to the Chester Pennsylvania Hospital, where he was cared for up to May 15, 1865, and then by the government was honorably discharged. He is now a resident of New Durham, N. H. Child: —

[849] ETHEL M. BOODEY, b. Nov. 28, 1868.

[226] **VI. 𝔏𝔦𝔷𝔷𝔦𝔢 𝔄.**[650] Meader, daughter of William and Hannah E. Leighton (B.) Meader, born March 24, 1843; married, April 15, 1875, Hiram Moors, born March 20, 1849. Child: —

[850] MAMIE L. MOORS, b. May 13, 1876; d. Sept. 2, 1877.

[184] **VI. 𝔄𝔯𝔦𝔞𝔫𝔫𝔞**[530] Boodey, daughter of Ira and Joanna (Sewards) Boodey, born Aug. 21, 1828 (twin sister of Sarah A.); married, July, 1848, Joseph O. Foss, born Sept. 20, 1822, of Barrington, N. H. Children: —

[851] ANNIE S. FOSS, b. Dec. 17, 1848; m. John J. Smith, of Great Falls.

[852] JAMES H. FOSS, b. Dec. 13, 1850; m. Lucretia Dill.

[853] FREDDIE E. FOSS, b. May 11, 1853; d. June 18, 1858.

[854] FRANK FOSS, b. July 12, 1855.

855 EMMA J. Foss, b. Jan. 31, 1858; m. May 15, 1879, Charles C. Hurd.

856 ELLA M. Foss, b. Jan. 31, 1858; m. April 17, 1877, Melvin A. Rogers.

857 OTIS E. Foss, b. May 31, 1860.

858 GEORGE F. Foss, b. July 26, 1863.

859 CHARLES H. Foss, b. April 17, 1866.

185 **VI. Sarah A.**531 Boodey, daughter of Ira and Joanna (Sewards) Boodey, born Aug. 21, 1828; twin sister of Arianna; married Robert N. Foss, of Barrington, N. H. He died Oct. 18, 1879. Children:—

860 FRANCES A. Foss, b. March 9, 1847; m. Sept. 31, 1868, Daniel McDuffy.

861 RUSSELL B. Foss, b. July 25, 1850.

862 MARTHA A. Foss, b. Sept. 25, 1852; m. July 19, 1868, Fred Wescott.   235

863 IRA BOODEY Foss, b. May 16, 1855.

186 **VI. Mary S.**532 Boodey, daughter of Ira and Joanna (Sewards) Boodey, born June 22, 1831; married Joseph Hill, of Barnstead, N. H. She died May 8, 1874. Children:—

864 SARAH C. HILL, b. July 14, 1848; m. June, 1867, Charles Huckins.   236

865 ELLEN F. HILL, b. Nov. 25, 1850; m. Charles Mooney.   237

866 GEORGE HILL, b. Dec. 16, 1860.

867 CLARA GRACE HILL, b. June 30, 1870.

186½ **VI. Martha**533 Boodey, daughter of Ira and Joanna (Sewards) Boodey, b. Sept. 16, 1834; married

George A. Caverly, May 16, 1854. They reside in Strafford, at the rural homestead of his father. He is both a mechanic and a farmer, full of energetic life and social good manners, which are sure to lead the way to life's joys and life's success. Children: —

[868] EMMA L. CAVERLY, b. in Strafford, March 29, 1856; d. April 23, 1856.

[869] ELLA E. CAVERLY, b. in Strafford, May 21, 1857, m. John D. Clark. **236**

[870] AZARIAH M. CAVERLY, b. in Strafford, Jan. 8, 1861; died Feb. 8, 1863.

[871] IRA A. CAVERLY, b. in Strafford, Jan. 8, 1861; d. Feb. 6, 1863.

[872] EVA A. CAVERLY, b. in Strafford, Aug. 10, 1863; d. Jan. 24, 1865.

[873] WILLIE F. CAVERLY, b. in Strafford, Dec. 13, 1868.

[187] **VI. Martha A.**[535] Boodey, daughter of Zechariah and Abigail (Watson) Boodey, born May 30, 1824; married, Nov. 23, 1842, Charles C. Woodman, of Strafford, N. H., born Nov. 12, 1814. Children: —

[874] SARAH A. WOODMAN, b. Aug. 25, 1843; d. June 23, 1844.

[875] ELIZABETH A. G. WOODMAN, b. June 10, 1845; d. Nov. 9, 1846.

[876] ZECHARIAH B. WOODMAN, b. Dec. 13, 1847; d. Dec. 7, 1849. **239**

[877] MARTHA E. WOODMAN, b. March 15, 1850; m. Nov. 13, 1870, J. F. Hanson.

[878] IDA F. WOODMAN, b. March 17, 1855; d. Dec. 25, 1858.

[679] GEORGE E. WOODMAN, b. Sept. 2, 1857.
[880] HOMER C. WOODMAN, b. April 1, 1860.

[188] **VI. Alonzo B.**[537] Boodey, son of Zechariah and Abigail (Watson) Boodey, born March 28, 1829; married Hannah F. Leighton, of Strafford, born Oct. 2, 1831. She died April 15, 1869. Children: —

[881] EVERETT S., b. Nov. 1, 1858.
[882] FREDERICK E., b. Oct. 30, 1860.
[883] FRANK A., b. Sept. 11, 1863; d. Oct. 2, 1863.

Alonzo married, 2d, Nov. 7, 1869, Mrs. Rosetta J. Foye, born Sept. 23, 1838.

[189] **VI. Elizabeth S.**[538] Boodey, daughter of Zechariah, of Strafford, and Abigail (Watson) Boodey, born Dec. 15, 1831; married, in 1847, Joseph F. Caverly, born May 27, 1820. He is an industrious farmer, now residing at Strafford, N. H. Children: —

[884] ROBERT B. CAVERLY, 2d, b. Oct. 17, 1848; clerk.
[885] FRANK P. CAVERLY, b. Jan. 23, 1853; lives at Haverhill.
[886] NANCY O. CAVERLY, b. March 26, 1859.

[190] **VI. George W.**[539] Boodey, son of Zechariah and Abigail (Watson) Boodey, born Nov. 22, 1834; married, Feb. 16, 1856, Ellen E. Ashby, of Bradford, N. H., born April 2, 1838. He was a musician for the Union army in the rebellion. Oct. 19, 1861, he went into the war with Fifth Regiment N. H. Volunteers. After an honorable discharge, in August, 1862, he again enlisted, Oct. 19, 1864, in the Post Band, at Hilton Head, S. C., and faithfully and honorably served his country to the end of the war.

"Honor to whom honor is due."

In the years 1873 and 1874 our veteran of the war was honored with a seat in the legislature of New Hampshire. He, as also his lady, is a distinguished musician, a master in

Music.

Orpheus' lute was strung with poets' sinews,
Whose golden touch could soften steel and stones,
Make tigers tame, and huge leviathans
Forsake unsounded deeps to dance on sands.

If music be the food of love, play on,
Give me excess of it; that, surfeiting,
The appetite may sicken, and so die.
That strain again, — it had a dying fall:
Oh, it came o'er mine ear like the sweet south,
That breathes upon a bank of violets,
Stealing and giving odor.*

Child of George W. and Ellen E. Boodey: —

887 WALTER R., b. June 22, 1866.

101 **VI. Asenath A.**540 Boodey, daughter of Zechariah and Abigail (Watson) Boodey, born Feb. 17, 1838; married, July 3, 1855, Seth W. Caverly, born Oct. 22, 1834, an active, industrious mechanic, who still resides on the homestead of his father, in Strafford, N. H. Children: —

888 MARY LIZZIE CAVERLY, b. in Strafford, Oct. 8, 1856.
889 JOSEPH LESLIE CAVERLY, b. in Strafford, April 19, 1860.
890 CARRIE ADELIA CAVERLY, b. in Strafford, Sept. 11, 1862.
891 ABBIE VINA CAVERLY, b. in Dover, July 8, 1866.

---

* From Shakespearian Dictionary, p. 249.

⁸⁹² CLARENCE C. CAVERLY, b. in Strafford, April 20,
1873.

⁸⁹³ ROBERT WILLIS CAVERLY, b. in Strafford, Oct.
21, 1875.

¹⁹² **VI. John ℗.**⁵⁴¹ Boodey, son of Zechariah
and Abigail (Watson) Boodey, born Nov. 27, 1842;
married, Nov. 27, 1863, Orissa D. Hanson, of Strafford,
N. H., born March 24, 1845. Mr. Boodey is an intelligent husbandman, and has done much in aid of these·
annals. He has been honored often to offices of trust.
Children: —

⁸⁹⁴ ERASTUS SHERMAN, b. Dec. 12, 1864.

⁸⁹⁵ EMMA EVERLYN, b. July 28, 1866.

⁸⁹⁶ ARIEL BLANCHE, b. Sept. 22, 1876.

¹⁹³ **VI. Elbridge G.**⁵⁵³ Boodey, son of Aaron
and Charlotte (Hill) Boodey, born Sept. 14, 1827;
married, Jan. 18, 1858, Mary A. Johnson, of Northwood,
born Aug. 23, 1832. Mr. Boodey now resides at (East)
Northwood, is in trade under the firm-name of Boodey
& Cate, they being dealers in lumber, flour, grain, etc.
He has long been honored in that town by many offices
of trust; has been called many times to preside at its
town-meetings; has been selectman more than once;
has served as its town treasurer, and for the years 1878
and 1879 was elected, and held, the office of representative to the legislature of New Hampshire. He has
given us much encouragement ih these annals.

¹⁹⁴ **VI. Charles B.**⁵⁵⁴ Boodey, son of Aaron
and Charlotte (Hill) Boodey, born Sept. 21, 1829;
married, June 2, 1851, Abby E. Fernald. He died Aug.
26, 1863. Children: —

897 ALBERT H., b. April 22, 1852.

898 CHARLES F., b. Nov. 2, 1856.

899 EDGAR S., b. Aug. 22, 1858; d. April 2, 1859.

900 MARY A.; b. Aug. 1, 1860.

195 **VI. Samuel B.**555 Boodey, son of Aaron, 2d, and Charlotte (Hill) Boodey; married Lucinda W. Patch; nobly served in the Union army of the rebellion in 1862 and 1863; was in the Massachusetts Heavy Artillery; was taken prisoner at Petersburg, was consigned to the Libby prison, escaped, and, being recaptured and imprisoned again, escaped and returned home; then, suffering from the effects of hardships and diseases there contracted, he died.

> Of God-like man!—if thus he e'er appears,
> 'Tis when his truth outlives declining years,
> Who ventures all in strength of youth or age,
> In deeds divine his energies engage;
> Who with one hand sustains a falling brother,
> Yet grasps his country's flag firm in the other;
> To flaunt its folds on freedom's towering height,
> In life's last hour still battles for the right;
> 'Tis such whose hand hath broken the galling fetter,
> 'Tis he whose life hath left the world the better,
> To him shall rise a fervid, loud acclaim;
> So beats a nation's heart at Lincoln's name;
> By whose true teachings treason lost its sway;—
> Then passed the good man from the world away.
> Still Greeley lives,—a Grant to lead the van,
> A Sherman bold, a gallant Sheridan.
> Hence shall the nation social pride maintain,
> In sovereign States shall sovereign order reign.
> Hail, glorious day! 'Tis wisdom's plan ordained,
> Above the storm is liberty proclaimed;
> The sun of peace resplendent shines again;
> O'er all the vale, it cheers th' abodes of men.*

---

* From my Epics, Lyrics, and Ballads, p. 387.

[196] **VI. John W.**[557] Boodey, son of Aaron and Charlotte (Hill) Boodey, born Dec. 16, 1835; died June 16, 1864, of wounds received in battle for the Union, at the Army Hospital in Washington city. He first enlisted in a New Hampshire regiment; served, and being honorably discharged, again enlisted in the 1st Mass. Heavy Artillery; was wounded in the battle at Spottsylvania. Previously he was in the murderous battle of

BULL RUN, JULY 19, 1861.

A constant cry of do or die
[On, on to Richmond! was the shout]
Evinced the spirit of metal and merit
To stamp the rebellion out.

The mass, all right, were full of fight;
Abram the people heeded;
But, sad for us, to quell the muss,
A marshal chief was needed.

With soldiers drilled, and squadrons filled,
A move at length was ordered;
With Scott at the head, McDowell led
The loyal army onward.

Up to Bull Run, the battle begun,
'T was ours for every reason;
But Johnston came and "blocked the game,"—
They called it "Patter's treason."

Fresh troops combined against the line,
And turned the tide of battle;
Both horse and foot reeled round about,
In broken ranks "skedaddle."

Our strong reserve had little nerve
To stay the massive numbers;
It lacked the spunk (for Miles was drunk)
To do such magic wonders.

Too much the foe had suffered now
   To follow up his chances;
Never force was frightened worse,
   Save panic-stricken Yankees.

And yet they fly; and in the sky
   Are rumblings, roar, and rattle;
Far down the way, wide scattered, lay
   Mixed implements of battle.

The Congress man, ah! how he ran!
   And the "London Times" benighted; *
'T would make you laugh, to see such chaff
   So fearfully excited.

O'er dell and ridge, and through Long Bridge,
   They urge their way in masses;
Both black and white, in equal fright,
   Among the mules and asses.

At Washington, they all had come,
   Exposed to every slander;
And little Mack was ordered back,
   To be their next commander.

He drilled the troop, and cheered high hope,
   In manners most inviting;
Favored of fame, he tried to train, —
   Brave in all — but fighting.

When the smoke disappeared from the battle-ground,
An officer over that field rode round;
And finding a "*run-away*" hid in a hole,
Beseechingly prompt he sought a parole,
         But heard no answer.
"March back," said the chief, "to your rightful ranks!
And away with all of your cowardly pranks!"
The soldier returned neither bullet nor blows,

* An editor of the Times was in their midst.

But sneeringly touched his thumb to his nose,
Exclaiming (as if to a clown or an elf),
       " No — you — don't,
Old fellow, you want this hole yourself! " *

195½ **VI. John M.**⁵⁵² Caswell, Capt., son of
Joanna (Boodey) and Enoch Caswell, born Oct. 27, 1827;
married, September, 1852, Mary E. Hunt; served as a
soldier in the Union army in the war of 1861; was
wounded at Chapin's Farm, Sept. 30, 1864, and died next
day, Oct. 1, 1864. He had resided at Manchester, N. H.
He commanded Co. A, 10th Regt. N. H. Volunteers.
Child : —

901   ADDIE E. CASWELL, b. March 14, 1853.

198 **VI. Elizabeth J.**⁵⁶³ Caswell, daughter of
Joanna (Boodey) and Enoch Caswell, born Jan. 6, 1829;
married James Going, born Nov. 12, 1823. He lived in
Manchester, N. H.   Children : —

902   FRANK K. GOING, b. Jan. 20, 1850.
903   JAMES C. GOING, b. June 30, 1852; d. Nov. 29,
         1854.
904   JENNY H. GOING, b. July 6, 1854; d. Sept. 13,
         1855.
905   JAMES H. GOING, b. Jan. 3, 1856.
906   LILY GOING, b. April 2, 1858; d. July 3, 1863.
907   FRED GOING, b. Nov. 6, 1860.
908   JOHN C. GOING, b. Dec. 13, 1865.
909   EDWARD GOING, b. Nov. 7, 1868.
910   AGNES GOING, b. Dec. 17, 1871; d. April 28, 1878.

198½ **VI. Alonzo M.**⁵⁶⁴ Caswell, son of Joanna
(Boodey) and Enoch Caswell, born April 26, 1832;

---

* From my Epics, Lyrics, and Ballads, p. 105.

married Margaret Poor, June 9, 1853; was valiant, and served in the Union army. For some time he held the place of quartermaster of the 1st N. H. Battery. Children: —

911 IMAGENE M. CASWELL, b. in M., Feb. 2, 1854.
912 EUGENE I. CASWELL, b. April 30, 1856.
913 ANNIE C. CASWELL, b. in M., Jan. 12, 1860.
914 ALONZO E. CASWELL, b. in M., July 10, 1861.
915 FRED M. CASWELL, b. in M., Dec. 13, 1872.

199 VI. Mary S.[567] Caswell, daughter of Joanna (Boodey) and Enoch Caswell, born Sept. 27, 1841; married, Jan. 1, 1874, William E. Boodey, born July 10, 1853. Child: —

916 CLARENCE W., b. in B., Sept. 4, 1874.

200 VI. Henry J.[569] Caswell, son of Joanna (Boodey) and Enoch Caswell, born Nov. 5, 1847; married, Dec. 15, 1867, Lydia A. Poor. Children: —

917 ARTHUR H. CASWELL, b. in M., June 7, 1869.
918 EDITH B. CASWELL, b. in M., June 6, 1876.

201 VI. Daniel Webster[572] Boodey, son of Daniel and Sarah (Wiggin) Boodey, born July 9, 1842; married, June 6, 1868, A. Marilla Furnald, b. Oct. 19, 1840. Children: —

918½ JOHN U., b. Feb. 20, 1869.
919 CHARLES W., b. March 9, 1878.

202 VI. Hannah B.[574] Huckins, daughter of Susanna (Boodey) Huckins and Israel, born July 18, 1828; married, Nov. 4, 1847, Frank Knowlton, born Oct. 11, 1824. Child: —

919½ WALTER F. KNOWLTON, b. Feb. 3, 1856.

33

203 VI. Azariah W.[575] Huckins, son of Susanna (Boodey) Huckins and Israel, born Oct. 3, 1831; married, Nov. 30, 1854, Betsey Paige. He was a twin brother of Zechariah B.; was a faithful soldier for the Union, in 3d Regt. N. H. Volunteers, and died in the service of his country, at Hilton Head, S. C., Aug. 20, 1862.

204 VI. Zechariah B.[576] Huckins, son of Susanna (Boodey) Huckins and Israel, born Oct. 3, 1831; married, April 30, 1864, Caroline Gear. She died June 21, 1872, aged 30 years. He was a twin brother of Azariah W. Huckins.

205 VI. Ruhana[577] Huckins, daughter of Susanna (Boodey) Huckins, born Sept. 18, 1835; married, in May, 1869, N. S. Bean, of Manchester, N. H. Child:—

920 N. S. BEAN, b. in M., Nov. 3, 1873.

206 VI. Warren[578] Huckins, son of Susanna (Boodey) Huckins and Israel, born May 10, 1838; married, May, 1869, Charlotte Carlton, of Davenport, Ia.; was a valiant soldier in the Union army in the war of 1861; was promoted through the various grades to the office of a captain in the 4th Regt. of the N. H. Volunteers; was in many conflicts, and, though once severely wounded, was not slain. Three children, one of whom was—

921 MINOT HUCKINS, b. Dec. 29, 1842; d. June, 1861.

207 VI. John S.[581] Boodey, son of John H. and Abigail R. (Smith) Boodey, born Sept. 2, 1845; married, Dec. 31, 1865, Nellie A. Wiggin, of South Newmarket, N. H. Mrs. Abigail died May 22, 1879, aged 31 years. Children:—

921¼ LAURA W., b. Nov. 21, 1866.

922 FRANK L., b. Oct. 10, 1869.

208 VI. Alfarata A.[582] Boodey, daughter of John II. and Abigail R. (Smith) Boodey, of Epping, N. II., born Aug. 21, 1849; married, Jan. 1, 1867, William II. Tilton, of Epping. Child: —

923 JOHN H. TILTON, b. Feb. 15, 1868.

209 VI. Daniel B. B.[588] Bartlett, son of Stephen and Cyrene (Howe) Bartlett (B.), born Oct. 31, 1843; married Amelia Moore, of Lowell, Mass. Children: —

924 ARTHUR BARTLETT, b. March 17, 1869.
925 BERTHA BARTLETT, b. Oct. 24, 1874.
926 HAYWARD BARTLETT, b. Aug. 25, 1877.

210 VI. Edwin W.[589] Bartlett, son of Stephen and Cyrene (Howe) Bartlett (B.), born April 11, 1845; married, Feb. 9, 1871, Sarah Hews, born May 22, 1849. Children: —

927 WALTER S. BARTLETT, b. April 11, 1872.
928 ALICE M. BARTLETT, b. March 8, 1875.

211 VI. Stephen E.[590] Bartlett, son of Stephen and Cyrene (Howe) Bartlett (B.), born Sept. 23, 1847; married, Jan. 13, 1873, Josephine Myers, of New York. Children: —

929 HARRY BARTLETT, b. in Lowell, May, 1876.
930 CHARLES M. BARTLETT, b. in Lowell, Sept. 24, 1878.

211½ VI. Charles F. Howe, Esq., son of Sarah and grandson of James Howe, Sen., born April 13, 1836; married, first, April 5, 1862, Emily A. Caswell, born May 29, 1838. She died. He married, second, Miss Helen M. Conihe, born 1841.

Charles F. is a distinguished lawyer, now (1880) a resident of the city of Lowell, Mass., and is still in the honorable practice of his profession. He long filled the office of Register in the U. S. Courts of Bankruptcy, in the Massachusetts district. He has been preferred as an alderman in the city of Lowell, and for a long time has been a master in Chancery under the laws of Massachusetts. His life thus far is a profitable success. In practice, he proclaims and verifies the axioms of the poet, that

> " We must not make a scarecrow of the law,
> Setting it up to fear the birds of prey;
> And let it keep one shape, till custom
> Make it their perch, and not their terror.
>   There is no power in Venice,
> Can alter a deed established.
> 'T will be recorded as a precedent;
> And many an error, by the same example,
> Will rush into the state.
> Let us, diligently in duty,
> Do as adversaries in the law,
> Strive mightily, — but eat and drink as friends."
>
> — *Shakespeare.*

²¹² **VI. B. Frank**⁵⁹¹ Boodey, son of Lot and Nancy (Evans) Boodey, born Dec. 14, 1848; married, May 9, 1874, the amiable Lura E. Hobbs, born Sept. 17, 1851, daughter of Samuel, Esq., and Caroline Hobbs, of Maine.

B. Frank is a native of Elizabeth, Jo Daviess County, Ill. When quite young he was adopted by Mr. and Mrs. Nelson, of Brighton, N. Y.; they educated him. He graduated with honors from the high school as well as from the Bryant & Stratton Business University, in

Rochester, N. Y. He is a nephew of Azariah Boodey, president, now or formerly, of the Toledo, Wabash & Western R. R. Company, has heretofore held the place of agent for the Western Coal and Mining Company, in Lafayette, Ind. Since 1878, his business and residence have been in Lowell, Mass., and at this period is connected with The Singer Manufacturing Company, under an agency. Practically, B. Frank is strong in business capacity, prompt, energetic, and industrious; and in years to come his noble race, at the end of his valiant career, may well anticipate a good account of him. Children: —

931 FRANK L., b. Feb. 26, 1875; d. Feb. 26, 1875.

932 SAMUEL H., b. March 27, 1877; d. March 27, 1877.

933 NELLIE EUDORA, b. Jan. 12, 1878.

213 **VI. Charlotte**594 Sias, daughter of Mary (Boodey) Sias and Jeremiah K., born Jan. 26, 1830; married, March 4, 1850, Edson G. Williams, born Feb. 20, 1829. He enlisted, a soldier for the Union, at Rochester, N. Y., in one of the first regiments for the war; and fighting for his country and its freedom bravely, he fell in the great battle at Antietam, Sept. 17, 1862. Children: —

934 AMBIA B. WILLIAMS, b. Dec. 28, 1852; m.   239

935 NELSON MORTIMER WILLIAMS, b. Aug. 10, 1854.

936 LILLIE CORA WILLIAMS, b. Jan. 5, 1858.

937 ELIZA EMARINE WILLIAMS, b. Nov. 25, 1859.

214 **VI. Mary M.**595 Sias, daughter of Mary (Boodey) Sias and Jeremiah K., born May 24, 1831; married, Dec. 7, 1853, George Gott, of Spencerport, N. Y. He served in a New York regiment of the Union

army throughout the rebellion. She survives him.
Child : —

 [938] GLENN GOTT, b. Oct. 22, 1856.

Mrs. Gott married, 2d, Dec. 12, 1871, Asa Conklin, a
successful merchant, of Chicago, Ill., born April 2, 1822.
Child : —

[939] ASA ROSCOE CONKLIN, b. Dec. 7, 1874.

215   VI.   Alonzo W.[596] Sias, son of Mary (Boodey)
Sias and Jeremiah K., born May 30, 1832; married,
May 30, 1863, the excellent Mary C. Tone, b. April 9,
1833, at Spencerport, N. Y.

"Westward the star of empire takes its way."

This then young man, Alonzo, born in the granite New
England, taking his life in his hand, in 1859, seeking to
make the most of his case in that life and youth and
health which the great God of Nature had given him,
turned his footsteps westward; weary were those footsteps at first and at times, but indeed they were sure
and steadfast. Single and alone, this untutored adventurer from the rock-bound coast of eastern New England,
had now reached the broad expanse of the western
prairie, a landscape strange and beautiful in verdure and
in flowers, but unknown of New England's variegated
native forest, or of the entrancing grandeur of the
mighty mountains afar off, which from the beginning of
the world hath lifted their cliffs above the sea. Here in
Minnesota, in the first years of its admission into the
American Union, upon the bleak prairie and upon soil
unbroken by the plow, and then, as yet, unhonored by the
wild forests of the world. At once the practical

idea of a nursery of fruit-trees, to be sown, grown, and transplanted there, fell upon the mind of this our young adventurer. Knowing or believing, as he did, that the same fertile soil which would feed the field would also feed the apple-tree, and would swell and feed, if sown, even the seeds of the wild forest, he at once advanced to sow the first seed, to plant the first tree in that prairie region of the new world. Then, more than half of all the populace of that place would scout the idea that a fruit-tree could be made to grow there. Then, a railroad to them had been unseen; and no fruit, to the most of that people, in the coming years, had been anticipated. Then, almost everything in the world's advancement, to that people, comparatively, seemed to be beclouded; no railroads, no highways, or conveyance by water; even the White Mountains of New England were as near as need be to the world's end; a bleak prairie extended everywhere. And yet our young kindred friend, in the faith of his God, and his own energies, built his cot there, plowed up the prairie, scattered broadcast into the furrows, seeds of the apple, the pear, the plum, and other fruits. In all these, in due time, he engrafted the various choicest varieties from the abundant fruits of all the earth; so that, from his vast nursery at a horticultural fair of the State of Minnessota, among other fruits, were exhibited by him "over sixty varieties of the common apple." He has long been one of the leaders in the Olmstead County Horticultural Society, and president of it; a treasurer, also, of the State Horticultural Society, and is still advancing farther onward and upward to the organization of a numerous society now in progress in that State, entitled and known as The Farmers' Institute. Thus it is

"Westward the star of empire takes its way."

Mr. and Mrs. Sias still reside on their pleasant homestead at Rochester, Minn.   Children : —

939½ GERTRUDE SIAS, b. June 18, 1867; d. Aug. 28, 1867.

940 EDGAR DANIEL SIAS, b. Oct 2, 1869.

940½ SARAH CORINNE SIAS, b. Nov. 10, 1871.

216 **VI. Daniel B.**[597] Sias, son of Mary (Boodey) Sias and Jeremiah K., born May 21, 1834; married, Jan. 27, 1865, Lucy H. Burgen, of Toledo, O., born April 13, 1842.   He went west at an early age.   For a long time has been in the employ of the Toledo, Wabash & Western R. R. Company, and has been their ticket-agent at Delphi, Ind.   They reside at the old homestead at Spencerport.   Children : —

941 RALPH B. SIAS, b. June 29, 1866.

941½ BLANCHE SIAS, b. March 16, 1868.

942 WILLIE A. SIAS, b. Feb. 13, 1870.

943 D. PURDY SIAS, b. Aug. 10, 1872.

944 CARLETON SIAS, b. Nov. 22, 1877.

945 Infant, b. Jan. 2, 1880.

217 **VI. Ira E.**[598] Sias, son of Mary (Boodey) Sias and Jeremiah K., born July 31, 1836; married Mrs. Martha Gerald, of Worcester, Mass.; died at their residence in Spencerport, N. Y., Dec. 31, 1878.

219 **VI. Roxanna M.**[601] Sias, daughter of Mary (Boodey) Sias and Jeremiah K., born Sept. 22, 1842. This lady graduated with high honors at the high school

at Rochester, N. Y. On the 25th of October, 1864, she intermarried with John D. Ostrom, Esq., then of New York City, born Feb. 14, 1832. He had graduated at Union College with the degree of A. B., and thence, May 20, 1859, he again graduated at the law department of the University at Albany, N. Y., with the degree of L. B.; was admitted to the practice of his profession in Minnesota, and advanced in it up to Oct. 2, 1871. Thence he removed to Texas, where he is accumulating a fortune in stock-raising. Children: —

[946] ORMY NELSON OSTROM, b. July 19, 1866.
[947] CLARK OSTROM, b. Jan. 11, 1868.

This far-off family, in this 104th year of our independence, stands like a beacon-light to the enterprising boys and girls of New England. It beckons every one of you to the fair fields of the earth where Nature has provided a congenial climate, and a soil deep in productive energies, everywhere bespeaking the promise of health, independence, and a. successful life. You, my young kindred, you who have lively, progressive hearts, who are endowed with noble, economical aspirations to become and to remain independent men and women, turn, turn yourselves towards Texas, or advance to some other garden of this our new and beautiful world, for there, most surely, will you find and obtain the livelihood of industrious, economical habits, as well as the flowery fields of independence, honor, and fame. Listen for a moment to an extract from the mother of this little Texas family. She had been besought by her cousin, "B. Frank," to furnish the record of herself and little ones for these annals. Thereupon she writes, and among other things, says: —

BRAZONIA, TEXAS, Jan. 7, 1880.

MY DEAR COUSIN FRANK:

You know I am, as of old, a most beautiful writer, but just at present have an abscess on the end of my first finger, which renders it difficult to make the usual display. I was right glad to hear from you, if it was (as you say) on business. Your letter sounded like you as you used to be. Ormy and Clark are now of the same age that you were when we went to Clover Light together. Ormy is a tall, quiet, studious boy, very reliable in every way, and is his mamma's special pride, because, I suppose, he has not one trait like myself. Clark is a little, roguish, fun-loving fellow, bright as a dollar, and everybody's favorite, especially his papa's. They are a great comfort to us. I was so glad, my dear cousin, that you have with you your mother, your wife, and your daughter. Cherish them all. You will never have but one mother! Little Nellie, kiss her for her cousin. Nannie wrote me how good a wife you had. Heaven has given you its best gift. You ask, "What in time we are in Texas for?" I wish you would come here, and you would never ask again. It is the most perfect climate in all the world. The finest oranges we ever saw. You cannot name a fruit or a flower that does not flourish here in the open air. We went four miles picnicking the other day, and brought home three barrels of the finest oysters we ever saw; fish and ducks, till you can't rest.

We like it, we do! Mr. and Mrs. Fale are near us. He and Mr. Evans have purchased a sugar plantation for $30,000. They had a vast sugar crop this year.

Now in regard to the Boodey book: I am so sorry I hadn't done something *smart*, so as to hand my name down (you know); but it's too late! If I live in Texas, perhaps I can do something yet. . . .

Give our regards to Mr. Caverly, and say to him we wish him great success. We will want the book. Hope in going back he won't come to a rope anywhere. . . .

Your Cousin, ANNA.

220 VI. Ambia A.[605] Gerald, daughter of Nancy (Boodey) Gerald and Carley, born April 2, 1849; married, Oct. 23, 1873, Clayton J. Benjamin, of Clyde, N. Y., born May 23, 1851. They now reside in San Francisco, Cal. Children : —

948 GERTRUDE A. BENJAMIN, b. Aug. 15, 1874.
949 LILLA CORA BENJAMIN, b. Sept. 27, 1876.

221 VI. Florence E.[610] Caverly, daughter of Leonard W. Caverly (B.) and Esther L., born Sept. 7, 1845; married, Aug. 17, 1865, Ephraim C. Benson. He officiates as real-estate agent in Boston, doing a successful business. Child : —

950 ELDON BENSON, b. June 8, 1870; d. July 31, 1870.

222 VI. Martha J.[619] Caverly, daughter of Cyrus, and granddaughter of Comfort, of S. (B.), born Dec. 31, 1852; married, Aug. 21, 1870, Almus Griffin, born Aug. 17, 1849; resides in Strafford, N. H. Children : —

951 ROLNEY A. GRIFFIN, b. April 27, 1872.
952 FANNY M. GRIFFIN, b. April 15, 1874.
952½ LILLIAN C. GRIFFIN, b. April 18, 1877; d. April 18, 1877.

222½ VI. Frank P.[630] Foss, son of Emily S. (Boodey) Foss and George W., born in Lowell, April 29, 1855; married, Oct. 23, 1875, Ida A. Carter, of that city. Child : —

953 SADIE A. Foss, b. Feb. 2, 1876.

224 VI. Albert R.[647] Leighton, son of Zechariah (B.) Leighton and Mishel (Bartlett) Leighton, born Dec.

8, 1849; married Jennie S. Martin, and resides in Haverhill, Mass. Child:—

[954]　FOREST A. LEIGHTON, b. 1878.

[225]　**VI. John F.**[648] Leighton, son of Zechariah (B.) and Mishel (Bartlett) Leighton, born May 6, 1853; married Katie H. Bean. Child:—

[955]　ARTHUR J. LEIGHTON, b. in the year 1879.

[227]　**VI. Samuel H.**[699] Hill, son of Azariah (B.) and Hannah (Hall) Hill, born in 1839; married, in 1862, Mary A. Swain, of Alexandria, N. H., born in 1837. Their residence is at Centre Strafford, N. H.

[228]　**VI. Charles M.**[700] Hill, son of Azariah (Boodey) Hill and Hannah, born Jan. 16, 1842; married, May 30, 1868, Mary E. Ricker, of Lebanon, Me., born Oct. 6, 1836. In trade at Strafford, N. H. Children:—

[956]　CHARLES F. HILL, b. June 1, 1872.
[957]　HENRY R. HILL, b. March 11, 1876.

[229]　**VI. Hiram S.**[701] Hill, son of Azariah (Boodey) and Hannah (Hall) Hill, born March 2, 1846; married, Oct. 31, 1872, Hattie I. Daniels, born June 16, 1854. They reside at Centre Strafford, N. H. Children:—

[958]　LEWIS D. HILL, b. March 23, 1874.
[959]　LILLA M. HILL, b. July 6, 1876.

[230]　**VI. Eva M.**[706] Chamberlain, daughter of Albert (B.) and Sarah (Hill) Chamberlain (B.), born in Brookfield, N. H., Sept. 29, 1853; married, March 10, 1875, Herbert H. Russell, of Waverly, Mass., born Nov. 7, 1849. Children:—

⁹⁶⁰ H. PERCY RUSSELL, b. July 23, 1876.
⁹⁶¹ CLARENCE A. RUSSELL, b. June 2, 1879.

231 VI. 𝕲𝖊𝖔𝖗𝖌𝖊 𝕭.⁷⁰⁷ Benton, son of Nancy Hill (B.) and Thomas H. Benton, born Feb. 12, 1824; married Mary T. Lathrop.

232 VI. 𝕾𝖚𝖘𝖆𝖓 𝕰.⁷²⁶ Clarke, daughter of Joseph T., the artist, and Betsey (Caverly) Clarke (B.), born Sept. 29, 1839; married, June 25, 1855, Charles E. Bacon, a thrifty, enterprising jeweller, of Dover, N. H., who now, (1880) in successful life, is still residing there. His lady is an artist in painting and music, and the son and daughter (surviving) give promise of health, strength, economy, usefulness, and long life. Children: —

⁹⁶² HORACE BACON, b. at Dover, June 8, 1858; d.
⁹⁶³ MARY ELIZABETH BACON, b. at Dover, March 19, 1861; d.
⁹⁶⁴ EDDY SANGER BACON, b. at Dover, March 8, 1863.
⁹⁶⁵ EMILY BACON, b. at Dover, Aug. 18, 1866.
⁹⁶⁶ HELEN AUGUSTA BACON, b. at Dover, Dec. 25, 1873; d.

234 VI. 𝕮. 𝕱𝖗𝖆𝖓𝖐⁷³⁸ Waterhouse, son of Charles H. and Nancy I. Caverly (B.) Waterhouse, born July 8, 1859; married Laura J. Hill, of Strafford, N. H. Child: —

⁹⁶⁷ HENRY D. WATERHOUSE, b. in Barrington, March 20, 1878.

Seventh Generation.

235 **VII. Martha A.**[862] Foss, daughter of Robert
N. Foss, of Barrington, N. H., and Sarah A. (Boodey)
Foss, born Sept. 25, 1852; married, July 19, 1868, Fred
Wescott. He died in 1872. Child: —

[963] HATTIE F. WESCOTT, b. March 11, 1870.

Second marriage, May 6, 1874, to Hiram Mace, of
Farmington, N. H., born Aug. 12, 1846. Child: —

[969] GEORGE D. MACE, b. Jan. 24, 1875.

235½ **VII. Martha E.**[877] Woodman, daughter of
Charles C. and Martha A. (Boodey) Woodman, born
March 15, 1850; married, Nov. 13, 1870, John F. Han-
son, of Strafford, son of John D. Hanson, of that
place. John F. is a good mechanic and a skilful musician.
Children: —

[970] HERMAN H. HANSON, b. April 6, 1876.
[971] AMY W. HANSON, b. May 11, 1879.

236 **VII. Laura C.**[864] Hill, daughter of Joseph,
of Barnstead, N. H., and Mary S. (Boodey) Hill, born
July 14, 1848; married, June, 1867, Charles Huckins.
Child: —

[972] ALBERT HUCKINS, b. in B., Dec. 13, 1867.

237 **VII. Ellen F.**[865] Hill, daughter of Joseph,
of Barnstead, N. H., born Nov. 25, 1850; married
Charles Mooney. Child: —

[973] J. M. MOONEY, b. July 14, 1877.

238 **VII. Ella E.**[869] daughter of George A. and
Martha (Boodey) Caverly, of Strafford, N. H., born May

21, 1857, in Strafford; married, March 30, 1875, John D. Clark. Child:—

⁹⁷⁴ ERNEST E. CLARK, b. in Strafford, May 28, 1878.

²³⁹ VII. 𝔄mbía 𝔅.⁹³⁴ Williams, daughter of Edson G. and Charlotte (Sias) Williams (B.), of Rochester, N. Y., born Dec. 29, 1852; married, May 24, 1871, James A. Wright, born Nov. 15, 1831. Children:—

⁹⁴⁰ EVA M. WRIGHT, b. Nov. 17, 1872.

⁹⁴² CHARLES E. WRIGHT, b. Sept. 1, 1874; d. Jan. 13, 1876.

⁹⁴³ MARY E. WRIGHT, b. Aug. 17, 1876.

⁹⁴⁴ J. NELSON WRIGHT, b. Oct. 17, 1879.

¹⁴³ V. John C.³⁵³ Peavey, Esq.,* son of Captain John and Mary (Caverly) Peavey, born Sept. 9, 1819; married, March 28, 1841, Mary A. Caverly, daughter of Daniel Caverly, Esq., born May 13, 1823. He is a husbandman, a skilful mechanic, and an inn-holder, residing at Bow Lake Village, in Strafford, N. H. Children:—

WILLIAM HENRY PEAVEY, b. Dec. 17, 1846.

GEORGE ALBERT PEAVEY, b. Aug. 24, 1849.

MARIETTA A. PEAVEY, b. Jan. 9, 1855; married Charles J. Daly, an active, intelligent gentleman, in trade at the Boston Highlands.

¹⁹³ VI. Elbridge G.⁵⁵³ Boodey,† born Sept. 14, 1827; married Miss Mary A. Johnson, of Northwood. Child:—

BLANCHE N., b. Feb. 11. 1859.

---

* A number omitted in the 5th generation (p. 226).

† A number in part omitted in the 6th generation (p. 252).

196¼   **VI.**   **Judith C.**[558] Boodey,* born Aug. 8, 1839; married Dudley P. Ladd, of Vermont.   Child:—

FRANK B. LADD, b. in Bradford, Mass., Sept. 6, 1869.

196½   **VI.**   **Edson B.**[561] Boodey,* born March 28, 1845; resides in South Berwick, Me.; married Abbie Savage, of New Market, N. H.   Child:—

FRED S., b. July 3, 1872.

---

* Numbers omitted in the 6th generation (p. 204).

Boodey Lineage.

AND now at Madbury, Oct. 19, 1880, at the grave of Zechariah, our remote New England ancestor, we, to the assembled generations, as the compiler of their Annals, orally address the following story of the ancestor, entitled

THE RECAPITULATION.

ARGUMENT.

1. The Divine Favor.—2. Faith of the Boy's Mother in the far-off France. 3. His incoming Sea-voyage.—4. New England seen from the Ship. 5. His Flight from Boston, and his Wanderings in the Wilderness. 6. His Concealment in the old Barn.—7. Freedom gained.— 8. The native Forest falls — Prompt Husbandry ensues — The Cot — The Better-half — Life's Years of Progress.—9. The Family full grown. 10. Nuptial Engagements, ceremonial. — 11. Old Age, and Life's Departure.—12. The Ancestor's Generations, and our Annals.

I.

Great Power above, who rules the sphere
    And sends the generations down,
That brought the panting pilgrim here,
And gave him grace and grateful cheer,
Crowning his life, through a long career,
    At Dover town;

Thanks! thanks to Thee who blest his birth
    Beyond the bleak Atlantic shore;
'Mid all the dangers and the dearth,
To brave the boist'rous waves of earth, —
    A pioneer.

To Thee who shaped the hand, the heart,
    For a lofty life and noblest thing;
To Thee whose power can ne'er depart,

35

Who guides the every aim and art
Of a purpose pure, — we bending bring
    Earth's best oblation;

A song of love, — oh, give it wing!
    Inspire the drowsy muse to sing
Of our progenitor, — his train,
His heart heroic, — his faith, — his fame,
    In the far-gone years;

Of the name divine, — the humble birth, —
    The advent strange, — the quaint old ways; —
Of meek good manners and of mirth,
His countless progeny on earth
    Proudly we praise.

How did he toil in age or youth,
    Pure ever at heart, — in deed or thought
How constant held the tongue to truth,
How through Earth's labors found, forsooth,
    Pure light and love.

Thence how he left, through faith and grace,
    Man's best example, which we trace,
And many a lesson to his race
Who've come to-day to fill his place,
    And learn of life.

II.

Look back afar to the native land,
    To a cottage stained of age and storm!
A mother there! — oh, see her stand,
Scanning the rolling sea, forlorn, —
    Her tearful eye!

A ship stands tossing on the strand;
  The sea-gale howls, portending woe;
"There's danger in that distant land;
Which youth untrained can ne'er forego,"
    That mother said it.

Three times she takes to the naval deck,
  Three times imploring prayers employ,
Against rebuke or kindly check,
All day she hangs upon the neck
    Of her beauteous boy.

Above the clouds her plaint arose,
  And from the skies a truthful Trust
(Our mothers had it from the first)
Lets down at length a calm repose,
    As sure it must.

Still *how* to sever the tender tie,
  Or how to yield, no heart could know
(The precept and the passions vie);
For him she'd lived, for him she'd die,
    In depths of woe.

She'd nestled him as does the dove
  (The midnight ghost proclaimed her love);
She'd cradled him, 'mid grief or joy,
Yet high her prayers o'erwhelm the boy
    Above the billows.   .

III.

No telegram the sea had gained;
  No photograph to find the face;
No steam-power then had been ordained,

Nor could Earth's bounty be obtained,
  Save through life's labor.

Still, did old ocean wave as now,
  The king of day stood beaming bright;
As now the pilgrim paid his vow,
And the star sent down pure, twinkling light,
    Sweet love at night.

Brisk now, the breeze inflates the sail,
  The parting waves their furrows fill;
Our God withholds the storm and hail,
And the boy made mighty at His will,
    Drinks inspiration.

Long were the weeks, with sail unfurled,
  Yet Heaven heeds both craft and crew;
High swelled the ship her journey through,
Till a towering wave lifts up to view
    New England, noble

IV.

NEW ENGLAND.

Oh, scan ye now both land and sea!
  Old ocean beats a beauteous shore,
While beast and wild-bird frantic flee,
To escape the craft they never did see
    On earth before.

Yet doth the wild-cat waul at will,
  The she-wolf, howling, much complains;
Still duteous life man must fulfil,
The King of kings is gracious still,
    Grandly He reigns.

Wide lakes reflect their limpid light,
  The landscape waves her grateful green;

In beauty and in grandeur bright,
The moon lets fall her joys at night,
And the mountains stand, sweet stars between,
    Vast — in the skies!

Light leaps the rill to fountains broad,
    Bright rolls the river to the sea;
Out from the cataract our God,
High pointing upward, lifts his rod,
    And the land is free.

Oh, beauteous Nature, given of Him
    To thrill the soul while thus we gaze,
Without a taint, without a sin,
To fill life's measure to the brim;
    To bless our days!

Parent of all, high favored now,
    As in thy kindness years of yore,
From far and near to bring the vow,
In multitude we humbly bow,
    Thee we adore.

v.

Held on the ship at Boston Bay;
    At dread despair the boy hath been;
Now bounding from the deck away,
Flying, his limber limbs obey
    A soul within.

Dangers thick-set are in the woods, —
    The catamount, the ravenous bear;
The savage roams the fen and floods;
Huge serpants tree-top move the buds,

And the Devil there, to spite the gods,
   Hath hidden a snare.

Detectives, stained of sin supernal,*
   Fiercely the panting boy pursues,
Through bush and brake, through midnight dews,
Or down declivities that bruise
   Their flesh infernal.

'Neath hemlocks high he fords the brook,
   Tears through and through the tangled vines,
Or seeks sweet rest 'neath rock or nook,
Or rambles through the plaintive pines,
   Wild, here and there.

At length the hill-tops promise joy;
   The evening zephyr whispers peace;
Sweet wood-nymphs greet the " sailor boy,"
As fierce he flies, — "Ahoy! ahoy!"
   Oh, take release!

Now, dark the hail-storm sweeps the wood;
   Loud thunders bolt terrific fire;
The mountain drives the fearful flood,
Yet God protects, as best he could,
   Our Zechariah.

Far now advanced, he hears no more
   The bay of blood-hound on his track;
Nor cry of vengeance, held in store,
At Boston, should they bear him back,
   To that dread doom.

---

* Tradition says, that the boy's comrade deserters, being arrested and returned to the ship, were at once executed.

A CASCADE (CROSSED OVER).

He seeks the garrison to shun,
  Some lurking foe might there betray;
More faith he had, the more he run,
Till Vic-to-ry, now nearly won,
  Lights up the way.

VI.

Now near Mahorimet* there stood
  A hovel old, rude, made of logs
(Its hay-patch small within the wood),
Unheld of garrison, men, or dogs;
  Of moonlight blest.

Coy, through its storm-stained rugged walls,
  Touched by the shades of the moving bough,
Soft creeping 'tween its timbered stalls,
The boy crawls breathless 'neath the mow, —
  The heart beats high.

Loud clatterings shake the crackled roof,
  Unseemly sounds are heard aloof;
Zigzag the lizard winds his way,
And dangers dire hang o'er the hay,
  'Mid cruel threatenings.

All through that night Mahorimet
  Is hooted by the boding owl;
And the wild old woods, disturbed, are set
With noisy beasts, that prey and prowl,
  Malignant mad.

VII.

Time hastens on, — the same old ship
  Hath swelled the sail for a foreign shore;

---

* Hick's Hill, which, cone-like, stands in its verdure near the resting-place of the ancestor, and which was called, by the Indians, Mahorimet.

And "the sailor boy," on every lip,
Is a hero now — pursued no more,
   Leaps forth for joy.

Out from the hidden hay to come,
   To drink the balmy woodland air,
Then from the skies a glorious sun
Beams bounteously, in beauty fair,
   To a lovely land.

Earth's landscape green in grandeur shone,
   Her mild October gilds the grove;
And sainted souls from Heaven's throne
Make messages of faith and love
   To the settler here.

VIII.

Rude nature now to faith must yield
   The rooted turf, the rocks that frown;
To clear the glebe and fence the field,
   The cloud-capped pines are coming down,
   And the wild old forest, bright or brown,
     Fated must fall.

Brave none the less, he builds a cot,
   And a better-half is brought to view,
To share the labors and the lot
   Of varied life its journey through,
     Its joys, its sorrows ; —

Of logs laid one above the other,
   Locked well together at their points;
With clay or mud, the one or t' other,
   To glut the hungry, gaping joints
     'Gainst wintry weather.

Obtained in truth, the cot, the wife,
  To husbandry the heart aspires;
Vast, vast the energies of life
  To duteous care, ambition fires
      Heroic zeal.

Warm, next anon, congenial spring
  Brings sweet rejoicings at their door;
Wild, here the feathered songsters sing,
As roundabout they duteous wing
      For a golden store.

Rudely the plowshare breaks the sod,
  And then the vernal seed is sown;
Prolific, hand in hand they plod,
They reap a harvest from their God,
      Rich made their own.

Thanksgivings loud went up that day,
  Devoutly from Faith's altar here;
And sainted sprites from heaven (they say),
Rejoicing loud, as well they may,
      Gave grateful cheer.

IX.

So rolled the years in days of old, —
  Dame, plenteous blest her vast domain;
Abundant in her flocks and fold,
Though less than now, in gifts of gold,
      She moved amain.

Forgetting not her Zechariah,
  She blessed him to a noble son ;
With eight dear daughters to admire,

Elizabeth and kind Kasiah,
　　As months moved on.

Prompt came his Hannah, good as new;
　Sweet Charity and Sarah, too;
Our Betty (Rowe) and Nabby (Drew); —
　And little Pet, — all prone to do
　　High, happy honors, —

To fill the sphere ordained of Heaven,
　To honor Him high first of all,
With fervent faith and reverence given
To father, mother, and neighbor even,
　　Obedient at call.

Such, such was life in the wilderness,
　To the pioneer of all our ways,
That fired the heart to manliness,
Entrancing earth to the blessedness
　　Of glorious days.

x.

Back let us look beyond the cloud,
　Portending rural distant time,
To scan the page that speaks aloud,
Of habits pure primeval proud,
　　Quaintly divine.

How then they framed the rude pavilion;
　How prompt to labor up and doing;
How whirled the wheel, — how each civilian
Wagged with his wife, upon a pillion,
　　Churchward moving.

How then, when Sabbath eve came on,
　As time advanced in lengthened lives,

Swains came to court, and wisely won
Six daughters from their native home,
    Prompt, frugal wives.

How proud the household to receive
    The advent of their nuptial guest;
How Nabby tittered in her sleeve,
With one and t' other taking leave,
And Betty, bashful, scarce could breathe,
    One of the best.

How Lizzie dropped a curtsey low;
    How mother acted, — just as though
She did not know 't was Hannah's beau;
And turned and went, as you must know,
Compulsion seemed to press her so,
    To "feed the fowls."

Of cattle fat, and fertile farm,
    The father stops "to talk 'em over";
Of "tater-bugs," then doing harm,
Of fleecy flocks, of "devilish dogs," —
But hastening away to "feed the hogs,"
    Relieved the lovers.

Then when the wedding hour had come,
    The parish door wide open speeds,
The household gathered, everyone,
Neat-dressed in webs, mother had spun,
In which the daughters all had done
    Their best of deeds.

The gray-wigged parson makes the prayer,
    With breeches blest, of scarlet dye, —
With buckles beaming silver fair,

With a gown begirt, and a cue of hair
    Close hanging by.

Grave, slow, and long the service run;
    True hand in hand the pledge they take;
Thereby the twain were made but one,
And wedded life is again begun, —
    Six tribes they make. '

At home still lived our Zechariah,
    In care for the parent prone to tarry,
To fill the crib and feed the fire;
To a kindred end our kind Kasiah
    Refused to marry.

XI.

Old Age comes crook'd in hateful garb,
    Oblivion hindmost, creeps concealed;
The scythe of Time is swinging hard,
And man's ambition, withering, marred,
    To fate must yield.

Hence did our honored father die;
    His household vanished out of sight;
Yet do we now through faith descry,
Up through the curtains of the sky,
    Most lovely light.

XII.

Our fathers, mothers, kindred kind,
    Who lived of old, down from the first,
We crave thy powers of might and mind,
Thy faith and fortitude combined,
    Thy pathways just; —

Not less of truth or blest renown;
　Not less of love, not less of cheer;
Out through the length of life's career,
Lead us to keep the conscience clear,
　　Craving the crown.

O look ye down to a kindred throng,
　To life and love, and sweet relations;
Here's youth and age and manhood strong,
Here's heart and hand, and the grateful song
　　Of generations.

We've come from where our mothers died,
　From where the pilgrim fathers rest;
Where wild, at morn or eventide,
The savage roamed the forest wide,
　　Beardless, half dressed.

Down where fair Hudson's waters pour,
　Out from old Ocean's coast we've come;
From where Niagara's rollings roar,
From California's golden shore,
　　We make but one.

Oh, grateful ties to truth entwined,
　Of myriad souls in earth or heaven!
Inspired of God, both man and mind
Filled up of the fruitfulness we find,
　　Vast, kindly given.

To thee, my listener, fain I'd bring
　Some golden garland; — but, more dear,
A book it is, — a precious thing,
To give thee light and give thee wing
　　To a lofty sphere.

Bright, shall it bring a balmy ray,
   A star to twinkle in thy crown:
Oh, live and learn!   For thee we pray,
While at thy footstool now I lay
      Your Annals down.

Farewell, my kindred, one and all;
   What hence shall be, no tongue can tell,
Yet what thy chances, what thy cup,
Heaven's kindly care shall hold thee up,
     Fare — fare thee well!

INDEX TO NAMES.

37